CONTEMPORARY
*B*lack
*B*iography

ISSN-1058-1316

CONTEMPORARY

*B*lack

*B*iography

Profiles from the International Black Community

Volume 79

 GALE
CENGAGE Learning™

Detroit • New York • San Francisco • New Haven, Conn • Waterville, Maine • London

GALE
CENGAGE Learning

Contemporary Black Biography, Volume 79

Kepos Media, Inc.: Derek Jacques, Janice Jorgensen, and Paula Kepos, editors

Project Editor: Margaret Mazurkiewicz

Image Research and Acquisitions: Leitha Etheridge-Sims

Editorial Support Services: Nataliya Mikheyeva

Rights and Permissions: Jackie Jones, Barb McNeil

Manufacturing: Dorothy Maki, Rita Wimberley

Composition and Prepress: Mary Beth Trimper, Gary Leach

Imaging: John Watkins

Gale
27500 Drake Rd.
Farmington Hills, MI, 48331-3535

ISBN-13: 978-1-4144-3972-3
ISBN-10: 1-4144-3972-5

ISSN 1058-1316

This title is also available as an e-book.
ISBN 13: 978-1-4144-5696-6
ISBN-10: 1-4144-5696-4
Contact your Gale sales representative for ordering information.

Printed in the United States of America
1 2 3 4 5 6 7 14 13 12 11 10

Advisory Board

Contents

Introduction

Contemporary Black Biography provides informative biographical profiles of the important and influential persons of African heritage who form the international black community: men and women who have changed today's world and are shaping tomorrow's. *Contemporary Black Biography* covers persons of various nationalities in a wide variety of fields, including architecture, art, business, dance, education, fashion, film, industry, journalism, law, literature, medicine, music, politics and government, publishing, religion, science and technology, social issues, sports, television, theater, and others. In addition to in-depth coverage of names found in today's headlines, *Contemporary Black Biography* provides coverage of selected individuals from earlier in this century whose influence continues to impact on contemporary life. *Contemporary Black Biography* also provides coverage of important and influential persons who are not yet household names and are therefore likely to be ignored by other biographical reference series. Each volume also includes listee updates on names previously appearing in *CBB*.

Designed for Quick Research and Interesting Reading

- **Attractive page design** incorporates textual subheads, making it easy to find the information you're looking for.
- **Easy-to-locate data sections** provide quick access to vital personal statistics, career information, major awards, and mailing addresses, when available.
- **Informative biographical essays** trace the subject's personal and professional life with the kind of in-depth analysis you need.
- **To further enhance your appreciation** of the subject, most entries include photographic portraits.
- **Sources for additional information** direct the user to selected books, magazines, and newspapers where more information on the individuals can be obtained.

Helpful Indexes Make It Easy to Find the Information You Need

Contemporary Black Biography includes cumulative Nationality, Occupation, Subject, and Name indexes that make it easy to locate entries in a variety of useful ways.

Available in Electronic Formats

Diskette/Magnetic Tape. Contemporary Black Biography is available for licensing on magnetic tape or diskette in a fielded format. Either the complete database or a custom selection of entries may be ordered. The database is available for internal data processing and nonpublishing purposes only. For more information, call (800) 877-GALE.

On-line. Contemporary Black Biography is available on-line through Mead Data Central's NEXIS Service in the NEXIS, PEOPLE and SPORTS Libraries in the GALBIO file and Gale's Biography Resource Center.

Disclaimer

Contemporary Black Biography uses and lists websites as sources and these websites may become obsolete.

We Welcome Your Suggestions

The editors welcome your comments and suggestions for enhancing and improving *Contemporary Black Biography*. If you would like to suggest persons for inclusion in the series, please submit these names to the editors. Mail comments or suggestions to:

The Editor
Contemporary Black Biography
Gale, Cengage Learning
27500 Drake Rd.
Farmington Hills, MI 48331-3535
Phone: (800) 347-4253

Rashied Ali

1935–2009

Jazz drummer, club owner, record-label founder

Rashied Ali played a major role in the development of free-form or experimental jazz. Although best known for his work as a drummer, particularly for saxophonist John Coltrane, he also wielded considerable influence as a club owner and record producer.

Ali was born Robert Patterson Jr. in Philadelphia, Pennsylvania. His birth date has been the subject of some controversy. At the time of his death in 2009, the *New York Times* listed his age as seventy-six. That information, if accurate, would place his birth in 1932 or 1933. According to the vast majority of sources, however, he was born July 1, 1935. The circumstances of his childhood, in any case, are not in dispute. Music was an integral part of life from his earliest days. His mother and her four sisters all sang and played the piano, often at a small Baptist church run by his grandmother. When his father and brother left that denomination and converted to Islam, Ali joined them, probably in the late 1940s. Among the most visible signs of his new faith was his adoption of a new name.

Well before his teens, Ali was taking formal lessons in voice, piano, and trombone. His interest in these quickly dissipated, however, when he discovered the drums. His love for that instrument eventually took him to the Granoff School of Music, a local institution known as an incubator of jazz talent. He also received considerable musical training during a three-year stint (1952–55) in the U.S. Army. William Grimes of the *New York Times* later attributed Ali's "crisp precision" on the drums to his work with several Army bands.

Upon his return to Philadelphia at the end of his military service, Ali found work as a drummer with a variety of blues and rock-and-roll bands. Jazz, however, remained his passion. The single greatest influence on his development was undoubtedly Coltrane. A native of North Carolina, the saxophonist had moved as a child to Philadelphia, where he lived only a few blocks from the Ali home. As his fame grew in the 1950s, his house attracted Ali and other young musicians, who would gather on the front porch just to hear him practice. It was not until 1958 or 1959, however, that the two actually met.

Among other advice, Coltrane urged Ali to move to New York City, the capital of the jazz world. Upon his arrival there in 1963, Ali worked for saxophonists Albert Ayler and Archie Shepp, among others. His first major recording credit, for Shepp's *On This Night,* came two years later. That album, and an impromptu jam session at a club one night, deeply impressed Coltrane, who offered Ali the chance to be the second drummer, behind Elvin Jones, on the album *Ascension* (1965). For a variety of reasons, including commitments to other musicians, Ali declined the invitation. Several months later, however, he joined the group in time to record 1965's *Meditations,* which became one of the hallmarks of his career and of the free jazz movement as a whole. Released from the task of keeping a steady beat, Ali and Jones were free to join Coltrane and the other band members in extended, sometimes discordant improvisations.

Shortly after *Meditations,* Jones moved on, leaving Ali as Coltrane's primary drummer, a role he retained until

At a Glance . . .

Born Robert Patterson Jr. on July 1, 1935, in Philadelphia, PA; died August 12, 2009, in New York, NY; married Patricia Bea Wyatt; children: nine. *Military service:* U.S. Army, 1952–55. *Religion:* Muslim. *Education:* Studied at the Granoff School of Music, 1950s.

Career: Independent musician, 1950s–2009; drummer for John Coltrane, 1965–67; Ali's Alley (jazz club), founder and owner, 1973–79; Survival Records, founder and owner, 1972–2009.

the saxophonist's death in 1967. In the interim, Coltrane released several major albums, including *Interstellar Space* (1967), a duet with Ali that Scott Yanow of AllMusic.com called "full of fire, emotion and constant abstract invention." Following the shock of his partner's death, Ali worked for a time with Alice Coltrane, John's widow, and had a prominent role in the success of her 1968 album *A Monastic Trio*. By the early 1970s, however, he had also developed a strong interest in the business side of the music industry. His first steps in this direction came in 1972, when he founded his own label and recording studio, Survival Records. For the artists who recorded on Survival, most of them relatively unknown, Ali served as a producer, sound engineer, and mentor. The studio had another purpose, however. By recording his own albums there, he had more complete artistic control over the music—and a larger portion of the sales revenues—than he would have had in a more traditional arrangement. Two of Ali's albums from this period, a duet with Frank Lowe entitled *Duo Exchange* (1973) and a live album called *New Directions in Modern Music* (1973), won particularly strong reviews.

A year after the establishment of Survival, Ali opened his own jazz club, Ali's Alley, in New York's SoHo district. Well aware that few of the city's music venues welcomed free jazz, Ali set out to create a haven for those who appreciated the new style. It remained open for six years, closing in 1979 during a prolonged economic downturn.

From his base at Survival, Ali pursued a wide variety of projects in the 1980s and 1990s. Many of these involved collaborations with other noted free jazz artists. In the mid-to-late 1980s, for example, he joined saxophonist George Adams, guitarist James "Blood" Ulmer, and bassist Sirone to form the influential but short-lived group Phalanx. He then moved on to Prima Materia, a quintet focused on exploring the legacies of Coltrane and Ayler, and to several collaborations with artists in other genres, including the spoken-word

performer Henry Rollins and, in an ensemble called Purple Trap, the rock guitarist Keiji Haino. In 2003 he began touring as the Rashied Ali Quintet, a name that recalled an identically titled album from 1973. Among his most significant recordings in this period were the two-volume *Judgment Day* (2005 and 2006) and a live album released in 2009.

On August 12, 2009, Ali died after suffering a heart attack. Surviving him were two brothers, his wife Patricia, and nine children.

Selected discography

Archie Shepp, *On This Night,* Impulse!, 1965.
John Coltrane, *Meditations,* Impulse!, 1965.
John Coltrane, *Live in Japan,* Impulse!, 1966.
John Coltrane, *Expression,* Impulse!, 1967.
John Coltrane, *Interstellar Space,* Impulse!, 1967.
John Coltrane, *The Olatunji Concert,* Impulse!, 1967.
Alice Coltrane, *A Monastic Trio,* Impulse!, 1968.
(With Frank Lowe) *Duo Exchange,* Survival, 1973.
New Directions in Modern Music, Survival, 1973.
Rashied Ali Quintet, Survival, 1973.
Phalanx, *In Touch,* DIW, 1988.
Prima Materia, *Meditations,* Knitting Factory, 1995.
Henry Rollins, *Everything,* Spoken Ear, 1996.
The Rings of Saturn, Knitting Factory, 1999.
Purple Trap, *Decided ... Already the Motionless Heart of Tranquility, Tangling the Prayer Called "I,"* Tzadik, 1999.
Sonny Fortune, *In the Spirit of John Coltrane,* Shanachie, 2000.
Moon Flight, Knitting Factory, 2000.
No One in Particular, Survival, 2001.
Judgment Day: Vol. 1, Survival, 2005.
Judgment Day: Vol. 2, Survival, 2006.
Live in Europe, Survival, 2009.

Sources

Periodicals

New York Times, January 6, 1988, p. C18; August 14, 2009.

Online

Jung, Fred, "A Fireside Chat with Rashied Ali," JazzWeekly.com, http://www.jazzweekly.com/interviews/rali.htm (accessed November 12, 2009).

Kelsey, Chris, "Rashied Ali: Biography," AllMusic.com, http://allmusic.com/cg/amg.dll?p=amg&sql=11:aifoxqr5ldte (accessed November 12, 2009).

"R.I.P. Rashied Ali (1935–2009)," InLog.org, August 13, 2009, http://inlog.org/2009/08/13/r-i-p-rashied-ali-1935-2009/ (accessed November 12, 2009).

Yanow, Scott, "*Interstellar Space*: Review," AllMusic.
com, http://allmusic.com/cg/amg.dll?p=amg&sql
=10:gzfwxqtgldte (accessed November 12, 2009).

—R. Anthony Kugler

Eugene Allen

1919—

White House maitre d'

In 1986 Eugene Allen retired from his post as maitre d' at the White House after thirty-four years of serving eight presidents and their families. A former country club waiter, Allen began working at the official residence of the American presidents in 1952 during Harry S Truman's last year in office, and went on to become the White House butler and then maitre d'. In 2009 a major Hollywood studio acquired the film rights to Allen's exceptional story. The media interest was sparked by a *Washington Post* profile that ran a few days after the historic 2008 election of Barack Obama as the nation's first African-American president. Allen "was on the job in the days President Dwight D. Eisenhower had to deal with the Little Rock desegregation crisis," noted *Washington Post* writer Wil Haygood, also observing that Allen served when Martin Luther King Jr. was assassinated in Memphis, that he traveled with President Richard Nixon to Romania, and that he "joined in on President Gerald Ford's birthday parties at the White House because his own birthday falls on the same day."

Waiter at Elite Clubs

Born on July 14, 1919, Allen came from a farming family near Charlottesville, Virginia, and grew up in a deeply segregated South. "We had never had anything," he recalled in the *Washington Post* interview with Haygood. "I was always hoping things would get better." From an early age Allen knew the backbreaking labor of making a living from the land. "I wanted a regular job," he told another interviewer, *Sunday Tele-*

graph journalist Helena De Bertodano. He found a job as a waiter at the Homestead, a luxury resort in Hot Springs, Virginia. In the early 1940s, he moved to the Washington, DC, area, where he became a waiter at a private golf and tennis club and met his wife Helene, whom he married in 1943. In 1952 an acquaintance mentioned that President Truman would be moving back into the White House soon after its renovation and would likely need additional household staff. "I wasn't even looking for a job," Allen recalled in the interview with Haygood. "I was happy where I was working, but she told me to go on over there and meet with a guy by the name of Alonzo Fields."

Fields was also an African American and had worked at the White House since the early 1930s. He gave Allen a tour and offered him a job as pantryman. Allen passed the extensive background check required for those who worked in such close proximity to U.S. presidents and their families and started work. In 1952 segregated schools were still legal in the United States, including the District of Columbia, which was home to the nation's capital but culturally still very much a Southern city. As elsewhere in the pre–civil rights era South, African Americans made up the majority of food-service professionals and domestic household workers.

As pantryman, Allen's duties included washing dishes and shining the White House silverware. In 1953 Dwight D. Eisenhower and his wife Mamie moved in as the new presidential family. Eisenhower used his con-

At a Glance . . .

Born on July 14, 1919, near Charlottesville, VA; son of a farmer; married in 1943; wife's name, Helene; children: Charles.

Career: The Homestead (Hot Springs, VA), waiter, early 1940s; waiter at a Washington, DC–area country club, 1942(?)–52; began at the White House in 1952 as a pantryman; promoted to butler; became maitre d', 1980; retired, 1986.

Addresses: *Home*—Washington, DC. *Agent*—International Creative Management, 825 8th Ave., New York, NY 10019.

stitutional power to desegregate the District of Columbia by executive order. The desegregation order included the District's public schools, which Allen's son, Charles, would shortly be attending, and predated the U.S. Supreme Court's landmark desegregation ruling in *Brown v. Board of Education* in May of 1954. Alonzo Fields retired during the Eisenhower years, and Allen was promoted to White House butler in his place.

Served through Eight Administrations

In 1961 John F. Kennedy and his wife, Jacqueline, brought their two young children to the White House, a major event for the White House staff. "When President Kennedy got shot was a terrible day," Allen recalled of the 1963 assassination in the *Sunday Telegraph* interview. Jacqueline Kennedy invited him to the president's funeral, he told De Bertodano, "but I said I'd stay at the White House as somebody had to be there to prepare for everyone coming back afterwards." Kennedy's successor, Lyndon B. Johnson, walked his daughter Lynda Bird Johnson down the aisle in the East Room in December of 1967, in the first wedding at the White House in fifty-three years. Allen stayed on the job through the presidency of Richard M. Nixon, who arrived at the White House in 1969. Nixon was elected to a second term in 1972, but was forced to resign in 1974. "The morning he left he got the whole staff on the second floor where he lived," Allen recalled in the *Sunday Telegraph* interview. "He said how sorry he was to leave the White House; he said if he was a millionaire he'd make all of us rich."

Following the Ford presidency, a school-age resident arrived at the White House in 1977 in the person of Amy Carter, daughter of former Georgia governor Jimmy Carter. During the Carter administration Allen

became the White House maitre d', which gave him responsibility for the frequent state dinners. He recalled working with First Lady Nancy Reagan, saying in the *Sunday Telegraph* interview, "I would ask her if she'd picked out the china for it and she'd say, 'No you do it, you know more about it than I do.'" Allen retired during the Reagan presidency, and the Reagans later invited Allen and his wife, Helene, to be their guests at a state dinner for West German chancellor Helmut Kohl.

Allen often worked six days a week, and at times those days stretched to sixteen-hour shifts making sure all events ran smoothly. It was a prestigious job, but not a lucrative one. "When I started out I was making $2,400," he told De Bertodano. "It was the same as my basic salary in my previous job but I made a lot more in tips before. When I left I was probably on $33,000." Allen retired in 1986 and spent the next two decades enjoying time with his wife at their home in northwest DC, where Allen's position had been a point of pride for the neighborhood. Both the Allens were interviewed by Haygood for the *Washington Post* article just a few days before the 2008 election, and they said they were looking forward to walking to the local polling station on November 4 to cast their votes for the first African-American presidential contender in U.S. history.

Invited to Obama Inauguration

Tragically, Allen made the journey by himself on Election Day. Helene, his wife of sixty-six years, died in her sleep on November 3, 2008. "She had a doctor's appointment at 9 o'clock," a grieving Allen said in the *Sunday Telegraph* interview. "I said 'It's time to get up.' She didn't reply. She couldn't. I knew she was sick but I didn't think she was sick like that. On Sunday night we both went to sleep and on Monday morning I woke up and she didn't." Haygood's *Washington Post* story ran on Friday, November 7. The moving tale of Allen's solo visit to the polls prompted a special invitation to the Obama inauguration from the Joint Congressional Committee on Inaugural Ceremonies. Allen attended with his son Charles, a State Department employee, and his daughter-in-law. "I've served a lot of presidents," Allen told Haygood on the chilly January day, "but I've never been to an inauguration."

Sources

Periodicals

Daily Variety, April 30, 2009, p. 2.
Sunday Telegraph (London), December 28, 2008, p. 11.
Times (London), January 19, 2009, p. 4.
Washington Post, November 7, 2008, p. A1; January 21, 2009, p. C1.

Online

"White House Worker Subject of Major Film," Smith-sonian Institution Traveling Exhibition Service, http://www.shows2go.si.edu/exhibitions/2008/11/white-house-worker-subject-of-major-film.html (accessed October 20, 2009).

—Carol Brennan

Lee Archer Jr.

1919—

Military pilot, corporate executive

Archer, Lee, Jr., photograph. AP Images.

Lee A. Archer Jr. is the only confirmed "ace" of the Tuskegee Airmen, a group of African-American pilots trained at Tuskegee Institute in Alabama for World War II. To have an ace record, a pilot must shoot down five enemy aircraft in one-on-one combat, which is confirmed by gun camera films. Archer also earned more than eighteen medals for heroism and received special citations from Presidents Eisenhower, Kennedy, and Johnson. After twenty-nine years of service to the U.S. military, he became a highly successful corporate executive.

Born on September 6, 1919, in Yonkers, New York, to Lee Archer Sr. and May Piper, Lee Archer Jr. grew up a few miles south of his birthplace in the New York City neighborhood of Harlem. After excelling in his studies in high school, Archer enrolled at New York University (NYU) to study international relations, but by 1941, war was imminent, and Archer became interested in flying for the military. However, Archer was barred from pilot training because the Army Air Corps (the precursor to the Air Force) was recruiting only white men. Archer took and passed the entrance tests—both physical and mental—but was relegated to being a regular enlistee in the Army. He was assigned to a training camp in Macon, Georgia, and became a specialist in field network communications.

Became an Ace Fighter Pilot

Archer realized his dream of flying through the efforts of the "Black Press," as it was then known, and to which he feels forever indebted. Editorials in publications catering to African Americans questioned why blacks could not be admitted to pilot training. As Archer recalled in an interview for the National Visionary Leadership Project, "they raised particular hell about it." By May of 1942, as Archer explained, President Roosevelt had issued an executive order to establish the Civilian Pilot Training Program (CPTP) at six historically black colleges. Of the enlistees in the CPTP, the Army Air Corps selected well-qualified African-American men to train at an air base that had been built adjoining Tuskegee Institute, a historically black college with a highly respected aeronautical engineering program. This was the birth of the Tuskegee Airmen, the first African-American military flyers.

Archer was one of two hundred applicants for the Army Air Corps; on the entrance exam, his score was the second highest. By July of 1943 Archer graduated first in his class, earned his wings, and became a Tuskegee Airman with the 302nd Fighter Squadron, 332nd Fighter Group. Naming his plane "Ina the Macon Belle" in honor of his wife, Ina, he flew one hundred and sixty-nine combat missions over more than eleven countries. While his "ace" status was not officially established until 1992, he was awarded the Distinguished Flying Cross, the Air Medal with 18 Oak

Leaf Clusters (meaning that he received this award eighteen times subsequent to the first), and the Distinguished Unit Citation. All three awards denote heroism in action. Archer also received Special Citations from Presidents Eisenhower, Kennedy, and Johnson.

Archer's distinguished military career continued after the war ended. He was assigned to the Tuskegee Army Air Field as chief of the Instrument Instructor School. Later, the army sent Archer to the University of California at Los Angeles to complete his bachelor's degree before assigning him to a variety of high-level international positions, including chief of protocol for the French Liaison Office, Supreme Headquarters Allied Powers Europe, and White House Air Force–France project officer.

Retired from the Military to Business

Archer retired from the military in 1970 and began a second career in business with General Foods Corporation that same year. His first position with the company was as a manager of urban affairs, and he was quickly promoted to director of urban affairs in 1971. General Foods then appointed Archer president of one of their small business investment companies, Vanguard Capital Corporation. By 1973 he was promoted again, this time to chairman and CEO of Vanguard Capital. By 1975 Archer was a vice president at General Foods and by 1980 he had attained full General Foods corporate vice president status.

In 1983 Archer joined with a group of other prominent African-American businessmen under the leadership of entrepreneur Reginald Lewis to purchase the McCall Pattern Company. Two years later the group acquired Beatrice International Foods, which became the largest minority owned and controlled business in the United States. In 1988 Archer founded two of his own companies: Archer Associates and Organization Publishing Company. Archer was formally recognized in 2006 for his pioneering achievements in minority business when he was given the ROBIE Lifetime Achievement Award by the Jackie Robinson Foundation. In 2009 Archer was again honored by being made a Millennium Member of the Reginald F. Lewis Foundation, a philanthropic organization that gives large grants to nonprofit organizations and is primarily involved with funding projects for African Americans.

When asked in an interview for the National Visionary Leadership Project what he believed were his greatest accomplishments, Archer first recognized his becoming a command pilot, noting that "to get there did some doing, especially under the conditions of it." Those conditions, of course, were segregation, discrimination, and racial prejudice. He then talked about his wife, the love of his life, to whom he was married for fifty-two years until her passing. He concluded the interview with a smile, remarking that another great accomplishment of his life was "especially the raising of four kids without them getting in trouble … yet." And his advice to youth? "Education, education. … It's the basis of all success."

Sources

Periodicals

Jet, March 27, 2006, p. 14.
Pitt Chronicle, February 11, 2008, p. 1.

Online

"Gala Luncheon, Saturday, June 13, 2009," Reginald F. Lewis Foundation, http://www.reginaldflewis. com/assets/June-13-Gala-Luncheon-Invitation.pdf
Lee Archer Collection, Veterans History Project, American Folklife Center, Library of Congress, http://lcweb2.loc.gov/diglib/vhp/bib/loc.natlib. afc2001001.44004.
"Lee Archer: National Visionary," National Visionary Leadership Project Oral History Archive, http:// www.visionaryproject.org/archerlee/

—Sandra Alters

Jennifer Baszile

1969(?)—

Writer

Jennifer Baszile left her post at Yale University to explore her family's history in *The Black Girl Next Door: A Memoir* (Simon & Schuster, 2009). Baszile's book recounts her growing up in the 1970s and 1980s in Southern California, where hers was one of just a handful of African-American households in her affluent community. Told from a child's point of view, the memoir exposes the outsider status Baszile suffered despite the financial and social success her parents had achieved. "The book is really about that period in American life when integration was made real by children, black and white," Baszile told Grace Laidlaw, a writer for the alumni magazine *Columbia College Today.*

Born in the late 1960s, Baszile was the younger of two daughters born to Janet, a schoolteacher originally from Detroit, and Barry Baszile, who came from rural Louisiana. Baszile's father was in sales and went on to launch his own metals business during her childhood. The family's fortunes improved steadily, and they moved from Carson, a predominantly black suburb south of Los Angeles where the smog was terrible during this era, to Palos Verdes, an peninsular ocean-front enclave. The lush and hilly landscapes of the Palos Verdes communities offered much better air quality and top-notch public schools for Baszile and her older sister, Natalie.

Stunned by Hate Crime

For years Baszile and her sister were the only African-American students in their schools. They first attended Vista Grande Elementary School, where Baszile began first grade in 1975, but in 1976 their parents bought a larger, much grander home in posh Palos Verdes Estates. "We had moved into a neighborhood so exclusive that it had neither sidewalks nor street lamps," Baszile writes in *The Black Girl Next Door.* "We moved up to live among new neighbors, dressed in golf shirts and tennis whites, who took their purebred dogs for after-dinner strolls. We all hoped that, with a move to the more exclusive town of Palos Verdes Estates, we had outrun race. We were sorely mistaken."

A few weeks after the Basziles moved in, someone painted the words "Go home" and a racial epithet on the front walk. "I had never experienced hatred in this way: plural, intimate, and anonymous at the same time," she wrote. "Fear seized my empty stomach and my eyes stung. My parents had taught me that people who used those words were white trash, rednecks, or crackers. Until that moment, I thought that they lived somewhere else." A few weeks earlier her parents had brushed off another incident, in which the cherub in their courtyard fountain was painted black, as a prank. This time, Baszile's father called the police and notified the local newspaper. The *Palos Verdes Peninsula News* ran a story, complete with a photograph of Baszile's father kneeling beside the graffiti. Baszile's mother—known in the household for her cool reserve and steely determination—affixed the story to a piece of poster board. "Then Mom taped her project on our mailbox for all the twilight dog walkers and evening

At a Glance . . .

Born 1969(?); daughter of Barrow (a business owner) and Janet (a teacher) Baszile; one son. *Education:* Columbia University, BA, 1991; Princeton University, PhD, 1999.

Career: Yale University, assistant professor of history and African-American studies, 1999–2007.

Addresses: *Home*—Connecticut. *Office*—c/o Author Mail, Simon & Schuster, Inc., 1230 Avenue of the Americas, New York, NY 10020.

strollers to read," Baszile wrote. "The paint was gone, but she wanted the community to bear the shame she refused to feel."

There were no more shocking hate crimes, but Baszile grew up feeling conflicted about her race. She had just one set of cousins in the Los Angeles area, and saw her parents' respective families on intermittent trips to Michigan and Louisiana. She recalled one particularly painful incident during her early teens—this one caused by her parents. Aboard a luxury cruise for a family vacation, Baszile and her sister had socialized with other teens the first few days. Their father seemed especially incensed that Natalie had been spending time with a boy who was white, and in a cabin-room dressing-down he railed against interracial dating. Then their mother informed the girls that they would not be allowed back into their cabin until they had introduced themselves to *every* other young black passenger on board the ship. After so many years of being told that race should never be a factor in their lives or achievements, "my parents flipped the script," Baszile wrote. "They were saying, 'We *know* that you are *not* black enough.'"

Drawn to History

That 1982 vacation prompted Baszile's parents to join together with some other African-American households in Palos Verdes to form the Black Heritage Association, or BHA. Baszile's mother served as youth coordinator for monthly teen meetings of about two dozen students from three area high schools. The group quickly emerged as an unofficial clique. "Even though most of us tried to play it fairly cool in the beginning, we were pretty glad to get together," she wrote in her memoir. The BHA seemed such a novel idea that the *Los Angeles Times* ran a story on it in 1985. Baszile, then in the tenth grade at Palos Verdes

High School, spoke about the presentations members delivered at meetings. The heritage of African Americans is "more than just slavery," the future history professor told reporter Ann Johnson. "There's a self-esteem in learning those things and a sense of importance."

Baszile's sister was the first African-American homecoming queen at Palos Verdes High School, and Baszile was the first black to be elected student body president. Her sister went on to college at the University of California in Berkeley, but Baszile yearned to distance herself from her parents' resolve to imprint on their daughters their own determination to succeed, which she found oppressive. "Rage and fury fueled my parents' intrepid drive for achievement as much as ambition did." After interviewing at several East Coast colleges, Baszile fell in love with Columbia University's urban campus and persuaded her parents to let her enroll there. She graduated from Palos Verdes High School in 1987, recalling that by that point "I barely felt anything except relief that it was over.... My days as the black girl next door had come to an end."

"I'd Lost My Passion"

Baszile graduated from Columbia and received her doctoral degree in history from Princeton University. From 1999 to 2007 she taught history at Yale University in Connecticut, becoming the first African-American woman in that department. In 2007 she left Yale and began work on her memoir. The idea for the book had come a few years earlier, Baszile explained in an interview for her book's Web site, The Black Girl Next Door, "when I recalled a picture of myself at age four or five and began to cry. I couldn't get the picture out of my mind. I was at a turning point in my career because my work as a college professor had become unfulfilling. I couldn't figure out why I'd lost my passion. Then I realized that I was a professional historian running from my past."

The Black Girl Next Door earned Baszile critical accolades. "The theme of self-definition runs throughout this memoir," wrote Sandra Lee Jamison in the *New York Times*. "The identity of 'the black girl next door' is thrust on Jennifer by circumstance. She struggles and ultimately achieves her own identity, perhaps not following the path envisioned for her but definitively finding her place in the world—a world that lies beyond the neighborhood her parents fought so hard for her to live in."

Selected works

The Black Girl Next Door: A Memoir, Touchstone/ Simon & Schuster, 2009.

Sources

Books

Baszile, Jennifer, *The Black Girl Next Door,* Touchstone/Simon & Schuster, 2009.

Periodicals

Los Angeles Times, May 26, 1985.
New York Times, January 9, 2009; February 8, 2009.
Publishers Weekly, September 15, 2008, p. 58.

Online

Laidlaw, Grace, "Jennifer Baszile '91 Teaches History Through Memoir," Columbia College Today, May/June 2009, http://www.college.columbia.edu/cct/may_jun09/bookshelf2 (accessed October 20, 2009).
"The Author," The Black Girl Next Door, http://www.theblackgirlnextdoor.com/author.php (accessed October 20, 2009).

—Carol Brennan

Big Daddy Kane

1968—

Rap musician, actor

Big Daddy Kane, photograph. Ray Tamarra/Getty Images.

Big Daddy Kane has played a prominent role in rap music since the 1980s. With witty rhymes and unabashed bravado, the New York native helped set the genre's dominant tone as it grew from a neighborhood pastime to a worldwide phenomenon. After a string of hit albums and several film roles, he largely withdrew from public life in the early 2000s. In the summer of 2009, however, he reappeared for a major concert in his hometown.

Kane was born Antonio Hardy on September 10, 1968, in the New York City borough of Brooklyn. Though he was raised in the struggling neighborhood of Bedford-Stuyvesant, known as Bed-Stuy, his family background was solidly middle class; his father worked as a truck driver and his mother as a registered nurse. Both parents were avid music fans, and it was through their record collection that Kane first experienced many of the artists he would later consider major influences on his own work. Chief among these was R&B singer Barry White, with whom he would later collaborate.

By the time Kane reached high school in the early 1980s, rap was spreading quickly. On street corners throughout Brooklyn, teens traded rhymes and rhythms. Kane was an enthusiastic participant in these contests, and his talent at rhyming and wordplay soon attracted attention. In 1984 he met the slightly older rapper Biz Markie, who became his close friend and mentor. It was in this period, too, that he adopted his stage name.

Within weeks of their initial meeting, Kane and Markie were appearing together at schools and community events around Brooklyn. With his friend's assistance, Kane met Marley Marl, a producer associated with Cold Chillin' Records and the Juice Crew; the latter was a loose rap collective, one of the most prominent members of which was Roxanne Shanté. Impressed with his rhymes and stage persona, Shanté asked Kane to accompany her on her 1985 tour. In addition to performing alongside her, he wrote a considerable portion of her lyrics. Following the tour he worked in a similar capacity for other members of the Juice Crew and for Kurtis Blow, one of the first rappers to achieve national fame. The success of those efforts, in turn, prompted Cold Chillin' to offer Kane a record contract in 1987. His first single, "Raw," appeared the next year, as did his debut album, *Long Live the Kane*.

At a Glance . . .

Born Antonio Hardy on September 10, 1968, in Brooklyn, NY; children: two.

Career: Rapper and writer for Roxanne Shanté, the Juice Crew, and Kurtis Blow, 1985–87; independent recording artist, 1987—; film actor, 1993—.

Awards: Grammy Award for Best Rap Performance by a Duo or Group, co-winner, 1990, for "Back on the Block."

Addresses: *Agent*—Red Entertainment Agency, 16 Penn Plaza, Ste. 824, New York, NY 10001. *Web*—http://www.officialbigdaddykane.com.

Noting, in particular, Kane's "articulate precision and locomotive power," Stanton Swihart of AllMusic.com would call the record "one of the most appealing creations from the original new school of rap."

Long Live the Kane reached number five on *Billboard* magazine's list of the nation's top R&B albums. Kane's follow-up effort, *It's a Big Daddy Thing,* did even better, peaking at number four and spawning no fewer than three hit singles ("I Get the Job Done," "Rap Summary (Lean on Me)," and "Smooth Operator"). In the album's wake, Kane embarked on a national tour with rap legends Public Enemy and LL Cool J. He also began appearing in the media in nonmusical contexts. Some of these were mildly controversial. In 1991, for example, he was photographed for *Playgirl* magazine. Similar photos appeared the following year in the pop star Madonna's book *Sex.* More troubling for some members of the public were the sentiments implicit in some of Kane's lyrics, particularly on the subject of homosexuality. Accusations of homophobia were relatively muted, however, and the controversy seemed to have little effect on Kane's popularity, either with critics or the public. In 1990 he won a Grammy Award for his work on "Back on the Block," a track on an album of the same name by the legendary impresario Quincy Jones. The song, an innovative mix of jazz, pop, and rap, was named the Best Rap Performance by a Duo or Group.

Kane's third album, 1990's *Taste of Chocolate,* had a more soulful, romantic sound than his earlier efforts, thanks in part to White's participation. While it sold well, as did his two subsequent albums (1991's *Prince of Darkness* and 1993's *Looks Like a Job for ...*), Kane struggled to match the critical and commercial success of his first albums. Perhaps in response to the pressure he faced, Kane took a break around 1993 to

focus on acting. He won significant roles in two Hollywood films released that year, a western called *Posse* and *The Meteor Man,* a comedy. After releasing another album, *Daddy's Home,* in 1994, he spent most of the next few years with his family. Then in 1998 he released *Veteranz Day,* his seventh major album. While it garned positive reviews, its sales were modest. Widespread rumors at the time suggested that Kane intended the album to be his last. That supposition gained credence some months later, when he moved with his family from New York to North Carolina.

Once settled in his new home, Kane pursued a variety of personal interests and business opportunities. Most of these were relatively low profile. Producers for music and film projects sought him out, however, and in 2007 he accepted a starring role in *Dead Heist,* an action movie from Swirl Films. The following year he appeared in *Love for Sale,* also from Swirl, and was the subject of a biographical documentary, *BDK*; the latter was directed by Anthony Marshall under the auspices of Scion Easy Ten, a film venture underwritten by Toyota Motor Corporation's Scion division. As of the summer of 2009, a clip from the film had been viewed more than seventeen thousand times on YouTube alone.

In August of 2009 Kane was profiled in the *New York Times* in conjunction with his appearance at Celebrate Brooklyn, a concert series held in that borough's Prospect Park. His first major public performance in a number of years, it attracted more than six thousand people. Whether the event marked a return to the music industry was unclear. Kane's interest in film projects, on the other hand, appeared as robust as ever; according to the Web site IMDB.com, he was involved in at least two films yet to be released.

Selected works

Albums

Long Live the Kane (includes "Raw"), Cold Chillin', 1988.
It's a Big Daddy Thing (includes "I Get the Job Done," "Rap Summary (Lean on Me)," and "Smooth Operator"), Cold Chillin', 1989.
Quincy Jones, *Back on the Block* (includes "Back on the Block"), Qwest, 1989.
Taste of Chocolate, Cold Chillin', 1990.
Prince of Darkness, Cold Chillin', 1991.
Looks Like a Job for ..., Cold Chillin', 1993.
Daddy's Home, MCA, 1994.
Veteranz Day, Blackheart, 1998.

Films

Posse, Polygram Filmed Entertainment, 1993.
The Meteor Man, MGM, 1993.
Dead Heist, Swirl Films, 2007.

Love for Sale, Swirl Films, 2008.
BDK (short documentary), Scion Easy Ten, 2008.

Sources

Periodicals

New York Times, August 10, 2009, p. A13.
Rolling Stone, January 10, 1991.

Online

"*BDK* Unofficial Teaser," Youtube.com, January 25, 2009, http://www.youtube.com/watch?v=aIJoAC eISDM (accessed November 13, 2009).

"Big Daddy Kane Biography," OfficialBigDaddyKane. com, http://officialbigdaddykane.com/ (accessed November 13, 2009).

"Big Daddy Kane," IMDB.com, http://www.imdb. com/name/nm0437263/ (accessed November 13, 2009).

"Big Daddy Kane" (interview), UrbanSmarts.com, April 17, 2004, http://www.urbansmarts.com/in terviews/bigdaddykane.htm (accessed November 13, 2009).

Huey, Steve, "Big Daddy Kane: Biography," AllMusic. com, http://allmusic.com/cg/amg.dll?p=amg&sql =11:difqxq95ld6e (accessed November 13, 2009).

Swihart, Stanton, "*Long Live the Kane*: Review," AllMusic.com, http://allmusic.com/cg/amg.dll?p= amg&sql=10:3pfrxqy5ldse (accessed November 13, 2009).

—R. Anthony Kugler

David Blackwell

1919—

Mathematician, educator

Professor David Blackwell has been at the forefront of mathematics for more than sixty-five years. A longtime chair of the statistics department at the University of California—Berkeley, his groundbreaking work in game theory has influenced developments in national defense, finance, and other fields.

David Harold Blackwell was born April 24, 1919, in Centralia, Illinois, a small town in the south-central region of the state. His father, Grover Blackwell, was a highly skilled worker on the engines of the Illinois Central Railroad. His mother, Mabel Johnson Blackwell, oversaw the household and the rearing of the couple's four children, of whom David was the eldest. Education was always a priority for the family, and care was taken to ensure that the children attended one of the area's few integrated schools, which were much better supplied and funded than the segregated institutions nearby.

Blackwell's talent in math was clear even before he reached high school. It was there, however, that his love for the subject really developed. A pivotal moment in that regard came in geometry class. In comments quoted in 1985 by Michael A. Guillen in the *New York Times*, Blackwell paid homage to the teacher in that course for helping him "see that mathematics is really beautiful." After finishing high school in three years, he entered the University of Illinois (UI), intent on a teaching career.

UI became the site of Blackwell's enthusiastic initiation into the esoteric world of higher mathematics. He received his bachelor's degree in the subject in 1938, a year early; his speed in completing the requirements was particularly remarkable given the numerous part-time jobs he had to take to defray tuition costs. After receiving a master's degree in 1939, he began work on a doctoral dissertation under the well-known mathematician Joe Doob. Two years later he received his Ph.D.

Blackwell's first position after UI was at the Institute for Advanced Study (Princeton, New Jersey), known internationally as the home of such luminaries as Albert Einstein. After serving there for a year (1941–42) as a Rosenwald Fellow, he began a systematic job search, a daunting task given the era's pervasive racism. Convinced that no integrated institution would consider him for a permanent academic position, he applied only to African-American schools. After a brief stint (1942–43) at Southern University in Louisiana, he spent a year at Clark College in Atlanta, Georgia, before moving to Howard University in 1944. He remained there for a decade, winning a rapid series of promotions. By 1950 he was a full professor and the chair of his department. His work, meanwhile, was increasingly focused on statistics and probability, particularly as they applied to games and game-like situations. His interest in game theory, as the field became known, was sparked by his work over three summers (1948–50) for the Rand Corporation, a prominent research organization with close ties to the federal government and the military.

While grateful to Howard for the success he had found there, Blackwell began to yearn for a position that better reflected his new interests. He found one in 1954, when the University of California at Berkeley

At a Glance . . .

Born David Harold Blackwell on April 24, 1919, in Centralia, IL; son of Grover Blackwell (a railroad worker) and Mabel Johnson Blackwell (a homemaker); married Ann Madison, 1944; children: eight. *Education:* University of Illinois, BA, mathematics, 1938, MA, mathematics, 1939, PhD, mathematics, 1941.

Career: Institute for Advanced Study, Rosenwald Fellow, 1941–42; Clark College, instructor, 1942–43; Southern University, instructor, 1943–44; Howard University, assistant professor, 1944–46, associate professor, 1946–47, professor and department chair, 1947–54; Rand Corporation, mathematician, 1948–50 (summers); University of California—Berkeley, visiting professor, 1954–55, professor (statistics), 1955–73, professor (statistics and mathematics), 1973–89, emeritus professor, 1989—.

Memberships: National Academy of Sciences; American Academy of Arts and Sciences; Institute of Mathematical Statistics; American Statistical Association.

Awards: John von Neumann Theory Prize, Institute for Operations Research and the Management Sciences, 1979; R. A. Fisher Lectureship, Committee of Presidents of Statistical Societies, 1986; Blackwell-Tapia Prize established in his honor, Mathematical Sciences Research Institute (University of California—Berkeley) and Cornell University, 2002; many honorary degrees.

Addresses: *Office*—c/o Department of Statistics, 367 Evans Hall, University of California–Berkeley, Berkeley, CA 94720-3860.

offered him a professorship in its statistics department. After a year as a visiting professor, he became a full professor in 1955. Aside from occasional sabbaticals and other temporary postings, Berkeley remained his home for the rest of his career. In 1973 his appointment was modified to give him joint standing in both the statistics and the mathematics departments. Sixteen years later, on his retirement from active teaching duties, he became professor emeritus.

Blackwell began publishing in mathematics journals in the 1940s. In the early 1950s he completed his first book, *Theory of Games and Statistical Decisions*, which he co-wrote with his friend and colleague M. A.

Girshick. In a sign of the book's lasting influence on college campuses nationwide, a revision was issued roughly twenty-five years after its initial publication in 1954. Blackwell also wrote a widely used textbook, *Basic Statistics* (1969), as well as dozens of papers and mathematical proofs. In about 1970 he published a game theory proof of the Kuratowski Reduction Theorem, an important concept in the branch of mathematics known as topology. In an interview included in the 1985 volume *Mathematical People*, Blackwell recalled the "real joy" he felt in "connecting these two fields [game theory and topology] that had not been previously connected."

Though difficult to quantify, the impact of Blackwell's work outside mathematics has been significant. The game theory he embraced in its infancy has been applied to a variety of fields, notably national defense—the reason for the Rand Corporation's early interest—and finance. An Internet search for "game theory" and "finance" in September of 2009 generated more than three quarters of a million hits.

Blackwell has received a host of awards over the years. In 1965 he was elected to the National Academy of Sciences (NAS), an honor given to only a tiny fraction of the nation's researchers. According to its Web site, the NAS was "chartered by Congress in 1863 as a private, nonprofit, non-governmental organization set up to advise the government and the nation on scientific and technological matters." Blackwell was the first African-American mathematician to be elected to its ranks. Other honors have included the 1979 John von Neumann Theory Prize, from what later became known as the Institute for Operations Research and the Management Sciences; the 1986 R. A. Fisher Lectureship, an annual award of the Committee of Presidents of Statistical Societies; and at least a dozen honorary degrees.

A dedicated and enthusiastic teacher, Blackwell was known throughout his career for his willingness to teach introductory courses as well as advanced seminars. His commitment to advising and mentoring activities, particularly among minority undergraduates, was recognized in 2002 when Berkeley's Mathematical Sciences Research Institute (MSRI), in conjunction with Cornell University, honored him (and fellow mathematician Richard A. Tapia) by establishing the Blackwell-Tapia Prize. According to MSRI's Web site, the biennial honor is given to "a mathematical scientist who has contributed significantly to his or her field of expertise, and who has served as a role model for mathematical scientists and students from under-represented minority groups."

In 1942 Blackwell married Ann Madison, with whom he had eight children. As of 2009, he resided, a widower, in northern California.

Selected writings

(With M. A. Girshick) *Theory of Games and Statistical Decisions,* Wiley, 1954.
Basic Statistics, McGraw-Hill, 1969.

Sources

Books

Albers, Donald J., and G. L. Alexanderson, *Mathematical People: Profiles and Interviews,* Birkhauser, 1985, p. 26.

Periodicals

New York Times, June 30, 1985.

Online

"Arlie O. Petters Receives First Blackwell-Tapia Prize," MSRI.org, July 25, 2002, http://www.msri.org/people/staff/meggin/pettersannounce.html (accessed November 12, 2009).

"Biography: David Blackwell," Berkeley.edu, http://www.stat.berkeley.edu/images/stories/docs/blackwell packet.pdf (accessed November 12, 2009).

"David Harold Blackwell: National Visionary," VisionaryProject.org, http://www.visionaryproject.org/blackwelldavid/ (accessed November 12, 2009).

"Frequently Asked Questions," NAS.edu, http://dels.nas.edu/dels/view.cgi?page=faq (accessed November 12, 2009).

Wilmot, Nadine, "An Oral History with David Blackwell", Berkeley.edu, 2003, http://digitalassets.lib.berkeley.edu/roho/ucb/text/BlackwellBook.pdf (accessed November 12, 2009).

—R. Anthony Kugler

Omar Bongo

1935–2009

Head of State

Bongo, Omar, photograph. Georges Gobet/AFP/Getty Images.

In the year of his death, 2009, Omar Bongo held the distinction of having been the world's longest-ruling head of state, excluding monarchs, and was the longest-serving president of any African country, having held this office in Gabon for forty-two years. During Bongo's years in power, he led his country to relative prosperity and political stability. At the same time, many of his political opponents died mysteriously, elections were said to be rigged, and he was accused of using his country's oil revenues to amass a vast personal fortune.

Entered Politics at a Young Age

The youngest of twelve children, Albert-Bernard Bongo was born in 1935 to peasant parents in what was then a French colony. He completed his primary and secondary education in Brazzaville, which was near his hometown of Lewai. After this schooling and some study of telecommunications at a technical college, he worked at the Post and Telecommunications Public Services in Gabon before beginning his military training. Ultimately Bongo achieved the rank of lieutenant in the French Air Force.

Gabon achieved its independence from France in 1960. Bongo immediately seized the opportunity to begin his political career in the now-independent nation, first working in the Ministry of Foreign Affairs under president Léon M'Ba. He used this position as a stepping stone to begin his ascent up Gabon's political ladder, subsequently attaining appointments to a series of junior cabinet posts. In 1966 M'Ba promoted the thirty-year-old Bongo to vice president. President M'Ba died the next year after a serious illness, and young Bongo succeeded him as president. In addition to serving as head of state, Bongo served as prime minister and held other cabinet posts concurrently with his presidency.

Shortly after becoming president, Bongo established a single-party system under the rule of the Parti Democratique Gabonais (PDG). The party's motto was "Dialogue-Tolerance-Peace," and the group's principles included national unity and the abolition of ethnic and tribal discrimination

Won Presidency under Single-Party System

In 1973 Bongo dissolved the National Assembly (the

At a Glance . . .

Born Albert-Bernard Bongo on December 30, 1935, in Lewai (now Bongoville), the territory of Gabon in French Equatorial Africa (now Gabon); died June 8, 2009, in Barcelona, Spain; name changed to El Hadj Omar, 1973; Ondimba added to surname, 2003; son of peasant parents; married Louise Mouyabi Moukala, 1955 (divorced 1959); married Marie Josephine Kama, a.k.a. Patience Dabany, 1959 (divorced 1986); married Edith Lucie Sassou-Nguesso, 1990 (died March 14, 2009); children: Pascaline Mferri Bongo Ondimba (born to first wife); Alain Bernard Bongo (president of Gabon 2009—) and Albertine Amissa Bongo (born to second wife); nine children born to third wife; approximately fifteen children born to other women. *Military service:* French Air Force, lieutenant, 1958–60. *Politics:* Gabonese Democratic Party *Religion:* Islam.

Career: Ministry of Foreign Affairs, 1960–62; assistant director of the presidential cabinet, 1962; director of the presidential cabinet 1962–65; presidential representative of defense and coordination, 1965–66; minister of information and tourism, 1966; vice president, 1966–67; president, 1967–2009; minister of the interior (1967–70); prime minister (1967–75); minister of planning (1967–77); minister of information (1967–80); minister of defense (1967–81).

sole legislative body at the time) and reestablished it with seventy members rather than its original forty-nine. He also increased the number of other government posts and appointed three new ministers. Although elections should have been held in 1974, seven years after Bongo took office, they were held in 1973, with Bongo the sole candidate for president.

Despite Bongo's autocratic rule, the Gabonese people were happy with the country's political stability and prosperity. Politically, the one-party system helped temper regional and tribal rivalries and promote unity. In addition, Bongo maintained a delicate ethnic balance in his administration. Rich natural resources—primarily oil—resulted in a relatively high standard of living for most people. To help funnel some of the oil revenues to the Gabonese people, Bongo's government demanded state participation in the foreign oil companies operating in Gabon, enforced the employment of native Gabonese people in managerial positions, and negotiated advantageous terms for the use of Gabon's natural

resources. All the while, Bongo, his family, and the upper class of his Bateke tribe appeared to be amassing personal fortunes from oil revenues. Nonetheless, under these conditions and the single-party rule, Bongo and all PDG candidates won the 1973 election by a landslide. These conditions prevailed for quite some time, and Bongo easily won re-election in 1979 as well.

After the 1979 election, the first organized, although illegal, opposition party surfaced. This group was called the Mouvement de redressement national, or Movement for National Restoration (MORENA). MORENA accused Bongo of corruption, personal extravagance, and favoring his own Bateke tribe; the group demanded that a multi-party system be restored. By 1982 thirty-seven MORENA members had been tried and convicted of offenses against state security, and Bongo remained committed to one-party rule.

Unrest Built among Gabonese

Although conditions within Gabon remained relatively favorable through the 1986 election, which Bongo and other PDG candidates won handily again, unrest built among the Gabonese. Conditions worsened as oil prices dropped precipitously and Gabon experienced a serious economic downturn. This downturn forced the government to impose compulsory reductions in public sector salaries in late 1988, which resulted in strikes by the staff of Air Gabon (the national airline) and other public sector employees. Negotiation resolved the situation, but labor unrest continued as the government was forced to introduce austerity budgets for 1989 and 1990. The undercurrent of unrest became a sizeable opposition movement.

In September of 1989 a conspiracy to overthrow Bongo involved senior members of the security forces and prominent public officials acting on behalf of Pierre Mamboundou, leader of a little-known opposition group based in Paris, the Union des peuples gabonais (UPG). Shortly after two leaders in the conspiracy plot died suddenly—reportedly from disease—the French Minister of the Interior expelled Mamboundou from France (France supported Bongo), and the opposition leader relocated to Senegal. By January of 1990 legal proceedings were ongoing against twenty-one Gabonese for their alleged roles in plots against Bongo stemming not only from the Mamboundou affair but also from an internal conspiracy led by a former Bongo aide.

Unrest continued to spread. Students boycotted classes at Universite Omar Bongo, protesting inadequate facilities and a shortage of academic staff. Doctors and teachers went on strike demanding better pay and conditions; they were joined by telecommunications workers and airport staff. President Bongo blamed the wave of strikes on reduced purchasing power, the result of austerity measures imposed at the insistence of the International Monetary Fund.

The continuing turmoil in Gabon forced Bongo and the PDG to establish a "special commission for democracy," in January of 1990. The establishment of this committee, however, was the beginning of the end of Bongo's single-party state, as the commission condemned the situation. In response, the autocrat promised that immediate political reforms would be introduced, shaped by a national conference to be held in March. Strikes continued.

Political Reforms Made

The March conference was attended by approximately two thousand delegates representing more than seventy political organizations, professional bodies, and other special interest groups. Conference participants voted for the immediate creation of a multi-party system and the formation of a new government to hold office until legislative elections were held in October of that year. Bongo agreed to abide by the decisions of the conference, realizing that continued anarchy would impede economic development and drive away foreign investors. Making several concessions, Bongo granted legal status to all opposition groups participating in the conference; thirteen groups immediately joined to form the United Opposition Front. Casimir Oye Mba, a prominent banker, was installed as prime minister, heading a twenty-nine-member transitional administration. Several members of opposition movements received ministerial posts.

As expected, the conference approved extensive political reforms, including the creation of a national Senate, which provided a second legislative body within the Gabon government. In addition, a transitional constitution was developed, which was later refined and revised by a constitutional committee. It provided the Gabon people with a bill of rights and a council to oversee the guarantee of those rights. It also provided for the transition to a multi-party system. The existing presidential mandate, effective through 1994, was to be respected. Subsequent elections would have more than one presidential candidate, and the presidential term of office was changed to five years with a limit of one re-election to the office.

In May of 1990 Joseph Rendjambe, a vocal critic of Bongo, was found dead in a hotel, reportedly poisoned. Rendjambe was a prominent business executive and secretary-general of the opposition group Parti gabonais du progres (PGP), and his death touched off the worst rioting in Bongo's twenty-three-year rule. Presidential buildings in the capital of Libreville were set on fire, and the French consul-general and ten oil company employees were taken hostage. A state of emergency was declared in Port Gentil, Rendjambe's hometown and a strategic oil production site. France sent in five hundred troops to reinforce the five-hundred-man battalion of Marines permanently stationed in Gabon to protect the interests of twenty thousand resident French nationals.

Won Presidency under Multi-Party System

The situation was somewhat under control by September of 1990, when the first multi-party elections under President Bongo's rule were held. However, control did not last long: in the first round of elections voters attacked election officials and smashed ballot boxes, claiming the election was rigged in favor of Bongo. The largest polling station, in the city hall in Libreville, was forced to close when angry voters ransacked the building, reportedly having discovered ballot boxes already stuffed as voting began. A second round of voting was suspended after the government acknowledged irregularities at a number of voting centers. Opposition groups claimed the government had halted voting in areas where the PDG appeared close to defeat.

Legislative elections were not completed until November, with the PDG winning sixty-three seats out of one hundred twenty. The largest opposition party, MORENA-Bucherons, won twenty seats. A total of eight parties were to be represented in the new legislature. On November 19, 2009, Prime Minister Oye Mba tendered the resignation of his transitional government, but he was re-appointed two days later by President Bongo. On November 26, 1990, a government of national union was announced, with the PDG holding one-third of the ministerial positions and the five largest opposition parties represented. After considerable unrest, difficulty, and debate, democratic pluralism had come to Gabon, with Bongo still as its president, his mandate effective through 1994.

Presidential elections were held in December of 1993. Bongo's primary rival was Roman Catholic priest Paul Mba Abessole. Once again, the elections were marked by fraud, strikes, riots, and death. The votes were counted in secret by the government. Bongo was declared the winner and Abessole the runner-up. Abessole immediately filed a lawsuit to have the election declared invalid, and he also set up an opposition government with himself as president. In the midst of this political turmoil in January of 1994, France suddenly devalued Gabonese currency, the CFA franc, by half. The inflation rate rose to 35 percent, and prices for imported goods soared. As summarized by the U.S. Department of State, "The controversy attending the presidential elections and reactions to the CFA devaluation led to clashes between [government] security forces and supporters of opposition parties during February [of 1994] and again in March. Security forces were directly implicated in the killings of at least 15 Gabonese and 70 foreign nationals (according to official figures) and were responsible for destroying an opposition radio station and the residence of opposition leader Abessole. The Government briefly held numerous persons without charge."

While social and civil disturbances raged, the court rejected Abessole's lawsuit. The situation was dire and led to the 1994 Paris Conference and Accords. These negotiations resulted in leaders of both the Bongo government and the opposition signing an agreement that allowed opposition members to join the government and establish an independent National Electoral Commission. Of twenty-seven ministerial posts, six were given to the opposition.

The arrangement between Bongo's government and opposition forces soon dissolved, and partisan politics ruled once again. In 1996 and 1997 elections were held for legislative and municipal positions; the PDG won handily in the legislative elections, but many cities elected opposition mayors. In the 1998 presidential election, Bongo won easily because the opposition vote was divided among many candidates and because his tight monetary policies—while unpopular at the time—had helped reduce inflation quickly. International observers noted that the election suffered from administrative problems, but they nevertheless declared the results valid. While the opposition did not accept the outcome as representative of the voters' wishes, there were no riots, bloodshed, or strikes in protest.

Allegations Made of Fiscal Corruption

By 2001 Bongo's government had managed to reduce inflation to 1.5 percent, but the country remained dependent on its dwindling oil revenues. In that same year Omar Bongo became a subject in a French corruption inquiry. Andre Tarallo, Africa manager for the oil firm Elf Aquitaine, was indicted by the French justice department for corruption in his dealings with various African leaders, including Bongo. "Commissions" were allegedly paid in return for oil rights and purchases. Bongo was said to have personally accepted Paris properties and money that Tarallo transferred to a secret Swiss bank account in Bongo's name. In November of 2003, a French court convicted Tarallo of the charges.

Also in 2003, as the end of Bongo's final term as president neared, he managed to succeed with what his opponents called a constitutional coup. The PDG-controlled National Assembly voted to change the constitution to permit the president to serve as many terms as the voters would allow. Subsequently, in elections that took place in November of 2005, Bongo easily beat his four opponents and secured another seven-year term in office. His election came as oil prices steadily rose again and Chinese President Hu Jintao showed continued interest in Gabon's oil—an interest that had been cultivated by Bongo. In addition, China was investing in Gabon in other ways, such as building a new Senate building, a multimedia center, and a port. As Bongo was sworn in to what would be his last term in office, Gabon was making clear economic progress and the country was relatively peaceful once again. President Bongo had even settled a long-

standing dispute with neighboring Equatorial Guinea over ownership of an island off the coast of both countries. The agreement was seen as a model of dispute resolution for other countries.

Other African nations were not as peaceful nor as economically stable as Gabon, and President Bongo was called in to mediate a peace conference in the Central African Republic in 2008. Like Gabon, this country had been a territory of French Equatorial Africa and gained its independence from France in 1960. As a result of the conference and the help of President Bongo, the Inter-Central African Global Peace Agreement was signed in June of 2008 in Libreville, Gabon.

On March 14, 2009, Bongo's third wife, Edith Lucie Sassou-Nguesso, died in a hospital in Morocco after a long illness. She was a practicing pediatrician with a specialty in HIV/AIDS. She and Bongo had been married for nearly twenty years, and Bongo was stricken with grief over her death. He suspended his official duties temporarily to mourn her passing.

Shortly thereafter, Transparency International France, an organization that tracks corruption, complained to the French government about alleged crimes perpetrated by three African heads of state, one of whom was Bongo. In early May, a French judge began an investigation of the corruption charges filed against the three men and discovered personal wealth that was suspected to belong to their counties' people, not to them personally. Bongo's incredible wealth included many extravagant properties in France.

Left Mixed Legacy

On May 21, 2009, Bongo was admitted to a hospital in Barcelona, Spain, with an undisclosed medical condition. He died on June 8, 2009, with the cause reported in various sources as a heart attack and as cancer. Bongo was remembered around the world in a variety of ways and from a variety of perspectives. Many remembered Bongo for his ability to compromise and facilitate conflict resolution with a goal of peace. In France, his death sparked controversy. Former French President Valery Giscard d'Estaing accused Bongo of illegally funding the presidential campaign of his rival, Jacques Chirac. Transparency International France threatened to sue Bongo's family members for funds they say Bongo embezzled from the government for personal use. Daniel Woolls of the Associated Press characterized Bongo just prior to his death as "ruling through a mixture of patronage and quiet intimidation," referring to Bongo's garnering political support in exchange for favors, contracts, or political appointments. Although Bongo led his country to relative peace compared to other African nations, and to a per capita income four times that of other African nations at the time of his death, a huge portion of the populace was poor. In addition, the country was still largely dependent on fluctuating oil revenues despite having a wealth of other natural resources.

The head of the Gabon Senate was sworn in as interim president the day after Bongo's death until a special election could be held. Bongo's son Ali Ben was declared the victor in an election on September 3, 2009, which was followed by unrest and accusations of electoral fraud. The next day Gabon's constitutional court verified the election results.

Sources

Periodicals

Business America, April 11, 1988; April 25, 1988; November 20, 1989.
Department of State Bulletin, October 1987.
Economist, June 2, 1990.
Jet, October 8, 1990.
New York Times, June 9, 2009, p. A20.
Time, May 21, 1990.
Times (London), June 9, 2009.

Online

"French Judge Wants to Investigate 3 African Leaders," Associated Press, May 5, 2009, http://abcnews.go.com/International/wireStory?id=7512614 (accessed November 4, 2009).
"Gabon Human Rights Practices, 1994," U.S. Department of State, February 1995, http://dosfan.lib.uic.edu/ERC/democracy/1994_hrp_report/94hrp_report_africa/Gabon.html (accessed November 3, 2009).
"Obituary: Omar Bongo," BBC News/Africa, June 8, 2009, http://news.bbc.co.uk/2/low/africa/8088399.stm (accessed October 29, 2009).
"Omar Bongo," *Telegraph* (London), June 8, 2009.
"Timeline: Gabon and Omar Bongo," Reuters, June 8, 2009, http://www.reuters.com/article/worldNews/idUSTRE55744Y20090608 (accessed November 3, 2009).

—David Bianco and Sandra Alters

Burning Spear

1948(?)—

Reggae musician, record-label founder

Burning Spear, photograph. AP Images.

A leading figure in the world of reggae, singer Burning Spear has helped to shape that genre since its emergence in the 1960s. Known for his distinctive, chant-like vocal style, he has long specialized in a variety called roots reggae, which combines danceable rhythms with a lyrical emphasis on the tenets of the Rastafari faith, the achievements of African culture, and the plight of the world's poor.

Spear was born Winston Rodney in St. Ann Parish, a large, mostly rural district in northern Jamaica. His date of birth has been variously reported. According to some sources, he was born March 1, 1945; others, however, have preferred March 1, 1948. There is no doubt, however, that he was raised in a strict, highly religious household. "I was brought up by my mother and father who were Pentecostal people," he told Douglas Heselgrave of *Music Box* magazine in 2005. "I had to go to church twice every Sunday. I went in the early morning and then had to wait and go back at two o'clock."

Surprisingly, Spear seems not to have had much interest in music in his youth. It was not until he underwent a mystical conversion to the Rastafari reli-

gion as a young adult that he turned to music, finding it an effective medium for expressing his new faith. A monotheistic creed with a deep pride in the cultural heritage of Africa and the African diaspora, the Rastafarian movement had begun to attract numerous adherents, particularly in Jamaica, by the 1960s. A major factor in its development was the growing popularity of roots reggae, a genre dominated by Rastafarians like Bob Marley.

It was a chance meeting with Marley, also a native of St. Ann, that sparked Spear's career. According to a biographical profile posted on the latter's Web site, BurningSpear.net, he was walking one day through the countryside when he encountered Marley. The two began to discuss reggae and Spear's dreams of a music career. Marley, whose own career had started a few years earlier, advised him to present himself to a producer named Clement "Coxsone" Dodd at Studio One, a well-known record label based in the Jamaican capital of Kingston. Spear's subsequent meeting with the producer resulted in a record contract. His first single, entitled "Door Peep Shall Not Enter," appeared shortly thereafter; the year was 1969.

At a Glance . . .

Born Winston Rodney on March 1, 1948 (some sources say 1945), in St. Ann Parish, Jamaica; married Sonia, early 1970s(?); children: at least five. *Religion:* Rastafari.

Career: Independent recording artist, 1969—; founder, Burning Music Production(s), 2003—.

Awards: Merit Award, Jamaican Federation of Musicians, 1990; Grammy Award, Best Reggae Album, 1999, for *Calling Rastafari*; Order of Distinction (Officer Rank), Government of Jamaica, 2007; Grammy Award, Best Reggae Album, 2008, for *Jah Is Real*.

Addresses: *Office*—c/o Burning Music Productions, P.O. Box 130187, Jamaica, NY 11413-0187. *Web*—http://www.burningspear.net/.

Over the next four years, Spear released three more singles and two albums through Studio One. He did so with the assistance of several backup singers, including Rupert Willington and Delroy Hinds, as well as an array of studio musicians. Spear himself has never been known as an instrumentalist, though he has often played the bongos or other drums on stage. Initially the name Burning Spear referred to the group, not its lead singer. With time and personnel changes, however, that distinction blurred, and Winston Rodney became Burning Spear. He had chosen the appellation after reading about the Kenyan leader Jomo Kenyatta (1893?–1978), whose nickname it had been.

The singer's first two albums, *Studio One Presents Burning Spear* (1973) and *Rocking Time* (1974), enjoyed strong reviews and sold well, though the market for reggae, particularly outside Jamaica, was still small. With a heavy, danceable beat, Spear's songs were popular at clubs and parties. The lyrics, however, were decidedly more thoughtful than those usually found in dance songs. His frequent praises of Jah, the divine force at the center of Rastafarian worship, lent a mystical quality to the music. Such overt religiosity, rare in dance music at the time, soon became one of roots reggae's essential features.

In 1975 Spear and his partners moved from Studio One to Island, a leading international label. The albums he recorded there over the next few years are considered some of the strongest of his career. Prominent among these was *Marcus Garvey* (1975), an homage to one of Jamaica's seven National Heroes. Garvey

(1887–1940), another native of St. Ann, was a leading proponent of what became known as black pride or Afrocentrism, a major theme in roots reggae. Spear's celebration of Garvey's life and thought became, in the words of AllMusic.com's Jo-Ann Greene, "a cornerstone of the entire roots movement."

After several more successes, Spear left Island in about 1980. Although he subsequently returned for a short period, most of the albums he recorded in the 1980s and 1990s were released by other labels. His relationship with those companies was often troubled, however, and in 2003 he formed Burning Music Production (or Productions) in order to maintain financial and artistic control over his own work.

Spear's recording output over the years has been impressive, with more than twenty major releases between 1973 and 2009. Albums such as *Marcus Garvey, Hail H.I.M.* (1980), and *Jah Kingdom* (1991) elicited strong praise from reggae critics and from his fellow musicians, who honored him with the Jamaican Federation of Musicians' Merit Award in 1990. Recognition from the broader music industry, however, was somewhat slower to arrive. That situation changed dramatically at the end of the 1990s, when Spear's record *Calling Rastafari* received a 1999 Grammy Award as the Best Reggae Album of the year. Nine years later he received another Grammy, this time for *Jah Is Real*. He has also been honored by the government of Jamaica, which awarded him the Order of Distinction (Officer Rank) in 2007.

As of 2009, the fortieth anniversary of his first single, Spear lived in the New York City borough of Queens with his wife, Sonia, who has had a significant role in the management of his career. As interest in roots reggae continued to grow, notably among fans not yet born when "Door Peep" was released, the singer showed little sign of slowing down. A frequent headliner at concerts and festivals worldwide, he was asked by the United Nations in 2007 to make a special appearance in Kenya to help cool rising political tensions there. Sixty-five thousand people of varied backgrounds and political leanings heard him play in the Kenyan capital of Nairobi. "They were hugging and jumping up together," Spear reported on his Web site. "One can see the force of the music."

Selected discography

Singles

"Door Peep Shall Not Enter," 1969.

Albums

Studio One Presents Burning Spear (includes "Door Peep Shall Not Enter"), Studio One, 1973.
Rocking Time, Studio One, 1974.

Marcus Garvey, Island, 1975.
Man in the Hills, Island, 1976.
Dry & Heavy, Island, 1977.
Hail H.I.M., EMI, 1980.
Farover, EMI, 1982.
The Fittest of the Fittest, EMI, 1983.
Mistress Music, Slash, 1988.
Mek We Dweet, Island, 1990.
Jah Kingdom, Island, 1991.
The World Should Know, Heartbeat, 1993.
Rasta Business, Heartbeat, 1995.
Appointment with His Majesty, Heartbeat, 1997.
Calling Rastafari, Heartbeat, 1999.
Freeman, Burning Music, 2003.
Our Music, Burning Music, 2005.
Jah Is Real, Burning Music, 2008.

Sources

Periodicals

Boston Globe, July 3, 2009.
Music Box, November 2005.

Online

"Burning Spear/BIO," BurningSpear.net, http://www.burningspear.net/docs/bio.doc (accessed November 12, 2009).

Greene, Jo-Ann, "Burning Spear: Biography," AllMusic.com, http://allmusic.com/cg/amg.dll?p=amg&sql=11:fifuxqq5ldfe (accessed November 12, 2009).

———, "*Marcus Garvey*: Review," AllMusic.com, http://allmusic.com/cg/amg.dll?p=amg&sql=10:gifexqwgld0e (accessed Noevember 12, 2009).

—R. Anthony Kugler

Mary Alice Chineworth

1917—

Catholic nun, educator

Sister Mary Alice Chineworth is a respected educator and administrator who has dedicated her life to teaching African-American youth and to fostering religious and racial tolerance. As a member of the Oblate Sisters of Providence, the oldest congregation of black Roman Catholic nuns in the United States, she daily puts into practice the mission of her order, which was founded more than three decades before the American Civil War for the purpose of educating black children. Throughout her long career, she has challenged traditional notions of how a nun should act, often speaking out on controversial issues of the day. She has been especially vocal in urging Catholic leaders to provide more opportunities for women and African Americans to advance within the church and to confront the issue of racism head-on.

Born on July 16, 1917, in Rock Island, Illinois, she was the second of four children of Alexander and Victoria Chineworth. She grew up in a biracial family: Her mother was white, the first child of a German family to be born in the United States, and her father was African American, the son of a slave from Madagascar. Although interracial couples were uncommon at the time—even illegal in some states—the family did not suffer greatly from the racism of their time, and Chineworth recalled her childhood as virtually "color blind," she noted in an oral history interview with Camille Cosby, a cofounder of the National Visionary Leadership Project. Both parents impressed on Chineworth the importance of education.

As a girl, Chineworth attended Catholic schools in which most of the students were white, and it was there that the seeds of her religious vocation were planted. She first felt called to the church at age four, inspired by the model of her kindergarten teacher, and she declared that she would grow up to "be a Sister just like Sister Mary Fidelis," as she notes on her vocation page on the Oblate Sisters of Providence Web site. That commitment stayed with her through high school, when she formally expressed her desire to enter the convent. When Chineworth was a junior, her guidance counselor asked her what order she planned to join. Her response, according to her interview with Cosby, was "What order? I didn't know there were other orders besides yours. Yours is the only order I know," she replied, speaking of the Sisters of Charity of the Blessed Virgin Mary, who ran her school. "You can't come to us because you're colored," the sister told her, as she and Chineworth began to cry.

At the time, Chineworth had only three options open to her if she wished to enter the convent, all of them black orders: the Sisters in Harlem, the Sisters in New Orleans, and the Oblate Sisters of Providence in Baltimore, Maryland. Chineworth chose the Sisters of Providence, describing her affection for the order as "love at first sight." At age nineteen, she boarded the train from Rock Island to Baltimore, accompanied by her father, to answer her religious calling.

Chineworth was attracted to the Sisters of Providence, in part, because of their remarkable history. They are the oldest order of black nuns in the United States, founded in 1829 by Father James Hector Joubert, a white priest of French heritage, and Elizabeth Clarisse Lange (known as Mother Mary Lange), a Catholic

At a Glance . . .

Born on July 16, 1917, in Rock Island, IL; daughter of Alexander Roth Chineworth and Victoria Schlicker Chineworth. *Religion:* Roman Catholic. *Education:* Catholic University, MS, educational psychology, PhD, higher education, 1970.

Career: St. Frances Academy, teacher; Mount Providence Junior College, president; Order of the Oblate Sisters of Providence, administrative positions, beginning 1973, superior general, 1989–93.

Memberships: National Black Sisters Conference.

Addresses: *Office*—c/o Oblate Sisters of Providence, 701 Gun Road, Baltimore, MD 21227-3828.

immigrant from Haiti, together with three other black women. From the beginning, the order focused on education as its primary mission. Upon arriving in Baltimore, Lange had been struck by the fact that the city's black children received no education. In fact, in the slave state of Maryland, it was then illegal to teach enslaved blacks to read or write. Using her own money, Lange started a school for black children in her own home, calling it the St. Frances of Rome Academy. The academy, now a high school called St. Frances Academy, remains under the care of the Sisters of Providence in the twenty-first century.

After completing her religious training with the Sisters of Providence and taking the black veil—the outward symbol of a member's permanent spiritual commitment to the order—Chineworth worked as a teacher for some thirty years at the St. Frances Academy, where her students came mainly from Baltimore's African-American neighborhoods. As her leadership talents became evident, she moved out of the classroom and into administrative positions, culminating in her appointment as president of Mount Providence Junior College in Baltimore. Beginning in 1973 Chineworth took on high-level administrative positions within the Order of the Oblate Sisters of Providence, finally attaining the rank of superior general in 1989, a position she held until 1993.

Throughout her religious career, Chineworth has defied traditional notions of how a nun should act, frequently speaking out about the role of women and African Americans in the church. In particular, she has been critical of the Catholic Church's leadership, which she argues did little to combat racism in its ranks until recently. "The bishops for decades have not insisted that priests fight [racism] and didn't compel them to

deal with it," Chineworth told the *Seattle Times* in 2001. "They just buried it." For Chineworth, it is essential that parishioners see themselves reflected in the church's leadership, so that they might find role models there. "It's very important to see one of your own in leadership positions in the black community. It's important to children to see what they can become. I've known some very wonderful pastors who are white, and who've done a wonderful job, but I wish that there were enough priests of color, African American priests, to serve," she said in an interview published in the 2004 book *A Wealth of Wisdom: Legendary African American Elders Speak*.

Like many religious communities, the Sisters of Providence struggle to maintain their membership as fewer women choose to dedicate themselves to religious life. At its peak in the 1960s, the order's membership numbered more than 300, with as many as eighteen young women entering each year. But by 2009 the order had dwindled to approximately eighty members. New novices are cause for celebration, as they are so rare—perhaps one each year. Although most of the sisters in the first decade of the 2000s were African American, the order also had many Latin American members and a handful of white sisters. The decline in membership concerns Chineworth, who is now one of the order's oldest sisters. Nonetheless, she remains committed to the order's goal of providing education: "As long as there are poor children—disadvantaged, marginalized children—to educate, we will be there," she told Cosby.

Selected works

(Editor) *Rise 'n' Shine: Catholic Education and the African American Community,* National Catholic Educational Association, 1996.
"My Little Vocation Story," Oblate Sisters of Providence, http://www.oblatesistersvocations.com/SrAlice.html (accessed September 22, 2009).
Oral history interview by Camille Cosby, National Visionary Leadership Project, http://www.visionaryproject.org/chineworthmary/ (accessed September 22, 2009).

Sources

Books

Cosby, Camille, and Renee Pouissant, eds., *A Wealth of Wisdom: Legendary African American Elders Speak,* Atria Books, 2004, pp. 63–67.

Periodicals

Los Angeles Times, March 27, 2009.
Seattle Times, September 1, 2001.
Washington Post, August 6, 1989, p. D3.

—Deborah A. Ring

Mamie Phipps Clark

1917–1983

Psychologist

Psychologist Mamie Phipps Clark conducted pioneering research in the early twentieth century on the effects of racism on the self-perceptions and self-esteem of African-American children. Working with her husband, Kenneth B. Clark, she challenged the notion that black children were inferior to white children in their mental and intellectual abilities—a common misjudgment in many public school systems at the time—showing instead that racial bias had a powerful and detrimental effect on black students' educational achievement. Used in trials in Delaware, South Carolina, and Virginia, the Clarks' research was crucial in ending school segregation during the 1950s. In 1954 their findings helped shape the U.S. Supreme Court's ruling in *Brown v. Board of Education of Topeka, Kansas* a landmark decision that overturned the doctrine of "separate but equal" education and declared segregation in public schools unconstitutional.

Mamie Katherine Phipps was born on October 18, 1917, in the racially segregated town of Hot Springs, Arkansas. Her father, Harold Hilton Phipps, was a respected local physician, and her mother, Katie Florence Phipps, assisted in his medical practice. Both parents encouraged their children to aim high professionally despite the racial barriers that stood in their way. Mamie attended the all-black Langston High School, graduating in 1934 and earning a scholarship to attend Howard University.

She enrolled at Howard intending to study physics and mathematics but found the faculty in both departments unsupportive, perhaps because of prejudices against

women in these fields. She soon met Clark, a graduate student in psychology and a teaching assistant. After taking his class on abnormal psychology, she became interested in the subject—and the instructor—and switched her major to psychology. This marked the beginning of a lifelong personal and professional collaboration between the two. Mamie completed her undergraduate degree in 1938, and on April 14 of that year, she and Kenneth married. She stayed on at Howard for another year to earn a master's degree in psychology in 1939.

Mamie Clark was keenly interested in the psychological development of African-American children and how racism influenced their self-image. Her master's thesis was an outgrowth of her work with black children in a segregated nursery school in Washington, DC, where she administered psychological tests to some 200 preschoolers. When presented with two identical dolls—one white and one black—the black children consistently demonstrated a preference for the white doll. Clark concluded from her study that children developed an awareness of their racial identity around the age of three, and that black children simultaneously acquired a negative self-image. Clark and her husband received a three-year fellowship from the Julius Rosenwald Fund to pursue this line of research on racial identification in African-American children, and they published three articles in the *Journal of Social Psychology* in 1939 and 1940. Their findings proved key in the evolution of the nascent field of developmental psychology.

Mamie Clark enrolled in the doctoral program at Columbia University, where her husband also was attending—they were the only two black students in the department. She completed her degree in 1943, becoming the first African-American woman to receive a doctorate in psychology from the university. She found, however, that job opportunities for a black woman with a doctorate in the 1940s were few. In 1944 she took a job as a research psychologist with the American Public Health Association, which she later described as distasteful and humiliating, and soon left to become a research associate at the New York Examination Center of the U.S. Armed Forces Institute, another unfulfilling job. Her initial career disappointment led her to conclude that "a black female with a Ph.D. in psychology was an unwanted anomaly in New York City," according to *Black Women Scientists in the United States* (1999) by Wini Warren.

In 1945, however, Clark began working as the chief psychologist at the Riverside Home for Children, a private agency that served homeless African-American girls. She was struck by the dearth of psychological services for black children, many of whom were incorrectly labeled as mentally retarded by the public school system. When she was unable to persuade any social service agency in the Harlem neighborhood in New York City to provide psychological services for such children, Clark and her husband opened the Northside Testing and Consultation Center, later renamed the Northside Center for Child Development, in the basement of the Dunbar Apartments in Harlem, where her family lived. Mamie Clark served as the center's executive director from 1946 until her retirement in 1980.

At first, the center was staffed by volunteers and served just over 100 clients, who were charged according to their ability to pay—most paid nothing at all. The Clarks soon clashed with the New York City public schools, which had classified a number of black students as mentally retarded and placed them in special education classes. Parents began to bring their children to Northside for psychological testing, and Mamie Clark found that many of the students were not in fact retarded but suffered from racial bias in the classroom that impeded their learning. Clark challenged the school system, and the students were reclassified. Nonetheless, Clark found that although most of the students made significant progress at Northside, their educational achievements could not be sustained in the public schools because the schools did not have the resources to help them.

As the number of clients at Northside grew, the Clarks were able to attract more funding from the philanthropic community. By 1968 they were serving 600 patients a year, had an annual budget of $450,000, and employed thirty-eight full-time staff members.

The Clarks' research provided crucial evidence in the fight to end school segregation, and they presented their findings at desegregation trials in Delaware, South Carolina, and Virginia. Most significantly, their work provided the foundation of the National Association for the Advancement of Colored People's argument in the *Brown v. Board of Education* case, which challenged the constitutionality of the "separate but equal" doctrine in education established by *Plessy v. Ferguson* in 1896. Writing the U.S. Supreme Court's unanimous decision in *Brown*, Chief Justice Earl Warren reasoned that the segregation of black children "generates a feeling of inferiority ... that may affect their hearts and minds in a way unlikely ever to be undone," citing the Clarks' research as evidence. The landmark ruling ended the legal basis for segregation in public schools in the United States.

A natural extension of her work in Harlem, Mamie Clark established and chaired the 110th Street Plaza Housing Development Corporation, which constructed the Schomburg Plaza, a 600-family housing complex for low- and middle-income families, and provided better facilities for the Northside Center. She served on the board of directors of numerous institutions, including the American Broadcasting Company, Mount Sinai Medical Center, New York Public Library, Museum of Modern Art, and Teachers College at Columbia University, and was a fellow of the American Psychological Association and the American Association of Orthopsychiatry. In 1966 Columbia University awarded Mamie and Kenneth B. Clark the Nicholas Murray Butler Silver Medal in recognition of their groundbreaking research.

Clark retired from her post at Northside in 1980. She died of cancer on August 11, 1983, at age sixty-five, at her home in Hastings-on-Hudson, New York.

Selected writings

(With Kenneth B. Clark) "Segregation as a Factor in the Racial Identification of Negro Pre-School Children," *Journal of Social Psychology,* vol. 8, 1939, pp. 161–163.

(With Kenneth B. Clark) "The Development of Consciousness of Self and the Emergence of Racial Identification in Negro Pre-School Children," *Journal of Social Psychology,* vol. 10, 1939, pp. 591–599.

(With Kenneth B. Clark) "Skin Color as a Factor in Racial Identification of Negro Pre-School Children," *Journal of Social Psychology,* vol. 11, 1940, pp. 159–169.

"Changes in Primary Mental Abilities with Age," *Archives of Psychology,* vol. 291, PhD diss., Columbia University, 1944.

(With Kenneth B. Clark) "Emotional Factors in Racial Identification and Preference in Negro Children," *Journal of Negro Education,* vol. 19, 1950, pp. 506–513.

(With Kenneth B. Clark) "What Do Blacks Think of Themselves?" *Ebony,* November 1980, p. 176.

Sources

Books

O'Connell, Agnes N., and Nancy Felipe Russo, *Women in Psychology: A Bio-bibliographic Sourcebook,* Greenwood Press, 1990.

Warren, Wini, "Mamie Phipps Clark," in *Black Women Scientists in the United States,* Indiana University Press, 1999, pp. 29–37.

Periodicals

American Psychologist, January 2002, p. 20.
New York Times, August 12, 1983.

Online

Brown v. Board of Education of Topeka, Kansas (1954), Cornell University Law School, http://www.law.cornell.edu/supct/html/historics/USSC_CR_0347_0483_ZO.html (accessed October 13, 2009).

Butler, Stephen N., "Mamie Katherine Phipps Clark (1917–1983)," Encyclopedia of Arkansas History and Culture, October 1, 2009, http://www.encyclopediaofarkansas.net/encyclopedia/entry-detail.aspx?entryID=2938 (accessed October 13, 2009).

"Mamie Clark," Columbia University Libraries, Oral History Research Office, http://www.columbia.edu/cu/lweb/digital/collections/nny/clarkm/index.html (accessed October 13, 2009).

"Segregation Ruled Unequal, and Therefore Unconstitutional," American Psychological Association, Psychology Matters, May 28, 2003 (revised July 2007), http://www.psychologymatters.org/clark.html (accessed October 13, 2009).

—Deborah A. Ring

Kenneth V. Cockrel Jr.

1965—

Politician

Cockrel, Kenneth V., Jr., photograph. AP Images.

Ken Cockrel Jr. was serving his third term on the Detroit City Council in 2008 when he became the sixty-first mayor of the city. As president of the council, Cockrel was designated by the city charter to serve as interim mayor in the event of the mayor's death, resignation, removal from office, or conviction for a felony offense. Cockrel succeeded Mayor Kwame Kilpatrick after Kilpatrick was forced to resign in a perjury scandal. Several months later a special mayoral election pitted Cockrel against area business leader and former professional basketball star Dave Bing, who won the race. Cockrel returned to his post as president of the city council, where his leadership and professionalism had earned him the respect of citizens and community leaders. "Cockrel is viewed as a voice of reason leading an elected group of people who often fight bitterly among themselves and with the mayor," asserted writer Brent Snavely in *Crain's Detroit Business.*

As a leader in Detroit politics, Cockrel inherited the legacy of his father, Ken Sr., who died prematurely in April of 1989. Ken Sr. was well known in Detroit as a civil rights attorney, community activist, and city council member. Ken Jr. was born in October of 1965 while his father was a student at Wayne State University Law School. Ken Sr. went on to a headline-making career as a defense lawyer in several high-profile cases involving police misconduct and institutionalized racial bias. Cockrel's mother, Carol, was a teacher; his parents later divorced. Some of his childhood was spent in the Jeffries Homes, a Detroit housing project; later the household moved to Highland Park, a small city which, along with the neighboring city of Hamtramck, is completely surrounded by Detroit. Cockrel graduated from one of Hamtramck's Catholic high schools.

As a child Cockrel was on the front lines with his father. Ken Sr. took him everywhere—to his law office, to the City-County Building, and to community meetings and organized protests. Cockrel followed his father to Wayne State University, earning a journalism degree and then working for the *Grand Rapids Press* and the *Cincinnati Enquirer.* In the spring of 1989 Ken Sr. died of a heart attack at the age of fifty. Three years later, Cockrel and his wife decided to return to Detroit, where Cockrel enrolled in the Michigan Political Leadership Program and was elected to the Wayne County Board of Commissioners in 1994. In 1997, twenty years after his father had done so, he won a seat on the Detroit City Counci. At thirty-two, Cockrel made history as the youngest person ever to be elected to the council.

In 2001 the scion of another African-American Detroit political family made history. Thirty-one-year-old Kwame Kilpatrick, the son of U.S. Congresswoman Carolyn Cheeks Kilpatrick, became the youngest person ever elected mayor of Detroit and one of the youngest mayors of any major U.S. city. Cockrel had supported his city council colleague Gil Hill in the race. Four years later Cockrel supported the incumbent Kilpatrick despite rumors of late-night carousing by the married father of three and a series of financial scandals.

Became Council President

In the meantime Cockrel had been reelected in 2001 to a second term on the city council, and in the 2005 election he had won the most votes among the nine successful candidates, thus promoting him to the post of city council president. Over his next ten years as council president, Cockrel emerged as a quiet, likable advocate for city residents and the business community alike. When the mayor was charged in a 2007 whistleblower lawsuit, Cockrel supported Kilpatrick. The case involved two Detroit police officers who claimed they were fired for investigating rumors of a party at the mayor's official residence in 2002 and the murder of an exotic dancer who had been involved with the alleged party. The fired officers also alleged that the mayor was having an extramarital affair with his chief of staff, Christine Beatty; both Kilpatrick and Beatty denied the charge under oath during the trial. A jury ruled in favor of the plaintiffs and ordered that the fired officers be awarded $6.5 million in damages. The city council authorized the payout, as well as another significant payment in a third whistleblower case.

Four months later the *Detroit Free Press* uncovered scores of text messages sent on city-owned communications devices that contradicted Kilpatrick and Beatty's sworn denials of a romantic relationship. Cockrel won praise for not calling for the mayor's resignation once the hundreds of salacious text messages were made public. "It's disappointing," the council president was quoted as saying by *Detroit Free Press* reporter Zachary Gorchow. "You look back at that trial that we went through which cost the city a lot of money. And we had to pay up with some money to settle. … In the overall scheme of the city's budget, $9 million is not a lot of money, but when you look at it for what it is and the principle of it, what $9 million could buy, in terms of being able to turn on streetlights, maybe purchase new police vehicles, it's a lot of money that could have otherwise been spent for something better."

Kilpatrick, disgraced but unbending, was charged with several felony counts including perjury and obstruction of justice, and he initially refused to resign as mayor. On September 4, 2008, he pled guilty to two of the felony counts and announced he would resign on September 18. Kilpatrick served 120 days in the Wayne County Jail, a new and vastly improved facility compared to the one whose conditions had been so atrocious in the late 1960s that Cockrel's father and other attorneys filed a lawsuit to force renovations.

Sworn in as Interim Mayor

Cockrel met with reporters immediately following the news of Kilpatrick's resignation. "This is a very sad day for the City of Detroit, but I think we also have to recognize that it is also a day of hope and renewal," Gorchow and another *Free Press* reporter, Robin Erb, quoted him as saying. "What we're going to have to focus on really is restoring the credibility of not only the mayor's office, but of the City of Detroit." Cockrel was sworn in as interim mayor at a low-key event on September 19, 2008, taking over a once-grand city that now counted more vacant property in square footage than it did occupied houses or businesses. Serving Detroit's nine hundred thousand residents, Cockrel oversaw fifteen thousand employees—many of them represented by powerful municipal unions—and a budget of $3 billion.

To provide an elected replacement for the remaining months of Kilpatrick's term, a special primary election was held in February of 2009, followed by a special mayoral election that May. In the mayoral election Cockrel went up against a formidable foe with equal name recognition in the city: local business mogul Dave Bing, also a onetime star with the Detroit Pistons basketball team. Bing had moved into the city to qualify for a spot on the ballot, a point that Cockrel emphasized on the campaign trail. Cockrel asserted that as a longtime Detroit resident he was the most attuned to voters' needs. Cockrel lost the election to Bing by four percentage points and returned to his post as president of the city council, where his stepmother Sheila Murphy Cockrel is a colleague. "We've got some history between us that isn't all good," Cockrel observed once in a *Free Press* interview, "but the thing that I appreciate about her and like about her is that when we come to this building and when we go out to that table, none

of it is evident. Professionally, she's been a good ally."

In the same interview, he reflected back on the legacy of his father. "There's not a day that goes by that I don't think about my dad, and don't wish that he was here to help me," he told Gorchow and *Free Press* colleague Suzette Hackney. "But I also recognize that I'm me, and I've got to do my thing."

Sources

Periodicals

Detroit Free Press, January 24, 2008; April 7, 2008; September 5, 2008.
Crain's Detroit Business, February 11, 2008, p. 1.

—Carol Brennan

Kenneth Vern Cockrel Sr.

1938–1989

Attorney, civil rights activist

Kenneth Cockrel Sr. was a well-known activist, attorney, and civil rights leader in Detroit for a quarter century. Cockrel held elected office only once—a four-year term on the city council—but he played a key role in guiding Detroit to become the first major American city to have blacks holding nearly every key leadership post. He died of a sudden heart attack in 1989 at the age of fifty, ending a stellar career that some had hoped would culminate in a successful mayoral run.

Kenneth Vern Cockrel was born in 1938 in Royal Oak Township, Michigan. Like many black Detroiters, he belonged to a family that had left the Deep South in search of automotive factory jobs in the northern industrial city. Royal Oak Township was located just across Detroit's northern border and had been hastily constructed to handle the city's housing crisis in advance of World War II, when a second wave of Southerners was drawn north, this time by work in the defense industry. By the age of twelve Cockrel was orphaned and went to live with an aunt and uncle. An indifferent student, he dropped out of the Detroit public schools system in eleventh grade and followed his brother into the U.S. Air Force.

Made Headlines as Marxist Lawyer

Cockrel was a nuclear weapons technician during his time in the Air Force. Returning to Detroit after his discharge, he entered Wayne State University, a state school located in the city, and earned a degree in political science in 1964. In 1967 he received his law degree from Wayne State University Law School. That July the city erupted in race riots that in some areas were quelled only by the arrival of U.S. Army troops authorized by President Lyndon B. Johnson. The riots of 1967 are commonly cited as the starting point for Detroit's decline, but in reality white residents had been steadily leaving the city for years, moving out to the newly built suburbs. Auto plant jobs were still plentiful, but racial tensions were flaring on the factory floor, and race-based economic injustice had not been addressed by the gains of the civil rights era.

Cockrel was part of a new generation of political activists in the city. A committed leftist, once out of school he joined a law firm that specialized in civil rights cases. He first made headlines when he defended a man accused of fatally shooting a Detroit police officer in a raid on a black separatist meeting held at the New Bethel Baptist Church in March of 1969. The pretrial hearing at Detroit Recorder's Court ended with the judge setting a bail amount of $50,000. "An infuriated Cockrel stormed from the courtroom and was quoted by the media as calling Judge Maher 'a racist monkey, honky dog fool, and a thieving pirate,'" according to Dan Georgakas and Marvin Surkin in their book *Detroit, I Do Mind Dying: A Study in Urban Revolution.*

Maher charged Cockrel with contempt of court, but the charge was thrown out and his client's bond reduced. Cockrel and his legal team won a stunning acquittal for their client in June of 1969. During the trial Cockrel

At a Glance . . .

Born on November 5, 1938, in Royal Oak Township, MI; died on April 25, 1989, in Detroit, MI; son of an autoworker; married Carol White (a teacher; divorced); married Sheila Murphy (a community activist and politician), 1978; children: (first marriage) Kenneth V. Jr.; (second marriage) Kate. *Military service:* U.S. Air Force, 1957(?)–59. *Education:* Wayne State University, BA, political science, 1964; Wayne State University Law School, JD, 1967.

Career: Partner in the law firm Philo, Maki, Cockrel, Rubb, Spearman, and Cooper after 1968; elected to the Detroit City Council, 1977.

Awards: Distinguished Achievement Medal, Detroit National Association for the Advancement of Colored People (NAACP), 1973; Frank D. Reeves Award, National Conference of Black Lawyers, 1976.

worked with Justin Ravitz, a partner at his firm, to show that the Wayne County jury selection process was rigged against black defendants. A large majority of defendants in Wayne County were African American, but prosecutors regularly packed the juries with white males from suburban Wayne County communities. Cockrel and Ravitz managed to obtain a new jury for the defendant, who was then exonerated. It would be the first of several important legal victories in Cockrel's career. A year later new jury selection rules helped Cockrel win another major acquittal, this time of a black autoworker charged with killing a coworker in July of 1970 at a Chrysler facility on Eldon Avenue in the city. The plant had already been the scene of several "wildcat" strikes, or walkouts by workers that were not authorized by the powerful United Autoworkers Union. The majority of the workers at the gear and axle manufacturing facility were black, while management and union representatives were white. The racism and working conditions at the plant were so dire, wrote Georgakas and Surkin, that Cockrel and the defense team "presented evidence that Eldon was one of the most dangerous plants in the United States and that the UAW was unable or unwilling to protect workers on the shop floor. As a climax to the defense, Cockrel took the entire jury to the scene of the crime so they could judge conditions for themselves."

Ran for City Council Seat

Cockrel was also intensely involved in the Detroit Revolutionary Union Movement, or DRUM, founded in

1969 at a largely black-staffed Chrysler plant. It was a Marxist-oriented group for UAW members dissatisfied with their current union representation, and it borrowed many of the core tenets and tactics of the Black Panther Party and other black militant groups. DRUM evolved into the League of Revolutionary Black Workers, which permitted non-autoworkers to join. The group was an integral part of the radical black left in Detroit, which battled with more moderate civil rights activists about the future of the city. Both coalitions, however, were adamantly opposed to a new unit operating inside the Detroit Police Department and known by its acronym, STRESS (Stop the Robberies and Enjoy Safe Streets). Trumpeted at its launch in 1971 as an elite crime-fighting unit, STRESS used decoys and plainclothes officers in its raids, and in two years of operation had shot and killed twenty Detroiters—seventeen of them black.

Cockrel led the crusade against STRESS, forming a citizens' group to oppose it and then defending an eighteen-year-old African-American man, Hayward Brown, who had been charged in the shootings of four STRESS personnel in December of 1972. It had taken nearly six weeks to arrest Brown, and two other suspects were gunned down in a police dragnet that had spread to Atlanta, Georgia. Cockrel won the case by putting the STRESS unit on trial, demonstrating the deficiency of tactics that permitted plainclothes officers to approach citizens in tense urban situations.

There were rumors in the spring of 1973 that Cockrel would run for mayor of Detroit that fall. To the surprise of some, he instead endorsed a labor leader and state senator, Coleman A. Young, for the post. Young was elected Detroit's first African-American mayor in a narrow contest that pitted him against the city's police chief. One of Young's first acts in office was to order the dissolution of the STRESS unit. Cockrel entered the political arena in 1977 when he won a seat on the Detroit City Council, which was then still called the Common Council. His name occasionally appeared in national news items, such as a notice in *Jet* in the summer of 1980 about an attempt by the Ku Klux Klan to march in the city with members of the American Nazi Party. "Let them march. Give them their constitutional rights," the magazine quoted him as saying. But Cockrel promised a counter-demonstration into the bargain. "I wonder what they would do if they were confronted by 10,000 people ready to kick their asses."

Cockrel did not run for a second term on the city council, leading some observers to think that he was preparing to challenge Young (who would in fact remain in office for a record five terms). Instead he returned to his law practice. His son, Ken Cockrel Jr., was elected to the city council in 1997 and became president of the council in 2005. By that time Detroit was in dire economic straits, with nearly all of the major automobile manufacturers and suppliers having relocated elsewhere. During his term on the council, the elder Cockrel had opposed Mayor Young's strategy to keep jobs in the city by granting generous tax abatements to businesses like Chrysler and General Motors. Cockrel's was the lone dissenting vote against one particularly generous 1981 deal approved by the council. "He was a prophet," labor activist Gene Cunningham said of Cockrel in the 1990 book *Detroit Lives*. "He kept saying, 'The more you give them, the more they'll want.'"

Sources

Books

Robert H. Mast, ed., *Detroit Lives,* Temple University Press, 1994, p. 316.

Georgakas, Dan, and Marvin Surkin, *Detroit, I Do Mind Dying: A Study in Urban Revolution,* 2nd ed., South End Press, 1998, pp. 11, 196.

Periodicals

Jet, June 26, 1980, p. 53.
New York Times, May 6, 1973, p. 154.

Online

"Ken Cockrel Sr.: Social Justice Advocate," WWJ-TV, http://wwjtv.com/etc/Ken.Cockrel.Sr.2.925550.html (accessed October 20, 2009).

—Carol Brennan

James E. Coleman Jr.

1948(?)—

Lawyer, law professor

James E. Coleman Jr. has had a prominent place in American law and legal education since the 1970s. The first African American to become a partner at Wilmer, Cutler, and Pickering (later WilmerHale), one of Washington's leading law firms, he gained a national reputation for his expertise in a wide range of issues, including legal ethics and capital punishment. He is perhaps best known, however, for his work at Duke University, where he has taught for several decades. His role in the school's investigation of the so-called "Lacrosse Team Rape Case" in 2006 led Peter Applebome of the *New York Times* to describe him as a "hero."

Few details are publicly available regarding Coleman's family background or early life. He is described in his faculty profile on the Duke Web site as "a native of Charlotte, North Carolina"; his birth date is uncertain. If he attended college at a traditional age, however, he was likely born in about 1948. In an interview with Melissa Block of National Public Radio in 2006, Coleman described the Charlotte neighborhood of his youth as "very poor." Despite this disadvantage, he was clearly able to excel academically, winning admission to Harvard University in 1966. After receiving his bachelor's degree four years later, he entered law school at Columbia University. When his studies there were complete in 1974, he began his legal career with a clerkship (1974–75) in Michigan under U.S. District Judge Damon J. Keith.

Following his clerkship, Coleman spent a year (1975–76) as an associate in a New York law firm (Kaye,

Scholer, Fierman, Hayes, and Handler) before moving to Washington, DC, where he worked as an assistant general counsel for the Legal Services Corporation, a federal agency that serves, according to its Web site, as "the single largest provider of civil legal aid for the poor in the nation." After several years there (1976–78), he moved briefly to the U.S. House of Representatives' Committee on Standards of Official Conduct, where as chief counsel he helped lead two high-profile corruption investigations. His success in that role drew the attention of Wilmer, Cutler, and Pickering (WCP), which hired him as an associate in 1978. Apart from several relatively brief leaves of absence, including a short stint as a deputy general counsel for the U.S. Department of Education (1980–81), he remained at WCP for the next eighteen years (1978–96). His work there in a variety of civil and criminal cases was highly regarded by both colleagues and clients, and in 1982 he was promoted to partner.

Major law firms like WCP have long encouraged their staff to volunteer a portion of their time to the *pro bono* (unpaid work "for the public good") cases of those unable to afford customary legal fees. Coleman embraced pro bono work with particular enthusiasm, notably in the area of civil rights enforcement. His efforts there won the praise of the NAACP Legal Defense and Education Fund, which presented him with its Pro Bono Award in 1987. A similar honor came fifteen years later, when Duke University's Samuel DuBois Cook Society gave him its Community Betterment Award for his civil rights outreach efforts.

At a Glance . . .

Born in about 1948 in Charlotte, NC; children: at least two. *Education:* Harvard University, BA, 1970; Columbia University, JD, 1974.

Career: Office of U.S. District Judge Damon J. Keith (Eastern District, Michigan), law clerk, 1974–75; Kaye, Scholer, Fierman, Hayes, and Handler, associate, 1975–76; Legal Services Corporation, assistant general counsel, 1976–78; Committee on Standards of Official Conduct (U.S. House of Representatives), chief counsel, 1978; Wilmer, Cutler, and Pickering, associate, 1978–80; U.S. Department of Education, deputy general counsel, 1980–81; Wilmer, Cutler, and Pickering, associate, 1981–82, partner, 1982–91, 1993–96; Duke University School of Law, professor, 1991–93, 1996—.

Memberships: American Bar Association; Alliance for Justice, board of directors; Lawyers Committee for Civil Rights Under Law, board of trustees; numerous state and federal bars.

Awards: Pro Bono Award, NAACP Legal Defense and Education Fund, 1987; named a Distinguished Teacher, Duke University, 1993; Community Betterment Award, Samuel DuBois Cook Society, Duke University, 2002.

Addresses: *Office*—c/o Duke University School of Law, Box 90360, Durham, NC 27708-0360.

Coleman's affiliation with Duke began in 1989, when he took a leave from WCP to teach a class at the university's school of law on the death penalty, one of his major interests. Two years later he joined the law school faculty full time. In 1993 he returned to WCP, although he continued to teach his capital punishment class as a visiting lecturer. He returned to Duke full time in 1996. His teaching duties there have included classes in ethics, wrongful convictions, criminal defense, and appeals. At times he has also held concurrent positions within the law school's administration, serving, for example, as its senior associate dean for academic affairs between 2002 and 2005.

Besides his official workload, Coleman has continued to play a significant role in legal affairs beyond the Duke campus, often in conjunction with his students. His activities in this area have largely focused on the legal needs of underserved communities, particularly with

regard to criminal defense. A founder of the law school's Innocence Project, a student-run organization dedicated to the exoneration and release of wrongfully convicted individuals, he has also been at the forefront of efforts to reform or restrict the death penalty, both locally, through his work with the North Carolina Joint Legislative Capital Punishment Commission, and nationally, through his membership on the American Bar Association's [Death Penalty] Moratorium Implementation Project Steering Committee. While on the North Carolina commission, he helped draft a law barring the state from exercising the death penalty if the prisoner in question showed evidence of mental retardation. That law became a model for similar legislation in other states.

Despite his growing prominence in legal circles, Coleman was not well known among the public until 2006, when three members of the men's lacrosse team at Duke were arrested for rape. The case drew intense media coverage, due in part to the racial and socioeconomic tensions it aroused. The accuser was an African-American woman who was unaffiliated with the school and had a modest, working-class background; the accused, all white, belonged to wealthy and well-connected families. With emotions running high on all sides, Duke named Coleman to a committee formed to monitor the situation and recommend a course of action. There were growing indications, meanwhile, that the prosecutor in the case, Mike Nifong, had failed to weigh the evidence in his eagerness to go to trial. All charges were eventually dropped, and Nifong was disbarred for his conduct. As the university and the community worked to put the incident behind them, Coleman won wide praise for his measured and resolute response to the crisis; according to Applebome of the *New York Times,* he was "the one Duke faculty member willing to take on Mr. Nifong."

As of 2009, Coleman held bar privileges in a large number of state and federal courts, including the U.S. Supreme Court. He has also served on the boards of several prominent nonprofit organizations, including the Alliance for Justice and the Lawyers Committee for Civil Rights Under Law.

Sources

Periodicals

Duke Law Magazine, Spring 2002.
New York Times, November 29, 2006; April 15, 2007.

Online

Block, Melissa, "Rape Accusations Prompt Introspection at Duke," NPR.org, April 7, 2006, http://www.npr.org/templates/story/story.php?storyId=5330847&ps=rs (accessed November 12, 2009).

Coleman, James E., Jr., "One System, Two Realities," HuffingtonPost.com, April 3, 2009, http://www.huffingtonpost.com/james-e-coleman-jr/one-system-two-realities_b_183030.html (accessed November 12, 2009).

"James E. Coleman Jr.," Duke.edu, http://www.law.duke.edu/fac/colemanj/ (accessed November 12, 2009).

"What Is LSC?" LSC.gov, http://www.lsc.gov/about/lsc.php (accessed November 12, 2009).

—R. Anthony Kugler

Michael B. Coleman

1954—

Mayor

Michael B. Coleman made history in Ohio in 1999 as the first African-American mayor of its state capital, Columbus. As the new leader of the fifteenth-largest city in the United States, Coleman pledged to continue the work he carried out as an eight-year Columbus City Council member, working to improve city services and revitalize its downtown district. "The secret of Coleman's success is his extreme mastery of the details of the city of Columbus," Democratic National Committee chair Joe Andrew told reporters for the *Cincinnati Enquirer.* "Watching him shaking hands and talking to people was amazing. He knew every street and every park that people talked about."

Became Dedicated to Helping Others

Coleman was born in 1954 in Indianapolis, Indiana, and moved to Toledo, Ohio, with his family when he was three. His father, a physician, installed the family in the black middle-class neighborhood centered around Prospect Avenue. Coleman had an idyllic childhood, recalling the Prospect Avenue area as a neighborhood "where everybody took care of everybody," he told *Toledo Blade* reporter Jack Baessler. "My whole future was shaped by that experience on Prospect. My values were established on Prospect. My mom and dad played the most important role. Both were strong people with strong values."

Coleman grew up with two brothers and a sister and attended St. John's Jesuit High School, where he was one of a handful of minority students. "I guess that is where I really learned to work with people," he said in the interview with the *Toledo Blade.* "I felt being in that kind of environment, which is reality, that you have to work harder, be more focused; you have to work with people." He maintained a B average in high school, but the school's counselor told him that he wasn't college material. His parents, however, would not accept the counselor's verdict and insisted that Coleman apply to various schools. He was admitted to the University of Cincinnati, where he studied political science, earning his degree in 1977. From there Coleman entered law school at the University of Dayton, graduating in 1980.

While he was still in school, Coleman was able to secure a summer clerkship at the White House. In Washington, DC, he had a momentous encounter with Thurgood Marshall. Coleman, who had idolized Marshall since childhood, giddily told the nation's first African-American Supreme Court justice that he was working toward his law degree. The legendary jurist was unimpressed, saying, "So what? What do you plan to do with it?" The encounter led Coleman to realize that his life's achievements would be measured by what he did for others.

Established Himself in Politics

After graduating from law school, he began his career as an attorney in the Ohio attorney general's office. Although most African-American attorneys in the office worked in the civil rights section, Coleman wanted

At a Glance . . .

Born Michael Bennett Coleman on November 18, 1954, in Indianapolis, IN; son of John (a physician) and Joan (a community activist) Coleman; married, Frankie; children: Kimberly, Justin, John David. *Politics:* Democrat. *Religion:* Baptist. *Education:* University of Cincinnati, BS in political science, 1977; University of Dayton School of Law, JD, 1980.

Career: Office of the Ohio Attorney General, antitrust section, attorney,1980–82(?); legislative aide to Columbus city councilman Ben Espy, 1982–92; Schottenstein, Zox & Dunn, attorney/partner, 1992–99(?); Columbus city council, 1992–99, president of council, 1997–99; Columbus mayor, 1999—.

Memberships: American Bar Association; National Conference of Black Lawyers; Ohio State Bar Association; National Conference of Black Mayors.

Awards: Community Service Award, Columbus Bar Association, 1989.

Addresses: *Office*—City of Columbus Mayor's Office, 90 W. Broad St., Columbus, OH 43215. *Web*—http://mayor.columbus.gov/.

to learn about business, so he requested an assignment in the antitrust division.

Although Coleman saw himself as an aspiring businessman, the world of politics called out to him. In 1982 he was hired as a legislative aide for Ben Espy, a Columbus City Council member. He served as a member of the Columbus Convention Center Citizens Advisory Group in 1986 and on the Retailers's Task Force of the Downtown Development Corporation's in 1987. He was also involved in the Community Housing Network, the Columbus Youth Corps, and the Central Ohio Transit Authority.

In 1992 he replaced Espy on the council when his boss was selected to fill a vacancy in Ohio's state senate. A year later, Coleman was elected to his own four-year term on the Columbus City Council. There he became known as a consensus builder and a scrupulous, diligent representative. He was reelected in 1997 by voters impressed with his commitment to improving the quality of life for Columbus residents. During his tenure, Coleman launched the Urban Recovery Fair to renovate inner-city housing, started a Volunteers Fair for a mentor program called Boys to Men, and served on the

Bikeway Advisory Committee, which gave the city popular bike paths. He was also commended for working cooperatively with the city's Republican mayor.

When Coleman was reelected in 1997, he also became president of the City Council. Shortly afterward, Cleveland Democrat Lee Fisher, a former state attorney general, chose Coleman as his running mate for the 1998 Ohio gubernatorial race. Fisher lost his bid, however, to Republican Robert Taft, a scion of one of the state's most famous political dynasties. Nonetheless, the failed run for lieutenant governor succeeded in raising Coleman's public profile.

Became Mayor of Columbus

In 1999 Coleman announced his long-rumored bid for the Columbus mayor's office. He bested his former boss, Espy, in the Democratic primary, and he entered into a heated campaign against Republican candidate Dorothy Teater, a county commissioner. "I see the job as mayor is to run an efficient government, pick up the trash, put the criminals in jail and provide basic city services and run an efficient, well-managed, financially stable government," he told *Business First–Columbus*. He also pledged to further his campaign to revitalize Columbus's city center. "I will make our downtown move from an eight-hour downtown to an 18-hour downtown at least—that's 18," he stressed in the same interview. "And I will create jobs in this community. I will invigorate the central city, and I'll take the whole city to the next level. We'll be a world-class city."

The campaign garnered more attention than would be expected for an off-year municipal election. The head of the Democratic National Committee visited Columbus to campaign for Coleman. Both candidates bombarded the airwaves with advertising, together spending a reported $3.7 million on their campaigns. Regardless of the winner, Election Day would be a historic moment: the Ohio state capital would select either its first African-American or its first female mayor.

On November 2, 1999, Coleman was elected Columbus's first African-American mayor with about 82,000 votes and a 60 percent majority. Perhaps even more significantly, he became the first Democratic mayor since 1971 in the capital city of a state known for decades as a Republican stronghold. Coleman was inaugurated on December 30, 1999, at the Franklin Park Conservatory, the place where he had married his second wife, Frankie, in 1984. As reported by the *Cincinnati Enquirer,* he told the crowd that day, "If we are going to be the 21st century city that we should be, I ask you to make the sacrifice and the personal commitment right now to do what none of us can do alone and what all of us can do together to meet these challenges."

Ran for Governor of Ohio

"When I was elected, the biggest thing that the press talked about was being the first African American mayor of [Columbus]—I mean, for a whole year," an exasperated Coleman told Gwen Ifill in her book on the new generation of African-American political leaders, the *Breakthrough*. However, Coleman's focus after the election was on bringing the community together, not emphasizing the differences. "I'm the one who teaches that diversity in the community is expected and accepted, not just tolerated," he told *Ebony*'s Nikitta Foston. "We have a very diverse community, and I thought it was important to bring the community together to say, 'Look, we're going to make this city the best city in the world to live, work and raise a family'."

The early focus of Coleman's administration was on quality-of-life issues, such as juvenile delinquency, demolishing abandoned buildings, building more bike paths, and attracting businesses to the city center. "Now, that doesn't have the stamp of race on it. But what it does, what that policy says, is rebuild the inner city. Bring it back," Coleman told Ifill. "We have this big hole in this donut. The hole in the donut is where a lot of people live. Many of them happen to be African American. But I'm not saying, 'Let's help black folks,' what I'm saying is, 'Let's fill this hole.'"

At a time when Coleman was trying to rebuild many of Columbus's neighborhoods, he wound up also having to rebuild his own home. No one was injured in a fire at Coleman's house in October of 2001, but the structure itself was razed, and the family lost "almost everything" they had. "It was a challenge to me both personally and professionally," he told Foston. "But the citizens of Columbus helped me and my family through that. They came to our aid, comfort and assistance."

Improved Quality of Life in Columbus

Despite the personal setback, Coleman continued to work hard to improve Columbus. In 2002 the Partnership for America's 21st Century City was established, securing more than $1 billion in private sector commitments to invest in targeted city neighborhoods in and near the city's downtown area. The city established special investment zones to give residents tax breaks if they built or renovated a home. Coleman established a partnership between the city and the Columbus Medical Association Foundation to spearhead Access HealthColumbus, an initiative to improve uninsured or underinsured residents' access to health care. In the face of a recession, Coleman fought to help Columbus retain jobs and tightened belts around City Hall.

Despite many difficulties, Coleman's work on behalf of Columbus was so popular that he was re-elected in 2003 without Republican opposition. In 2004 Coleman was at the pinnacle of his popularity. According to *Ebony* magazine, Columbus had the nation's second-hottest job market and was one of the most affordable places in the country for home ownership. That year *Black Enterprise* selected Columbus as one of the top ten cities in the country for African Americans to work and live, and a 2001 BET Nightly News study had declared Columbus "the number one city in America for Black families." In the midst of all these accolades, Coleman was on a media blitz, appearing on talk shows to talk about the economy, terrorism funding, and the presidential election and addressing the Democratic Convention in Boston, where he delivered one of the nominating speeches for the party's presidential candidate, John Kerry. While making media appearances as a Kerry surrogate was intended to help the Democratic candidate win the battleground state of Ohio, it was also the case that Ohio governor Taft, who had thwarted Coleman's 1998 bid to be lieutenant governor, was restricted by term limits from running for a third term in office. In 2006 the governor's mansion could be wrested from the Republicans, and Coleman wanted to be in a position to do so.

In February 2005 Coleman was the first Democrat to declare himself a candidate for governor. His popularity was so great, and his fund-raising prowess so respected, that for months he had the field to himself. The only opponent who emerged to challenge Coleman in the Democratic primary was six-term congressman Ted Strickland. Although Coleman remained a favorite to get the party's nomination, chinks began to appear in his armor. Right wing talk show host Glenn Beck targeted Coleman after an incident in a Columbus public school in which a developmentally disabled student was sexually assaulted. During a contentious interview with Beck, Coleman lost his patience when he believed the host was impugning his manhood.

Second Gubernatorial Run Derailed

Then in June, the National Conference of Black Mayors held their annual meeting in Columbus. The event was a natural showcase for Coleman, but it was marred by controversy. He was criticized first by conservatives when it was learned that Nation of Islam leader Louis Farrakhan would be addressing the conference, then by his fellow mayors when he elected not to attend the conference the evening of Farrakhan's speech. Farrakhan savaged his absent host in his speech. As quoted in the *Columbus Post,* he said, "You're the mayor of the city, but you're afraid because you want to be governor so you scratch where you don't itch and you bend and you bow. It's you. It's not white people. It is your fear of them that keeps you under control." The conference attendees applauded.

However, the bad publicity of the Beck and Farrakhan incidents paled in comparison to the scandal that came in October, when Coleman's wife, Frankie, lost control of her car and hit a parked pickup truck in a Columbus suburb. Her blood alcohol level was more than three times the legal limit at the time of the accident, and her subsequent arrest was captured on a police dashboard video camera.

A month later, with just under a year left until the general election, Coleman withdrew from the governor's race. He cited the needs of his family—his son, a Marine Lance Corporal, had recently returned home after his company sustained heavy losses in Iraq—and his workload as mayor as reasons for quitting the race. Of his wife, Coleman was quoted in the *New York Times* as saying, "Throughout her life, she's been taking care of others. Now she's taking care of herself. I'm going to be there to support her." His wife pled guilty to driving while intoxicated and served a three-day jail sentence.

Elected to a Third Term as Mayor

After withdrawing from the race, Coleman was energetic in his support for Strickland, and he helped his former rival capture the governor's office in 2006. Coleman was tapped to chair the new governor's transition team, and his wife helped in the effort to prepare the Strickland team to hit the ground running after their inauguration. Strickland's lieutenant governor—Coleman's former running mate, Lee Fisher—subsequently gave Frankie Coleman a job with the Ohio Department of Development.

The job led to a second major scandal. Frankie Coleman had been criticized for lateness and absenteeism during her time with the transition, and matters came to head when one of her supervisors at the Department of Development refused to sign her timesheet because it credited her for days she did not work. The supervisor was then fired, and the incident became public. Frankie Coleman resigned her position and entered a substance abuse program. The state investigation of the scandal led to charges being filed by against her by city prosecutors for filing false timesheets. In August 2007 Frankie Coleman entered a no contest plea to two misdemeanor charges and received a suspended one-year sentence, with five years' probation and a $1,000 fine. The Colemans' marriage survived two more years before the couple announced that they were undergoing an amicable divorce.

Frankie Coleman's sentencing came just a few months before her husband stood for re-election. This time, he was not running unopposed. Republican attorney Bill Todd ran on a platform centered on direct mayoral control of the Columbus public schools, but his campaign was remembered mainly for its publicity stunts and negative advertisements. Less than two months before the election, Todd sued the Columbus School District, alleging that the disparate funding of various public schools in the system amounted to an unconstitutional violation of students' rights. One Todd radio ad, which a *Columbus Dispatch* editorial endorsing Coleman labeled as "one of the most repellent political ads in decades," featured the sound of a woman screaming as if being raped. Coleman beat Todd handily in the election.

In his third term, Coleman's main challenge was dealing with the nationwide economic downturn. Like most major cities, Columbus was facing rising unemployment and revenue shortfalls; Coleman had to juggle budget and service cuts in order to keep as many police and firefighters on the streets as possible. In 2009 Coleman advocated, and voters approved in a special election, an income tax increase to prevent layoffs of public safety personnel.

Despite the urgency of the economic crisis, Coleman continued to champion quality of life issues. In 2008 the city imposed a curfew on all minors in an effort to combat juvenile delinquency. Coleman also pushed for mass transit investments, particularly streetcars to service the downtown area. Throughout his time in public service, Coleman has been adamant that he be judged by his accomplishments on behalf of Columbus's residents, not the symbolic value of his office. As he told Ifill, "I'm proud to be an African American, and I'm proud to be a mayor, but if my legacy was to be the first [black mayor of Columbus], then I would have failed as a mayor. I want my legacy to be, 'He's the best mayor that ever has been in the city of Columbus.'"

Sources

Books

Ifill, Gwen, *The Breakthrough: Politics and Race in the Age of Obama,* Doubleday, 2009.

Periodicals

Business First–Columbus, October 29, 1999, p. 1.
Cincinnati Enquirer, February 10, 1998; May 5, 1999; October 16, 1999; November 3, 1999; December 31, 1999; November 5, 2003.
Columbus Dispatch, June 12, 2007; October 14, 2007; October 17, 2009.
Ebony, March 2003, p. 154.
Toledo Blade, February 22, 1998, p. B1.

Online

"Biographical Information for Columbus Mayor Michael B. Coleman," *Office of the Mayor, Columbus, Ohio.* http://mayor.columbus.gov/biography.aspx?id=1456&menu_id=442 (accessed November 25, 2009).

—Carol Brennan and Derek Jacques

Danny K. Davis

1941—

Politician

Davis, Danny K., photograph. Scott J. Ferrell/Congressional Quarterly/Getty Images.

A survivor of combative, racially polarizing political conflict within the Chicago City Council from 1983 to 1986, Danny Davis emerged in the 1990s as one of the leaders of the city's large and influential African-American community. In 1996, after two previous attempts, he was elected to the U.S. Congress and has retained this post for many terms, winning re-election every two years with more than 80 percent of the vote. In 2008 Davis won his seventh consecutive term.

Far from mellowing politically, the pro-choice advocate of gay rights and health care reform continued to be a staunch defender of government social programs and proved effective in protecting some of them against budget cutters. Also a strong proponent of second-chance programs for those convicted of crimes, Davis was instrumental in the passage of the Second Chance Act of 2007, which was signed into law by president George W. Bush on April 9, 2008. The legislation provided transitional assistance for ex-offenders as they re-enter civilian life.

Davis was born in Parkdale, Arkansas, on September 6, 1941, the son of a cotton farmer. In 1961 he graduated with a bachelor's degree in history from Arkansas Agricultural, Mechanical, and Normal College, now the University of Arkansas at Pine Bluff. Davis then moved to Chicago's West Side, where he took a job as a postal clerk. Davis pursued a career in education, teaching, and serving as a guidance counselor in Chicago's public schools during the 1960s. In 1968 Davis received a master's degree in guidance from Chicago State University. Married with two children, he established deep roots within his West Side community and served as a deacon of the New Galilee Missionary Baptist Church.

Became Health Care Administrator

A strong commitment to his community prompted the idealistic Davis to switch careers, putting him on a path that would ultimately lead him into politics. He became a health care administrator at the community level, serving as director of training at the Martin Luther King Neighborhood Health Center between 1969 and 1971, and then earned a doctoral degree in public administration from the Union Institute in Cincinnati in

At a Glance . . .

Born Daniel K. Davis on September 6, 1941, in Parkdale, AR; son of a cotton farmer; married to Vera; children: Jonathan, Stacey. *Politics:* Democrat. *Religion:* Missionary Baptist. *Education:* Arkansas AM & N College (now University of Arkansas at Pine Bluff), BA, history, 1961; Chicago State University, MA, guidance, 1968; Union Institute, PhD, public administration, 1977.

Career: Chicago Post Office, clerk, 1961–65; Chicago Public Schools, teacher and counselor, 1962–69; Martin Luther King Neighborhood Health Center, director of training, 1969–71; Westside Health Center, executive director, 1972–79; Chicago City Council, alderman, 1979–90; Cook County Board of Commissioners, 1990–96; House of Representatives, U.S. congressman, Seventh District of Illinois, 1997—.

Memberships: Congressional Black Caucus, secretary; Community Health Centers Caucus, co-chairman; Congressional Sugar Caucus, co-chairman; Progressive Caucus; Democratic Socialists of America; Congressional Postal Caucus, chair; Northeastern Illinois Planning Commission; Ways and Means Committee; Alpha Phi Alpha Fraternity, life member.

Awards: Best Alderman Award, Chicago City Council, 1980–81, 1981–82, and 1989–90; Leon M. Despres Award, 1987; six honorary doctorates.

Addresses: *District office*—3333 W. Arthington St., Ste. 130, Chicago, IL 60624. *Suburban office*—2301 Roosevelt Rd., Broadview, IL 60155. Washington *Office*—2159 Rayburn House Office Building, Washington, DC, 20515-1307.

1977. Davis become the executive director of the Westside Health Center, a post he held until 1979, and served as president of the National Association of Community Health Centers.

Davis combined his health care career with a commitment to grassroots community organizing, founding and becoming president of an organization called the Westside Association for Community Action. A run for the Chicago City Council was the next step. Davis was elected in 1979 as alderman of the Twenty-Ninth Ward, a district on the city's western edge. He served

on the council through some of its most turbulent years, emerging as a key ally of mayor Harold Washington, who was elected on a groundswell of African-American support in 1983 to become Chicago's first African-American mayor. Finding that Washington's initiatives were frustrated by entrenched white council members, Davis received an education in the difficulty of bringing about political change through established channels.

With an eye to the future, Davis challenged veteran U.S. Representative Cardiss Collins twice in primary elections, in 1984 and 1986. He was unsuccessful both times but in 1990 was elected to the Cook County Board of Commissioners, the legislative body for the county that included the city of Chicago. He ran for mayor of Chicago in 1991 against the extremely popular Richard Daley Jr. Although he lost the election, Davis broadened his name recognition, and he went on to build his influence within the Chicago-area Democratic Party. In 1992 he became a state co-chair of Bill Clinton's successful campaign for the presidency. Clinton, in return, named Davis to the board of directors of the National Housing Partnership, and he continued to serve on the county commission.

Won a Seat in the House

In 1996 Collins finally retired, and Davis entered a ten-way race for the Seventh District Congressional seat. A campaigner with a booming voice and a stately personal presence that contrasted favorably with the other, more flamboyant candidates in the race, Davis offered a liberal platform that called for increased spending on urban concerns and health care and for a rise in the federal minimum wage to $7.60 an hour. Running, according to the *Progressive,* on a slogan of "jobs, justice, equality, and peace," Davis called for cuts in defense spending and argued for the maintenance of affirmative action programs, a favorite target of Republicans. He also led journalists on tours of Chicago's public housing projects during the Democratic National Convention. Davis won the primary by a margin of thirteen percentage points over his nearest competitor and cruised to victory in the general election in his overwhelmingly Democratic district.

One of the most liberal members of the House, Davis maintained both his long-standing Democratic affiliation and ties with a small left-wing organization called the New Party. Although Davis might have been expected to have his liberal influence severely circumscribed in the Republican-dominated House of the late 1990s, he brought his considerable persuasive skills to bear on his fellow House members. He voted against a 1997 tax cut bill, arguing, according to the *Almanac of American Politics,* that "[w]e cannot have a great, civilized and humane nation without paying the cost; if all we can do is cut, cut, cut, all that we will get is blood, blood, blood." On that issue and on many other votes, Davis ended up in the minority.

However, on other issues, Davis enjoyed more success. He worked with the House Transportation Committee leadership on a bill to increase funding for services that would transport inner-city workers to suburban jobs. This issue gained importance in the late 1990s as the economy flourished and suburbs grew dramatically. Inner-city workers, many of whom did not own cars, were unable to commute to jobs that often went unfilled. Davis sponsored new funding for neighborhood health care centers and worked with fellow Chicago representative Bobby Rush to secure emergency help for the perennially strapped Chicago Housing Authority.

Challenged Supreme Court Hiring Practices

During the late 1990s Davis took a strong stand on several controversial issues. He vigorously opposed the charter school movement and was quoted by the *Almanac of American Politics* as saying that it was "a sinister move to dismantle public education." In 1998 Davis was the first to point out that the U.S. Supreme Court employed very few minority lawyers on its staff of clerks. Although this situation went virtually unchanged, Davis earned national recognition within progressive circles. That same year, Davis took the lead in resisting Republican-inspired budget cuts aimed at home-improvement loans for low-income Americans and at summer jobs programs for urban youth. "Having [young people] on our streets instead of working is a crazy plan that is detrimental to their futures and to our communities," Davis told *Jet.*

Over the next decade, Davis won his congressional seat every two years, always garnering more than 80 percent of the vote. In 2004 he generated criticism when he helped to organize a religious ceremony in the Dirkson Senate Office Building honoring the highly controversial reverend Sun Myung Moon. Davis personally crowned the religious leader and his wife as the king and queen of peace, carrying the crown to them on a pillow. Many lawmakers were extremely angry about the crowning event, which had caught them by surprise. The ceremony had been integrated into an awards ceremony honoring nearly one hundred people from all over the nation, which is what the lawmakers thought they were attending. When questioned, Davis explained that he did not agree with many of Moon's religious teachings and that the money Moon's associates contributed to his campaigns had nothing to do with his support of Moon.

Davis was the focus of additional controversy in 2005 when traveled to Sri Lanka to help determine whether U.S. relief funds were being distributed properly after the December 2004 tsunami. The trip was reportedly paid for by a Sri Lankan separatist rebel group, the Tamil Tigers, which the United States considered a terrorist group. Davis explained that he thought the trip was paid for by a Tamil cultural organization based in Illinois.

Won Seventh Term in Congress

On April 28, 2008, Davis was rewarded for his many years of work on second-chance programs for ex-offenders when the Second Chance Act of 2007 was signed into law by President George W. Bush. The law provided funding for programs Davis believed were necessary to help ex-offenders live in the world outside of prison. The funding would provide job training, substance abuse counseling, and services to help provide family stability. Davis told *Jet,* "No single piece of legislation is going to solve the re-entry crisis we are facing, but the Second Chance Act is a good start. I hope that with the passage of this bill we will begin a new era in criminal justice."

A few months later, in November of 2008, Davis captured his seventh term in Congress. The following month he was propelled to national attention when Illinois governor Rod Blagojevich asked Davis if he would accept appointment to the Senate, filling the seat that Barack Obama had vacated when he won the presidency. Blagojevich was mired in controversy at the time, having been arrested on corruption charges earlier in the month and being accused of previously trying to sell the Senate seat. Davis turned down the offer from Blagojevich but suggested that the governor might ask Ronald W. Burris, the state's former attorney general. Meanwhile controversy raged, and senators claimed they would not seat anyone appointed by the governor due to the serious allegations against him. Neither would they, however, hold a special election. Burris was eventually seated as a U.S. senator from Illinois.

By July of 2009, Davis had become worried about the status of local government in Illinois, particularly in Cook County. According to the Associated Press, Davis sought to bring a "level of stability" to government in Cook County, and so was considering running for president of the Cook County Board of Commissioners. If elected to this position, Davis would preside over seventeen commissioners and could help direct county legislation in one hundred and twenty-eight municipalities, including Chicago. However, Davis was barred by law from running for both Congress and the Board of Commissioners at the same time.

Cook County appeared to be in need of a strong leader, and polls showed that Davis would be a formidable opponent against the weak incumbent, Todd Stroger. However, by November of 2009 the field had become crowded with other strong candidates, and new health care legislation had been passed by the House. Excited by the prospect of health care reform, Davis decided to seek his eighth term in Congress, telling the Associated Press that he wanted "to be around [the U.S. House of

Representatives] to help." In addition, Davis was a member of the influential Ways and Means Committee, and with his Congressional seniority, believed that he could be most useful to his constituents by retaining his congressional seat.

Selected works

(With Philip M. Crane) "US Postal Service Privatization," *American Legion,* May 2003, p. 56.

Sources

Periodicals

Chicago Sun-Times, November 9, 2009.
Chicago Tribune, November 1, 2009.
Ebony, January 1997, p. 64.
Jet, April 8, 1996, p. 40; August 3, 1998, p. 32; April 28, 2008, p. 12.
New York Times, December 31, 2008, p. A1.
Progressive, November 1996, p. 25.
Washington Post, June 23, 2004, p. A1.

Online

"Congressman's Sri Lanka Trip Questioned," UPI, August 24, 2006.
"2 More Canadians Arrested in Tamil Tigers Investigation," CBC News, August 24, 2006, http://www.cbc.ca/canada/story/2006/08/23/tamil-weapons-bust.html (accessed November 9, 2009).

—James M. Manheim and Sandra Alters

Charles H. Ellis III

1958(?)—

Religious leader

Ellis, Charles H., III, photograph. Scott R. Galvin/UPI/Landov.

Charles H. Ellis III inherited the pastorship of the Detroit's Greater Grace Temple of the Apostolic Faith in 1996 and has since built it into the city's largest congregation. In 2005 its four-thousand-seat auditorium hosted the funeral of civil rights leader Rosa Parks, and in late 2008 Ellis gained international media attention for bringing three sport-utility vehicles to its stage during a special Sunday service as Detroit was waiting to hear Washington's decision on bailing out the city's Big Three automakers. "For those who do not believe that this is a spiritual message," he declared, according to *New York Times Magazine* writer Jonathan Mahler, "I would suggest to you that it was the automobile industry that proved to be a catalyst for an underprivileged man, unlearned not due to his intellect but in large part due to the inequities of an educational system in a segregated society."

Greater Grace Temple is a part of the Pentecostal Assemblies of the World (PAW) Christian denomination, a network of black Pentecostal churches founded during the 1920s following a split with the majority-white Southern Pentecostal organization. Ellis's grandfather was founder and pastor of the Indiana Avenue Pentecostal Church of God in Chicago. Ellis's father, David, relocated to Detroit with his family in the early 1960s to take over New Bethel Temple, a Pentecostal church started as a home church by the Rev. Ellington Forbes in the 1920s. One of seven children in the family, Ellis was a toddler at the time of the move. Brought up and educated in Detroit, he prepared to follow his father into the ministry.

Ellis attended Wayne State University and earned a bachelor's degree in business administration. When his father died suddenly from a heart attack in 1996 at the age of sixty, Ellis took over as pastor of the church, now named Greater Grace Temple. He soon announced a plan to fulfill his father's vision of building a "City of David" for the community, and by 2002 a massive new complex was completed on the city's west side, on a nineteen-acre site that was once home to an amusement park. Facilities included an imposing dual-spiral modern church, a charter school, a day-care center, senior citizen housing, a television studio, a banquet hall and conference center, and a funeral home. "What we're creating is a campus which we call the city of David," Ellis told Marti Benedetti in an interview for *Crain's Detroit Business.* "When we built this church,

At a Glance . . .

Born 1958(?); son of David L. Ellis (a minister); married; wife's name, Crisette Michelle (a cosmetics salesperson); children: Kiera Monet, Charles Haywood IV, and Kirsten Maria (died, 1994). *Religion:* Pentecostal Assemblies of the World. *Education:* Wayne State University, BA, business administration.

Career: Pastor, Greater Grace Temple of the Apostolic Faith, 1996—; board member for the Booker T. Washington Business Association, Young Men's Christian Association (YMCA) of Metropolitan Detroit, and Sinai-Grace Hospital.

Addresses: *Home*—Bloomfield Hills, MI. *Office*—Greater Grace Temple, 23500 W. Seven Mile Rd., Detroit, MI 48219.

we thought of it being a city that would offer all kinds of activities." Ellis's complex even included a golf course purchased from the city of Detroit, whose finances were in far worse shape than those of Ellis's efficiently managed church. "The 18-hole course was originally built in 1914 by prominent members of the Jewish community," wrote Benedetti. "Since Greater Grace bought it, it is the only black-owned and -operated golf course in the state and one of a few in the country."

Greater Grace Temple served as the spiritual home for Ellis's congregation, which numbered between six thousand and eight thousand members. It seated four thousand and hosted gospel-music festivals and other social and cultural events. The temple also offered community services that were much needed in the area, including scores of youth, teen, adult, and senior outreach programs. Youngsters came for free haircuts and school supplies on annual Back to School Day, there was a summer job training program for teens, and financial education classes were on offer. An entrepreneurial ministry assisted Detroiters in launching their own businesses. Apart from casinos and sports venues, few other projects of this size were launched in the city during this era.

A media-savvy pastor, Ellis led services with a theatrical flair. The church's Easter Week passion play featured live animals, and a multimedia presentation called "To Hell and Back" was designed to provide a glimpse of the Pentecostal vision of the sinner's afterlife. In the fall of 2008, with the U.S. economy in the throes of an economic downturn, Ellis's sermons took on a more urgent-care tone. The mortgage crisis and credit crunch that affected all Americans was especially dev-astating to the Motor City, where the remnants of the automobile industry still provided one source of steady, full-time, union-protected jobs.

In December of 2008 Congress debated whether to assist General Motors and Chrysler via the Troubled Asset Relief Program (TARP), and Detroiters braced themselves for the worst. Ellis chose a Sunday to bring three hybrid-fuel sport-utility vehicles on stage at Greater Grace Temple, and he invited senior officials from the United Autoworkers Union (UAW) to speak. Then he took the pulpit with a sermon entitled "A Hybrid Hope," in which he urged parishioners, Detroiters, and the rest of America to have both faith and hope. He asked his congregation to pray for a turn-around for the automobile manufacturing industry, and for a strong future for the Big Three and hybrid-technology vehicles. Then Ellis turned to the topic of the upcoming Congressional vote on using TARP government-bailout funds to help the Detroit automakers. "We have never seen as midnight an hour as we face this coming week," *New York Times* journalist Nick Bunkley quoted Ellis as saying. "I don't know what's going to happen, but we need prayer. When it's all said and done, we're all in this thing together."

African-American autoworkers are the backbone of Ellis's congregation, and the once-secure manufacturing jobs offered by the Big Three were partly responsible for making Detroit in the 1970s the first U.S. city with a majority-black population to be fully governed by elected African-American leaders. Ellis was interviewed by Mahler for a lengthy *New York Times Magazine* article entitled "G.M., Detroit and the Fall of the Black Middle Class." Speaking from an office chair crafted from the seat of a Cadillac Escalade sport-utility vehicle—a gift from one of his flock—he said that many of his congregants were facing layoffs that could turn out to be permanent. Because of job losses they were being hit by foreclosure notices, utility shutoffs, and other setbacks. "The problem that I have is that most people, because of pride, don't want to tell me they're in trouble," Ellis explained. "They come here on Sunday morning in a suit, and I say, 'How you doing?' 'I'm blessed and I'm highly favored of God,' they answer. I don't know they're 30 days from being evicted. If I know early enough, I can help them make the most out of a bad situation. Now there's nothing I can do except help them get a U-Haul truck and find a place to store their stuff."

Sources

Periodicals

Crain's Detroit Business, August 13, 2007, p. D4.
New York Times, December 8, 2008, p. A19.
New York Times Magazine, June 28, 2009.

Online

"Bishop Charles H. Ellis," Northeast District Council, Pentecostal Assemblies of the World, http://ndcoun cil.org/index.php?option=com_content&view=ar ticle&id=32%3Abiobishopcharleshellis&catid=11% 3Aabout&Itemid=37 (accessed October 20, 2009).

"The Late Bishop David Ellis," A Place Called Agape, http://agapeworldwide.wordpress.com/apostolic-le gends/the-late-bishop-david-ellis/ (accessed October 18, 2009).

—Carol Brennan

Vernon Forrest

1971–2009

Boxer, business owner

Forrest, Vernon, photograph. David Livingston/Getty Images.

A three-time championship title-holder, Vernon Forrest was one of the great boxers of the 1990s and into the twenty-first century. He reached his professional peak in 2002, when he defeated "Sugar" Shane Mosley—then undefeated and considered by many the best pound-for-pound boxer in the world—in consecutive World Boxing Council (WBC) championship bouts, a feat that earned Forrest *USA Today* and *Ring Magazine*'s Fighter of the Year awards. Forrest was thwarted in his attempt to capture his third welterweight title the following year, when World Boxing Association (WBA) champion Ricardo Mayorga defeated him. However, Forrest rebounded after two losses to Mayorga and several major injuries to capture the WBC junior middleweight championship in 2007 and again in 2008.

Outside of the boxing ring, Forrest was known for his sound business acumen and charitable work. In 1998 he established a charitable foundation to provide housing for people with disabilities, and his philanthropic efforts led him to become the first active boxer honored with the Boxing Writers Association of America's Marvin Kohn "Good Guy" Award in 2003. Forrest was fatally shot in July 2009 during a robbery in his hometown of Atlanta, Georgia.

Abandoned College for the Olympics

Vernon Forrest was born on January 12, 1971, in Augusta, Georgia, where his father worked as a mechanic and his mother worked as a nurse's assistant. He was the sixth of eight children in the family. He began boxing as a nine-year-old and demonstrated enough talent that he continued to train throughout his teenage years and eventually earned an athletic scholarship to Northern Michigan University (NMU).

Forrest attended NMU for two years as a business administration student but dropped out to pursue his Olympic ambitions. Having already taken the U.S. junior welterweight title in 1991 and the junior welterweight world amateur champion title in 1992, Forrest seemed to be a good bet to make the team. At the Olympic trials, however, he encountered a formidable opponent in Shane Mosley. Standing six feet tall, Forrest had a formidable height and reach advantage on the five foot, eight inch Mosley. However, Mosley's

At a Glance . . .

Born January 12, 1971, in Augusta, GA; died on July 23, 2009, in Atlanta, GA; children: Vernon Forrest Jr. *Religion:* Baptist. *Education:* Attended Northern Michigan University.

Career: Amateur boxer, 1980–92; professional boxer, 1992–2008; Destiny's Child group homes, owner, 1999–2009; Champions Limousine Service, owner, 2002–09.

Awards: U.S. junior welterweight national champion, 1991; junior welterweight world amateur champion, 1992; International Boxing Federation welterweight champion, 2001–02; *USA Today* Fighter of the Year, 2002; *Ring Magazine* Fighter of the Year, 2002; World Boxing Association welterweight champion, 2002–03; Phoenix Award, City of Atlanta, 2002; Edward J. Neil Trophy, Boxing Writers Association of America, 2002; Marvin Kohn Good Guy Award, Boxing Writers Association of America, 2003; World Boxing Association junior middleweight champion, 2007–08.

great speed and punching power made them an even match. In the end Forrest took the fight by a 6–4 decision and made the U.S. Olympic Boxing Team.

Considered a gold medal favorite, Forrest was stricken with food poisoning shortly before his first-round bout at the Barcelona Games and left the competition without a medal. As he later remembered in a 2000 *Los Angeles Daily News* profile, "I walked around Barcelona like a zombie." After returning from the games, Forrest moved to Atlanta and prepared for his debut in the professional ranks. Forrest finished his amateur career with a record of 225 wins against just 16 losses.

Forrest made his professional boxing debut on November 25, 1992, when the twenty-one-year old went up against Charles Hawkins in Las Vegas. Forrest won the fight on a technical knockout (TKO) when the referee stopped the fight in the first round. In 1993 Forrest had five bouts, each of which he won on a TKO. None of the fights went beyond the third round. The following year Forrest emerged with two more wins, one with his first outright knockout in the first round against Randy Archuleta. Forrest expanded his unbeaten streak through 1995 with seven more victories and added three knockout wins in 1996. In 1997 he continued his string of victories with five more wins.

Waited for Title Fight

After winning three bouts in 1998 and another four matches in 1999, Forrest's professional record stood at 30 wins and no losses, leading many boxing experts to ask why he had not yet been given a chance at a title bout. One explanation was that Forrest, while a great fighter, was not a great entertainer. His fighting style—intelligent, precise, technical boxing—was appealing to purists, but didn't fill the arenas the way some of the sport's more reckless and popular brawlers did. Outside the ring, Forrest carried himself with quiet dignity in a sport that rewarded aggression, flash, and showmanship. As a Los Angeles *Daily News* article headlined in January of 2000, "Forrest's Problem: He's Too Nice." Jon Wertheim of *Sports Illustrated* put it a little differently: "Forrest is about as flashy as the gray sweats he wears for his workouts." Citing the fighter's lack of gimmicks, tattoos, nicknames, and bombastic pre-fight press conferences, Wertheim went on to write, "Forrest forsakes one of boxing's most important commandments: Thou Shalt Have Schtick."

A more significant factor in Forrest's long wait for a shot at the title may have been his reluctance to be under contract to a major boxing promoter such as Don King or Bob Arum. The big promoters were the gatekeepers to boxing's championship fights, but Forrest wanted to determine his own fate. As he told Coyote Duran of the *Dog House Boxing* Web site, "Let it be known that I'm an independent fighter. I'm not contracted with anybody and the reason why I like it like that is because I don't want to be in no one's stable of fighters. I don't wanna be pushed on a shelf or pushed behind for someone else."

During his long wait for a title shot, Forrest applied his energies to pursuits outside the boxing ring. Forrest's interest in the mentally disabled began when he witnessed an autistic child struggle to tie his shoes while visiting a friend who worked with people with disabilities. "If you sit there and watch a person take about an hour to tie his shoestrings, then you realize that whatever problems you got ain't that significant. A light went on in my head," he told the New York Times in 2006. In 1997 Forrest, his mother, and his girlfriend, Toy Johnson, began training to operate group homes for mentally disabled adults. They were certified by the state of Georgia in 1999 to operate residential facilities and together founded Destiny's Child Inc. (DCI) with one group home in Atlanta. Within three years DCI expanded to six group homes and fourteen employees. "The state tells you not to get attached to the clients," Forrest told *Sports Illustrated*. "Real quick, you realize that if you're going to give them enough love and support and attention, it's impossible not to get attached. I feel as if they're my thirty brothers." In recognition of his efforts in working with the mentally challenged, Forrest received the Phoenix Award from the city of Atlanta in April of 2002. In addition to his management of DCI, Forrest also started Champions Limousine Service in 2002.

Became Welterweight Champion

On August 26, 2000, Forrest finally got his first shot at a title match when he faced Raul Frank in Las Vegas for the International Boxing Federation (IBF) welterweight championship. The long-sought title bout quickly turned sour, however, when the referees stopped the fight in the third round for an alleged head-butting incident between the fighters. Although the infraction was later ruled an accident, the fight was declared a no-contest match. As a result the IBF title remained vacant for another nine months until Forrest and Frank boxed again in a second title fight. This time Forrest took the fight in a twelve-round decision that gave him the IBF welterweight title. Forrest held the title for less than a year, however, as he gave it up in order to fight in another championship match for the WBC welterweight title early in 2002. The fight matched him against Shane Mosley, the boxer he had defeated for a spot on the Olympic boxing team ten years before.

In going up against "Sugar" Shane Mosley in New York City on January 26, 2002, Forrest faced one of the most popular fighters of the day. Mosley not only had the crowd on his side going into the bout, but odds-makers favored him by as much as seven to one to take the match. In the second round, however, Forrest sent Mosley down with an uppercut, the first time the Mosley had been knocked down during his professional career. At the end of the bout, Forrest was declared the winner by a unanimous decision of the judges and became the WBC welterweight champion. "I've been preparing for this day for twenty-one years," the new champion told the *Atlanta Journal-Constitution* shortly after winning the bout, "This is what I envisioned how boxing would be when I was nine years old."

Although Forrest enjoyed his newly won title, he faced the immediate challenge of a rematch with Mosley, which was set for July 20, 2002, in Indianapolis. The media hype over the rematch dwarfed the interest in their previous match, with Mosley boasting that he would retake the title. Their second bout again went the full twelve rounds, and although the judges' scores were closer this time, Forrest retained his title by maintaining solid defensive techniques throughout the fight. "[Mosley] came out with a different strategy for this fight, but I was still able to get some shots off," Forrest explained to the *New York Times* after the fight. "When two great fighters are in the ring together, you can't fight with reckless abandon. I had to be careful. His shots didn't really stun me, but I knew he was a sharp puncher." After retaining his title Forrest also gained a lucrative, six-bout contract with the HBO cable network, which put him in an elite league of fighters that included Oscar De La Hoya and Lennox Lewis.

Lost Title to Mayorga

In the first fight under his HBO contract Forrest faced Nicaraguan fighter Ricardo Mayorga, a boxer managed by promoter Don King. Known as a slugger, Mayorga's style contrasted greatly with Forrest's more deliberate technique. During the January 2003 fight, however, Forrest abandoned the disciplined strategy that had served him so well in the past and attempted to match Mayorga punch for punch. The switch in tactics was disastrous, and Forrest suffered a TKO in the third round. "I abandoned my ability and engaged in a shootout," Forrest told Gregory Leon of the *Boxing Talk* Web site after the fight, "And anytime you get into that with a guy who throws wild haymakers like that, someone is going to get hit. And he caught me before I caught him." "It was the biggest mistake I ever made in my career," Forrest told the *Atlanta Journal-Constitution,* "Everybody makes bonehead mistakes. That was my one bonehead mistake. I've made it, I've suffered for it, and now I'm moving on."

Forrest's rematch with Mayorga was scheduled for July, and the former champion trained in seclusion, cutting off communication with the press and even his own family for three months prior to the bout. Despite his intensive preparations and renewed dedication to his disciplined fighting style, Forrest was unable to wrest the title from his nemesis. He didn't suffer the indignity of another knockout, but Mayorga boxed well enough to secure a majority decision from the judges. "I felt like someone had ripped my heart right out from my chest," Forrest told Geoffrey Gray of the *New York Times.* "I was in love with boxing, and it broke my heart."

Made Comeback as Junior Middleweight

For the next two years, Forrest's career was effectively derailed. He had chronic shoulder pain in his left arm, which for years he had treated with stopgap cortisone shots whenever he was preparing for a bout. After the second Mayorga fight, however, Forrest learned that years of wear and tear had resulted in bone spurs and a torn rotator cuff, which would require several major reconstructive surgeries on his left shoulder and elbow.

Forrest's path to recovery was arduous. Even after he was medically cleared to fight again, he found that after a two-year layoff he had to prove once more that he was a legitimate title contender. After he won two warm-up fights against low-ranked opponents by knockout, Forrest took on former champion Ike Quartey in August of 2006, winning a ten-round decision. Finally, in July of 2007—four years after his second defeat to Mayorga—Forrest got a title shot, fighting Carlos Manuel Baldomir for the vacant WBC junior middleweight title. Forrest won an easy unanimous decision against Baldomir to become a world champion again.

After a successful title defense in December, Forrest was shocked to lose his title to Sergio Mora in June of

2008. Afterward, Forrest was candid that overconfidence lay at the root of his loss. Contrary to his normal behavior, Forrest had been openly contemptuous of Mora, a fighter whose primary claim to fame coming into the fight was that he had won the boxing reality show *The Contender.* In a pre-fight conference call, Forrest mocked Mora, calling him "The Pretender," and stating, "I promise they're going to take you out on a stretcher." After Mora won a tight majority decision, Forrest was more gracious, assuring his opponent that the mockery had not been personal, and making no excuses for his loss. "Congratulations to Sergio," he said in a post-fight interview. "He fought a very good fight, a really technical fight, and he was the better man tonight."

For all his kind words, Forrest was not done with Mora. He exercised his contractual right to a rematch, and had the twenty-seven-year-old champion back in the ring just three months after their first bout. This time Forrest was dominant, stunning his opponent in the fifth round and knocking him down in the seventh, on the way to an easy unanimous decision victory.

Shot to Death in Robbery

This time, Forrest did not have the opportunity to defend his title. Early in 2009 he suffered a rib cage injury while preparing for a tune-up fight. The injury had not healed by the time that Forrest was required to make a mandatory defense of his title, so the WBC stripped him of the championship he had won from Mora.

Forrest had not finalized plans to fight again at the time of his tragic death. On the night of July 25, 2009, Forrest stopped at an Atlanta gas station to fill the tires of his car. According to the *Atlanta Journal-Constitution,* an armed man approached Forrest, demanding the boxer's watch and ring. Forrest, who was also armed, chased the robber, and the two men exchanged gunfire. Forrest had given up the pursuit and was on his way back to his car when one of the robber's accomplices shot him multiple times in the back, killing him. The Atlanta police acted quickly to apprehend the suspects in Forrest's murder, making three arrests within a month of the slaying with help of surveillance camera footage and the cooperation of the community.

Meanwhile, the world of boxing mourned the death of one the sport's true class acts. Charles Watson, Forrest's longtime trainer, was unsurprised that his friend would resist a robbery attempt. "Vernon always was the type of guy who wasn't going to let anybody take anything from him," Watson told the *Atlanta Journal-Constitution.* "He would give you the shirt off his back, but if you tried to take something from him, he was going to fight you for it." HBO Sports president Ross Greenburg told the Associated Press that Forrest "was one of the most gracious and charitable fighters in boxing and he will be missed by the entire boxing community. ... Maybe Vernon's lasting legacy will be for Americans everywhere to rise up and end this kind of senseless violence."

Sources

Periodicals

Atlanta Journal-Constitution, January 27, 2002, p. E1; January 30, 2002, p. C2; April 4, 2002, p. F5; January 27, 2003, p. D3; March 2, 2003, p. D4.; July 26, 2009; August 25, 2009.

Daily News (Los Angeles), January 17, 2000, p. S21.

Dayton Daily News, July 22, 2002, p. D1.

Los Angeles Times, July 19, 2002, p. D1.

New York Post, December 12, 2001, p. 72.

New York Times, July 21, 2002, p. 6; January 23, 2003, p. D4; July 16, 2003, p. D6; August 5, 2006; July 27, 2009, D8.

Sports Illustrated, February 4, 2002, p. Z2; July 29, 2002, p. 52.

Online

"Former Champion Forrest Shot to Death," ESPN. com, http://sports.espn.go.com/sports/boxing/news/story?id=4356715 (accessed November 25, 2009).

"Interview with Vernon Forrest," *Dog House Boxing,* http://www.doghouseboxing.com/Duran/Coyote102105.htm (accessed November 25, 2009).

"Mora in Search of Respect against Forrest," ESPN. com, http://sports.espn.go.com/sports/boxing/news/story?id=3424644 (accessed November 25, 2009).

"Vernon Forrest," HBO, http://www.hbo.com/boxing/fighters/forrest_vernon/bio.html (accessed November 25, 2009).

"Vernon Forrest Career Record," *About.com Boxing,* http://boxing.about.com/library/bl_forrest.htm (accessed November 25, 2009).

—Timothy Borden and Derek Jacques

Andrew Foster

1879–1930

Professional baseball player, baseball manager

Foster, Andrew, photograph. National Baseball Hall of Fame Library/MLB Photos via Getty Images.

Jackie Robinson is well known for breaking the color barrier in modern baseball after the 1945 season, when he became the first African-American player to sign with a major-league team. Fewer baseball fans know about the important contributions that Texas-born player, manager, and Negro National League founder Andrew "Rube" Foster made to the integration of the game, paving the way for Robinson and other minority players a generation later. On the mound, Foster was a dominant pitcher, described by some as the best in the game, black or white. As a manager, he made the Chicago American Giants the top team in black baseball, rivaling the white major-league teams for fans. Most important, he established the Negro National League in 1920, one of several leagues of African-American teams in existence before the integration of baseball, and the first to last for more than a single season—an achievement for which he is known as the father of black baseball. Foster constantly reminded his players that integration was on the horizon, although he did not live to see the day. He was inducted into the National Baseball Hall of Fame in 1981 in recognition of his extraordinary contributions to the game.

Foster was born on September 17, 1879, in Calvert, Texas, the son of Andrew Foster Sr. and his wife Evaline. Andrew Sr., a serious and devout man, was the presiding elder of the African Methodist Episcopal Church in the area and the minister of the local congregation. He preached against drunkenness and smoking, and discouraged his son from playing baseball. Young Andrew faithfully attended his father's services every Sunday morning but spent every Sunday afternoon on the baseball diamond, in spite of his father's wishes and an affliction with chronic asthma. He is said to have organized his first team by the age of eight, and his enthusiasm for the game grew.

Became Best Pitcher in Black Baseball

Foster left school after the eighth grade, running off to Waco, Texas, to play baseball. He began his career in 1897 pitching for the Waco Yellow Jackets, an independent black team that traveled across Texas and neighboring states. The team found few fans among fellow African Americans, who looked down on base-

At a Glance . . .

Born on September 17, 1879, in Calvert, TX; died on December 9, 1930, in Kankakee, IL; son of Andrew (a minister) and Evaline Foster; married Sarah Watts, October 29, 1908; children: Sarah, Earl Mack.

Career: Chicago Union Giants, 1902; Otsego Independents, 1902; Cuban X-Giants, 1903; Philadelphia Giants, 1904–06; Chicago Leland Giants, player-manager, 1907–10; Chicago American Giants, player-manager and owner, 1911–26; Negro National League, president, 1920–26.

Awards: National Baseball Hall of Fame, 1981; Texas Sports Hall of Fame, 1999.

ball players as "low and ungentlemanly," Foster said, according to Robert Peterson, author of *Only the Ball Was White.* Foster also pitched during batting practice for white major-league teams that held their spring training in Texas.

Early in his career, Foster gained a reputation for his fastball, sharp curveball, and screwball. In 1902 he was invited to join Frank Leland's all-black Chicago Union Giants for a salary of $40 a month and a stipend of 15 cents per meal. Although Foster pitched a shutout in his first game, he struggled by midseason and left the team. He headed north to join the Otsego Independents, a white semiprofessional team in the Michigan State League, and after a rocky start—he lost his first five outings—he defeated every team on the circuit. By the end of the 1902 season, Foster had signed with the Cuban X-Giants of Philadelphia, then the best team in black baseball. He earned the nickname "Rube" after defeating white Hall of Fame pitcher Rube Waddell of the Philadelphia Athletics in an exhibition game that year.

By 1903 Foster was considered the best black pitcher in baseball. He took the X-Giants to the postseason to win the black championship against the Philadelphia Giants, five games to two; Foster won four games himself. The next season he switched teams to sign with the Philadelphia Giants, winning twenty games—including two no-hitters—setting a new record for single-game strikeouts, and again bringing his team a championship title. According to some accounts, Major League Baseball (MLB) manager John McGraw wanted to sign Foster to the New York Giants in 1904 but league rules would not permit African-American players. Instead, McGraw hired Foster to tutor the Giants pitching staff. Hall of Famer Christy Mathewson is rumored to have learned his fadeaway pitch—a screwball—from Foster.

Shifted into the Manager's Position

Foster joined the Chicago Leland Giants in 1907 as a player-manager, guiding the team to a 110–10 record (including a reputed forty-eight-game winning streak) and a Chicago city league title. As his physical skills began to decline, particularly after he suffered a broken leg in 1909, Foster became a keen student of the game and easily shifted into the manager's position. In 1910 he assembled one of the finest teams in black baseball history, which included players such as Bruce Petway, John Henry Lloyd, Pete Hill, and Grant "Home Run" Johnson. The team went 123–6 overall that season and 11–0 against the top black teams.

By this time, Foster had total control over the club, having parted company with team owner Leland. For the 1911 season, Foster renamed the team the Chicago American Giants (often called simply the American Giants), and formed a partnership with John M. Schorling, the white son-in-law of Chicago White Sox owner Charles Comiskey. The American Giants drew incredible crowds, often outselling the city's white MLB teams, the White Sox and the Cubs. The American Giants dominated Chicago's semiprofessional circuit and national black baseball, winning Negro League championships in 1914 and 1917 and sharing the title with the New York Lincoln Stars in 1915. Altogether, they won five pennants under Foster's leadership.

The American Giants were known as much for their style as for their talent: Players traveled in private Pullman cars, wore a different set of uniforms each day, and used a variety of bats and balls. Foster was a shrewd manager, paying his players the highest salaries in the league while setting high standards for professionalism, conduct, and appearance. His style of play emphasized speed, bunting, power hitting, and defense. Adept at promoting his team as well, Foster once hired boxing heavyweight champion Jack Johnson to hand out souvenirs to female fans.

Founded the First Viable Black League

Foster made what is perhaps his greatest contribution to baseball in the offseason in 1920, when he assembled a group of team owners for a meeting at the YMCA in Kansas City, Missouri. There, he organized the Negro National League, a coalition of eight teams that played in the South and Midwest from 1920 to 1931. Attempts had been made to organize a formal black league in 1887 and in 1906 but none had ever come to fruition. The Negro National League was notable because it was the first of several leagues that were organized before the integration of baseball in the late 1940s, and because it was the first viable league, lasting twelve seasons. Foster served as president of the league until 1926—while continuing as manager of the American Giants—and ruled with an iron fist. He acted as the booking agent for the teams, set player salaries, hired the umpires, and even directed teams on their rosters and style of play. But he also had a benevolent side, often advancing loans to teams to meet payroll out of his own money and helping players who were in financial need.

In May of 1925, Foster was nearly asphyxiated by a gas leak in his hotel room in Indianapolis, and had to be dragged to safety. Although he recovered, he began to suffer health problems, and his behavior became increasingly bizarre and erratic. The following year, he retired as manager of the American Giants and president of the Negro National League, and was confined to a state asylum in Kankakee, Illinois. He died at the asylum of a heart attack on December 9, 1930, at age fifty-one.

In the absence of Foster's strong leadership, the Negro National League faltered, and the organization finally folded in 1931. Foster was inducted into the National Baseball Hall of Fame in 1981 in recognition of his talents as a player, manager, and league founder.

Sources

Books

Cottrell, Robert Charles, *The Best Pitcher in Baseball: The Life of Rube Foster, Negro League Giant,* New York University Press, 2001.

O'Toole, Andrew, *The Best Man Plays: Major League Baseball and the Black Athlete, 1901–2002,* McFarland, 2003.

Peterson, Robert, *Only the Ball Was White,* Prentice-Hall, 1970; reprint, Oxford University Press, 1992.

Whitehead, Charles E., *A Man and His Diamonds: A Story of the Great Andrew (Rube) Foster, the Outstanding Team He Owned and Managed, and the Superb League He Founded and Commissioned,* Vantage Press, 1980.

Periodicals

Austin (TX) American-Statesman, January 26, 1999, p. C1.
Newark (NJ) Star-Ledger, September 17, 1997, p. 21.

Online

"Andrew Rube Foster," Negro League Baseball Players Association, http://www.nlbpa.com/foster__andrew_-_rube.html (accessed September 24, 2009).
"Rube Foster," Baseball Library, http://www.baseballlibrary.com/ballplayers/player.php?name=Rube_Foster_1888 (accessed September 24, 2009).

—Deborah A. Ring

Lloyd Gaines

1911–1939(?)

Student, civil rights activist

Gaines, Lloyd, photograph. AP Images.

Student Lloyd Gaines played a major role in the long struggle to desegregate the nation's schools. After the University of Missouri School of Law denied him admission on racial grounds in 1936, the Mississippi native filed a lawsuit that reached the U.S. Supreme Court. His victory there in 1938 helped set the stage for the landmark desegregation decision *Brown v. Board of Education* sixteen years later. His contributions would undoubtedly be better known had he not vanished in March of 1939. Decades later, the circumstances surrounding his disappearance continued to be a focus of speculation and controversy.

Lloyd Lionel Gaines was born in 1911 in Water Valley, a small town in northern Mississippi. His parents were sharecroppers who lived in considerable poverty. In 1926 Gaines moved with his mother and siblings to St. Louis, Missouri, where they hoped to find better jobs and living conditions. A diligent, articulate student, Gaines excelled at Vashon High School, graduating in 1931 as valedictorian of his class. He spent a year at nearby Stowe Teachers College before transferring to Lincoln University in the state capital of Jefferson City. He went on to earn a bachelor's degree in history from the latter in 1935.

Gaines's education took place under arduous conditions. Money for tuition was a constant worry. He got by with several small scholarships, help from friends and family, and a number of part-time jobs, most of them poorly paid. Money was also a serious problem for the schools he attended, all of which to this point had been segregated. Although the U.S. Supreme Court had mandated, in the 1896 decision *Plessy v. Ferguson,* that educational facilities for African Americans be "equal" in quality to those reserved for whites, they rarely were. Gaines and his classmates had to cope constantly with old textbooks, substandard equipment, and other problems brought on by years of inadequate funding.

Despite these handicaps, Gaines had notable success at Lincoln, winning honors for his work in history and serving as president of his senior class. He had long planned to attend law school, but the University of Missouri School of Law, the only public institution of its kind in the state, denied him admission on explicitly racial grounds, even as it acknowledged his academic

At a Glance . . .

Born Lloyd Lionel Gaines in 1911 in Water Valley, MS; disappeared March 19, 1939, in Chicago, IL. *Education:* Lincoln University, BA, history, 1935; University of Michigan, MA, economics, 1938(?).

Career: Held a variety of part-time jobs to pay for his education.

Memberships: Alpha Phi Alpha.

Awards: Scholarship named in his honor, University of Missouri School of Law, 1995; University of Missouri—Columbia, Black Culture Center renamed the Lloyd L. Gaines–Marian O'Fallon Oldham Black Culture Center, 2001; honorary law degree (posthumous), University of Missouri School of Law, 2006; license to practice law (posthumous), Missouri Bar, 2006.

qualifications. In lieu of admission, university administrators offered to pay his tuition in a neighboring state. Rejecting this solution, Gaines resolved to sue. With the help of the NAACP and noted civil rights lawyer Charles Hamilton Houston, he filed suit in circuit court in 1936. After losing there, he appealed to the state supreme court, where he lost again. A second appeal brought the case, known as *Gaines v. Canada* (Sy Woodson Canada was the university's registrar) to the U.S. Supreme Court, which heard oral arguments on November 9, 1938.

Gaines suffered considerable hardship while the case was making its slow progress through the court system. A quiet, reserved person by nature, he was by all accounts deeply uncomfortable amid the intense publicity the suit generated. Reporters hounded him, and he routinely faced threats and taunts from angry whites. To keep busy, he enrolled in graduate school at the University of Michigan, which did not bar African-American students. There, about 1938, he earned a master's degree in economics. Money, meanwhile, remained a problem. In an effort to find better-paying work, he moved from Michigan to Chicago, Illinois, where he took a room in a house belonging to Alpha Phi Alpha, his undergraduate fraternity.

On December 12, 1938, Gaines learned that he had won his case. In a ruling that foreshadowed its more sweeping decision in *Brown v. Board of Education* sixteen years later, the Supreme Court declared that Missouri had to admit Gaines or build a separate law school for African Americans; merely declaring a willingness to pay out-of-state tuition was not an accept-

able solution under the separate-but-equal doctrine enshrined in *Plessy v. Ferguson*. As Hamilton noted before the Court, traveling out of state would have imposed a significant burden in terms of time, money, and convenience. While the justices stopped short of overturning the 1896 case, as they would do in *Brown v. Board of Education*, they revealed their increasing skepticism over the feasibility of the Plessy doctrine. As Hamilton's protégé Thurgood Marshall would argue in 1954, separate facilities were inherently unequal. Gaines's suit helped to push the Court, and white Americans in general, toward a belated recognition of that fact.

In the immediate aftermath of the decision, however, the state of Missouri continued to oppose Gaines's admission. Choosing the alternative offered by the Court, state administrators announced the creation of a segregated law school at Lincoln. The new program opened in January of 1939 with several dozen students in ill-equipped classrooms. Gaines did not attend. Deeply frustrated by the situation, he spent his days in Chicago, looking for work and reconsidering his career plans. His lawyer, meanwhile, was preparing to challenge the state's response to the earlier suit. When he summoned his client for a preliminary deposition, however, there was no response. Gaines, it seemed, had vanished.

A few details of the disappearance slowly emerged. On the evening of March 19, 1939, Gaines told his housemates at the Alpha Phi Alpha dormitory that he was going out to buy stamps. He never came back. Because he had not always been careful about notifying friends and family of his whereabouts, his failure to return home was not immediately reported. That delay proved costly. Despite intense media coverage and a concerted effort by NAACP branches nationwide, he was never seen again.

Gaines's fate has been a subject of intense speculation for decades. A variety of theories have been proposed, many involving suicide; murder at the hands of racial extremists; or a simple desire to begin life again somewhere else, perhaps in Mexico. While it seemed unlikely in 2009 that the truth would ever be known, there was an increased recognition that the mystery of his disappearance, intriguing though it was, should not obscure his contributions to civil rights. One of the first signs of that recognition had come in 1995, when a scholarship for minority students was established in his honor at the University of Missouri School of Law, the institution that had denied him admittance. Six years later, the Black Culture Center at the university's flagship campus in Columbia was renamed the Lloyd L. Gaines–Marian O'Fallon Oldham Black Culture Center (Marian O'Fallon Oldham was another student denied admission on racial grounds). Then in 2006 came two singular, posthumous honors: a degree from the school of law and a license to practice from the state bar association. As Mike Middleton, Missouri's deputy chancellor, said at the time, in comments quoted by *Jet* magazine, "This University has benefited greatly from what Lloyd Gaines did for us, for the state of Missouri, and for the nation."

Sources

Periodicals

Black Issues in Higher Education, January 3, 2002, p. 14.
Diverse Issues in Higher Education, May 4, 2006, p. 8.
Jet, May 15, 2006, p. 33.
New York Times, July 12, 2009, p. A19.
Riverfront Times, April 3, 2007.

—R. Anthony Kugler

Keith Glover

1966—

Playwright, director, actor

American playwright Keith Glover has been hailed as the successor to August Wilson for his forthright and lyrical portrayals of black life in America. After starting out as an actor and making the rounds of regional theater, Glover eventually turned to playwriting, first to provide better roles for himself, and later to give voice to stories informed by his upbringing in rural Alabama. Glover's plays are powerfully influenced by jazz and the blues. In works such as *Thunder Knocking on the Door* and *In Walks Ed,* he skillfully weaves together dialogue and music to create a hybrid genre that is part play, part musical. Called a "playwright to reckon with" by Alvin Klein in the May 18, 1997, *New York Times,* Glover is considered one of the most inventive authors writing for the contemporary stage.

Experimented with Jazz and Storytelling

Glover was born in 1966 in Birmingham, Alabama, the son of Earnestine Glover and Jimmy Akines. He grew up in nearby Bessemer, raised primarily by his grandmother, Evelyn Glover. As a boy, he absorbed the family lore that his grandfather and uncles told, and learned the value of storytelling as an art form. "In Alabama, the spoken word is something that is paramount," he explained in a 1999 interview with Vincent F. A. Golphin of *About ... Time* magazine. "Being able to tell stories to explain your experiences or the experiences of others was something that was taught, but also held in high esteem." Glover was introduced to another art form—the art of jazz—by his stepfather,

Woody Phifer, a guitar player and luthier (a maker of stringed instruments). Taking up the trumpet, Glover hoped to become the next Miles Davis but found that his talent did not live up to his enthusiasm. Nonetheless, jazz remained a powerful inspiration that would shape his artistic vision later in life.

Glover moved to New York City in 1980. At age fifteen, he began studying with the legendary acting coach Lee Strasberg at his Manhattan institute, where Glover was the only black student. He found that there were few good roles for African-American men—for lack of any other role, he was cast as black heavyweight boxing champion Jack Jefferson (based on the real-life Jack Johnson) in a production of *The Great White Hope.* The experience prompted Glover to try his hand at playwriting. "I'm not ready to be Jack Johnson, so I started writing my own scenes," he told Golphin. "It wasn't like, 'Let me sit down and write this great epic,' it was, 'I want to write something that is more appropriate for me to act, something that I'm connecting to.'" At age seventeen, he submitted a script to the Young Playwrights Festival in New York and received encouragement from founder Gerald Chapman.

After graduation from Murry Bergtraum High School, Glover headed to college, putting aside writing for acting. He left school before being graduated, however, to return to New York to try his luck as an actor. Soon he landed the role of Kenny Hathaway on the soap opera *As the World Turns,* staying with the show for a year and a half. He appeared in the film *Jacknife* (1989) with Robert De Niro, and had turns on the NBC

At a Glance . . .

Born on February 18, 1966, in Birmingham, AL; son of Earnestine Glover and Jimmy Akines; married Veronica Grant; children: Alena Ryan. *Education:* Lee Strasberg Theatre and Film Institute.

Career: Stage, television, and film actor, 1980s—; playwright, 1995—.

Memberships: Dramatists Guild; New Dramatists Playwright Organization.

Awards: Pew Charitable Fellowship/Theatre Communications Group Grant, 1996; M. Elizabeth Osborn New Play Award, American Theatre Critics Association, 1997, Helen Hayes Award for Outstanding Resident Musical, 1997, both for *Thunder Knocking on the Door;* Lois and Richard Rosenthal New Play Prize, Cincinnati Playhouse in the Park, 1997, for *In Walks Ed,* and 2001, for *Dark Paradise.*

Addresses: *Literary agent*—Bret Adams, Ltd., 448 W. 44th St., New York, NY 10036-5205.

drama *Law & Order* and Fox's *New York Undercover.* Most notably, he performed at regional theaters across the country, appearing in productions of Wilson's *Fences* at Capital Repertory Company and *Two Trains Running* at Center Stage in Baltimore, as well as Samuel Kelley's *Pill Hill,* directed by Marion McClinton, and William Shakespeare's *The Merchant of Venice,* directed by Mark Lamos, both at Hartford Stage.

Turned from Actor to Playwright

The tedium of life on the road prompted Glover to turn once again to writing, and that became his passion. His first play, *Dancing on Moonlight,* premiered at the Joseph Papp Public Theater in 1995, directed by McClinton. Set in Harlem in 1935, the play portrays black men and women gambling and running numbers backstage at the Apollo Theater as a woman dies while giving birth to a child. The father flees, accused of cheating. The action of the play, which is modeled on Greek tragedy, centers on the child, who, twenty-five years later, has inherited the gambling operation and finds himself caught between the family business and his desire for a clean life.

Critics hailed Glover as a promising playwright and praised his innovative use of language but generally found the play's plot and dialogue too predictable. Ben Brantley of the *New York Times,* for example, noted in 1995 that "there are moments when Mr. Glover achieves a distinctive, searing poetry in his blend of street vernacular and oracular mysticism… . More typically, though, the dialogue smacks of B-movie melodrama."

Glover's second play, *Coming of the Hurricane,* the story of a freed slave turned bare-knuckle boxer in the post–Civil War South, was produced by the Denver Center Theatre Company (1994), Penumbra Theatre Company in St. Paul, Minnesota (1995), and Arena Stage in Washington, DC (1996). It was a finalist for the American Theatre Critics Association's award for best play in 1995 and a runner-up for the Theodore Ward Prize for African-American playwrights.

Rewrote the Musical Genre

He soon followed up with *Thunder Knocking on the Door,* which originated at the Alabama Shakespeare Festival and underwent significant revisions in subsequent productions at Baltimore's Center Stage, the Dallas Theater Center, and the Yale Repertory Theatre during the 1996–97 season. The play, which Glover subtitled "A Bluesical Tale of Rhythm and the Blues," is set in 1966 in Bessemer and features ten original compositions by blues musician Keb' Mo'. It tells the story of the Dupree family, whose patriarch, the guitar-playing Jaguar Dupree, died some twenty years ago. When mystery man Marvell Thunder comes to town to challenge the two children of his onetime musical rival to a "cuttin'" competition (a guitar duel), he resurrects Dupree's spirit and, in the process, helps Dupree's children reclaim their blues legacy.

The dialogue of *Thunder* is written in the twelve-bar blues scale, leaving the actors free to improvise, so that each performance is unique. "I wanted to attack the ways we write musicals," Glover explained in a 1997 interview with *American Theatre* magazine. "When I saw musicals as a child, it seemed that the book [the dialogue] was always an afterthought. I wanted to blur the line between music and book, so that the two parts really melded together." *Thunder Knocking on the Door* earned the American Theatre Critics Association's Osborn Award in 1997 and the Helen Hayes Award for outstanding resident musical. It received an off-Broadway production at the Minetta Lane Theatre in 2002.

Glover earned critical acclaim for his fourth play, *In Walks Ed,* which premiered at the Long Wharf Theatre in New Haven, Connecticut, in 1997, directed by the author. In the play, the title character returns to his old barroom hangout after fifteen years of working for the mob to settle an old debt. Again, the dialogue is mixed with rock and roll, jazz, and blues music. Glover garnered a Pulitzer Prize nomination for *In Walks Ed,* as well as the Cincinnati Playhouse in the Park's Richard Rosenthal New Play Prize. Glover's other works for the stage include *Dark Paradise: The Legend of the Five-Pointed Star* (2001), *Rose of Corazon: A Texas Songplay* (2004), and *Jazzland* (2006).

Glover's portrayals of black life in America have earned him comparisons with Wilson, as well as Lorraine Hansberry. But the author is quick to reject such comparisons—although he certainly was shaped by Wilson's and Hansberry's seminal work, his plays stand apart in their form, rhythm, and consciousness. He told Golphin, "August ... is one of the true people who knew the time before civil rights and afterwards.... . I was born in Birmingham in 1966. I'm a child who had to be taught that rather than to know it first-hand. My life is shaped by different things. If you try to put the rhythms of August or Hansberry on my stuff, it doesn't work."

Selected works

As playwright

Dancing on Moonlight, 1995.
Coming of the Hurricane, 1995.
Thunder Knocking on the Door, 1996.
In Walks Ed, 1997.
Dark Paradise: The Legend of the Five-Pointed Star, 2001.

Rose of Corazon: A Texas Songplay, 2004.
Jazzland, 2006.

Films

Jacknife, Cineplex/Odeon, 1989.

Television

As the World Turns, CBS, c. 1981.

Sources

Books

Craghead, Anissa L., "Keith Glover," in *Twentieth-Century American Dramatists,* 3rd series, ed. Christopher J. Wheatley, *Dictionary of Literary Biography,* Vol. 249, Gale Group, 2002, pp. 85–91.

Periodicals

About ... Time, September/October 1999.
American Theatre, October 1995; January 1997, p. 12.
Back Stage, July 5, 2002, p. 7.
New York Times, April 24, 1995; May 18, 1997; December 7, 1997; April 16, 2000, p. 12.

—Deborah A. Ring

Isaac H. Green

1959—

Investment advisor

President and CEO of Piedmont Investment Advisors Isaac H. Green came up through the ranks of money managers to found his own very successful investment firm. Piedmont is known for its team approach to money management, for its record of strong returns and minimal volatility in its funds, and for its commitment to the African-American business community. Green's firm has been highly successful in managing portfolios of large institutional clients, including state retirement systems and trade unions, among others. Its excellent track record was rewarded in 2009 with a contract to help manage a portfolio worth $218 billion that the U.S. Treasury purchased from troubled financial institutions as part of the TARP Capital Purchase Program—an unprecedented contract for a minority-owned money management firm.

Raised in North Carolina

Isaac H. Green was born in Henderson, North Carolina, in 1959. His father, James P. Green, a physician, had been born and raised in Henderson and returned to his hometown with his wife, Carolyn, to become a country doctor and raise his three children. Although his father was a physician and both his siblings went to law school, Isaac sought something different. He chose money management because, as he told David Bailey, "It's an industry that black folks aren't participating in and don't know about." He firmly believed that access to money and financial institutions were key to African-American empowerment.

After graduating with a BA in history and economics from Duke University in 1982 and an MBA from Columbia University in 1984, Green began his career as an analyst with North Carolina National Bank in Charlotte, which eventually became Bank of America. After working there for four years, he took a pay cut to return to Durham—or, as he said, "coming back to play for the home team"—and work as research director at N.C. Mutual's NCM Capital Management, a large African-American-owned investment firm. He became the chief research officer and then senior vice president and director of investments at the firm, learning the ins and outs of money management at all levels.

In 1993 Green moved on to Loomis Sayles & Co., an investment firm in Detroit, taking a position as a portfolio manager—one of an estimated twenty African-American portfolio managers in the nation at that time. Because his ties to North Carolina were so strong, it was difficult for him to leave home. His parents, he told one reporter, cried when he told them the news. While at Loomis, Green managed seven funds with $10 billion in assets and quickly rose to the rank of director of the value equity management division. However, he regretted not having a direct role in money management decisions, a factor which spurred him to found his own company in 2000 with two colleagues from Loomis Sayles. He wanted to put into practice an investment strategy that would minimize investors' risk. He told Charles Keenan of *Institutional Investor,* "At a big firm one has no choice but to dance to the music that is being played. We didn't want to run money that way. We wanted to articulate a new

At a Glance . . .

Born Isaac H. Green in 1959, in Henderson, NC; son of James P. Green (physician and state legislator) and Carolyn Marie Smith Green; married Pamela; children: two. *Politics:* Democrat. *Education:* Duke University, BA, history and economics, 1982; Columbia University, MBA, 1984.

Career: North Carolina National Bank, 1984–88; North Carolina Mutual Capital Management Group, 1988–93; Loomis Sayles & Co., 1993–2000; Piedmont Investment Advisors, 2000—.

Addresses: *Office*—Piedmont Investment Advisors, LLC, 411 West Chapel Hill Street, Suite 1100, Durham, North Carolina, 27701. *Web*—http://www.piedmontinvestment.com/.

investment product." He had come to disagree with the dominant view that stocks should be picked primarily on the basis of growth—those valued above market averages—or long-term value—those valued below market averages. Instead, he wanted to concentrate on developing diversified portfolios designed to produce steady returns over long periods of time without wild ups and downs.

Returned to Durham

Green moved his new company, Piedmont Investment Advisors, back to Durham in 2001 in large part to be part of the "Black Wall Street" on Parrish Street, home to several black-owned financial firms. His roots in North Carolina also pulled him back to the city: his great-grandfather was one of the founders of the nation's oldest and largest minority-owned insurance company, N.C. Mutual, as well as one of the founders and first president of North Carolina Central University. Green told Lee Weisbecker of the *Business Journal—Serving the Triangle's Business Communities,* "In the back of my mind, I always knew I'd come home one day. I came back for myself, for the community, for the future." He wanted his new investment firm to serve the black business community in North Carolina. He told Anne Fawcett of the *Herald-Sun,* "In many ways, this company is a product of that [black professional] community. Now these guys are able to reap some of the harvest from seeds they planted, and I'm here to plant more seeds."

To make the move back to Durham possible, Green struck deals with N.C. Mutual and Mutual Community

Savings Bank, each of which bought shares in the new investment firm in exchange for investment services. Despite founding the company during a prolonged bear market, Piedmont managed to beat the S&P 500 index by an average of 300 points in each of its first three years. The company was then selected to manage pieces of the North Carolina state retirement system. In 2007 Piedmont was selected by the Teachers' Retirement System of the State of Illinois to manage $25 million as part of the system's emerging managers program, as well as by the California Public Employees' Retirement System (CalPERS) to manage $100 million as part of its emerging managers program. Those investments helped push the assets Piedmont had under management to $1.5 billion. CalPERS also invested directly in the firm, buying part of the stake previously held by N.C. Mutual. The firm had steadily grown and by 2009 had twenty-three employees.

In 2009 *Black Enterprise* listed Piedmont number ten among black-owned asset managers. By June 2009 the firm had $2.4 billion in assets under management. In addition, Piedmont was selected along with two other firms by the U.S. Treasury Department to manage a portfolio purchased from troubled financial institutions as part of the TARP Capital Purchase Program worth $218 billion. Orim Graves, executive director of the National Association of Securities Professionals, told Jeffrey McKinney of *Black Enterprise* that it was the first time that the federal government had hired a minority-owned firm to manage such a large amount of money.

Sources

Periodicals

Black Enterprise, August 1, 2002; October 1, 2006; June 1, 2008; May 1, 2009; May 15, 2009.
Business Journal—Serving the Triangle's Business Communities, October 12, 2001, p. 3.
Business—North Carolina, December 1, 1991, p. 20.
Herald-Sun, October 11, 2001; February 27, 2007; March 7, 2007.
Institutional Advisor—Americas, January 16, 2004.
News & Observer, October 18, 2001, p. D1; December 2, 2001, p. E1; March 9, 2007, p. D3.
Pensions & Investments, May 28, 2007.
U.S. Fed News, May 14, 2007.

Online

Piedmont Investment Advisors, LLC, http://www.piedmontinvestment.com (accessed October 15, 2009).

—Melissa J. Doak

James Harris

1947—

Professional football player, sports executive

Harris, James, photograph. Paul Hawthorne/Getty Images.

James "Shack" Harris was one of the first African-American starting quarterbacks in professional football. He made his rookie debut in 1969 with the Buffalo Bills, then endured a few doleful years when his career seemed to languish. "Shack was the only quarterback I knew who had a stronger arm than me," U.S. Congressman and former Bills quarterback Jack Kemp told William C. Rhoden in a 2007 article for ESPN.com. "He was a tremendous talent, a diamond in the rough. You look at the quarterbacks of today ... and Shack Harris was as good as any of them. But at the time, he was undeveloped."

Born in 1947 and a native of Monroe, Louisiana, James Larnell Harris was recruited to play for the legendary football program at Grambling State University in his home state in 1965. The Grambling Tigers were a powerhouse in black college football under coach Eddie Robinson, who holds the record for the most football wins at a Division I school in the National College Athletic Association (NCAA). Robinson produced scores of future pro football stars, and Harris joined the team when the longstanding racial barriers in both college and professional sports were beginning to erode. "Right after he signed me," Harris told writer George Vecsey in the *New York Times,* Robinson "went to New York for a coaches conference where everyone asked if he was *ever* going to produce a black quarterback for the pros. He took it to heart. After four years, I was prepared to compete."

Sat Out 1968 Draft

During Harris's era the Grambling Tigers won or tied four Southwestern Athletic Conference (SWAC) conference titles. In his senior year Harris was featured in the television documentary film *Grambling College: 100 Yards to Glory,* which aired on ABC in January of 1968. In the film, broadcaster Howard Cosell and sportswriter Jerry Izenberg claimed that top Grambling players such as Harris and Henry Davis were as good as any college players coming up in that month's pro football draft and that they deserved starting positions. Grambling had lost just one game that year, and Harris had been named the Most Valuable Player at the 1967 Orange Blossom Classic, a traditional match-up between the Florida A&M Rattlers and the top-ranked historically black college or university team.

At a Glance . . .

Born James Larnell Harris on July 20, 1947, in Monroe, LA.

Career: Starting quarterback with the Buffalo Bills of the American Football League, 1969; released from contract, 1972; worked for the Office of Minority Enterprise at the U.S. Department of Commerce; Los Angeles Rams, quarterback, 1973–77; San Diego Chargers, quarterback, 1977–79; Tampa Bay Buccaneers, West Coast college scout, late 1980s; Baltimore Ravens, director of professional personnel, 1997–2002; Jacksonville Jaguars, vice president for player personnel, 2002–08; Detroit Lions, senior personnel executive, 2009—.

Awards: Orange Blossom Classic, Most Valuable Player, 1967; named to AFC-NFC Pro Bowl team, 1974, and Most Valuable Player; Southwestern Athletic Conference Hall of Fame; Grambling University Athletic Hall of Fame; Louisiana Sports Hall of Fame.

Addresses: *Office*—Detroit Lions, Inc., 222 Republic Dr., Allen Park, MI 48101.

The New York Giants were reportedly interested in taking Harris in the 1968 Common Draft—as the event was known in the era before the American Football League (AFL) and National Football League (NFL) merged—but didn't want him to play quarterback. He declined the offer and waited for the next year's draft. In January of 1969 the AFL's Buffalo Bills picked him in the eighth round as a quarterback. Running back O.J. Simpson, fresh out of the University of Southern California, was the No. 1 draft pick that year and was also signed by the Bills. Harris was peeved at being passed over by so many teams and almost refused the offer, but Coach Robinson urged him to reconsider. "He said if I didn't go, we might not ever have a black quarterback in the pros," Harris recalled in the *New York Times* interview with Vecsey.

The hurdle wasn't cleared, however, as Harris discovered when he reported to Buffalo to sign his contract. Speaking with ESPN.com's Rhoden, Harris recounted how team executives now told him that he would be playing a receiver position instead. "Now, when I stepped into that office, I'd never had a conversation with white people before. Coming from the South, I didn't look anybody in the eye. I looked down at the floor. They said they needed me to sign this contract. If I didn't, I was going to have to go to Canada." He asked

to make a phone call, and called Robinson. "I don't know what he told them," Harris recalled, "but they backed down."

A Dismal Rookie Season

The indignities Harris endured did not end with his contract negotiations. "They took me to my room," he told Rhoden. "Had me staying at the YMCA for six dollars a night. When O.J. came to town, he was staying in a suite at the Hilton. They gave me a job, working in the equipment room, putting laces in shoes." He later shared an apartment with another significant African-American player of the era, Marlin Briscoe, who had just joined the Bills' line-up that year.

In September Harris and O.J. Simpson were both put in the starting backfield. Harris made NFL history as the first starting African-American quarterback in a season-opening game. But by ill luck he was injured that day and forced to sit out much of the 1969 season. Then in 1970 he was cut during training camp. "I read about it in the paper," he told Rhoden in the ESPN. com profile. "In those days, they could cut you and bring you back, but I didn't know that. I left, went home to my apartment in Buffalo. I'm home, watching the news, and I hear I'm missing. Next thing I know, Marlin's knocking on the door. Marlin was hot. He could feel my pain." Briscoe had warned him about the dangers of being "the first"—in 1968, playing with the Denver Broncos, Briscoe had been the first black quarterback to start in a game.

The Bills suffered through a few losing seasons, and Harris lost some of his earlier confidence. "I withdrew into a shell," he told sportswriter Joe Marshall in an article for *Sports Illustrated* a few years later. After the 1972 season opener, the Bills released him from his contract. Years later teammate Briscoe would tell Rhoden that the Rust Belt city had not been a good match for Harris, as compared to Briscoe's historic start in Denver. "James got death threats and negative publicity. … Buffalo was more of a melting pot. You had ethnic groups bumping up against one another." After leaving the Bills, Harris worked for a time with the Office of Minority Enterprise at the U.S. Department of Commerce. In the meantime Briscoe was urging Paul "Tank" Younger, the famed scout for the Los Angeles Rams and a Grambling alumnus, to take a look at Harris—he did, and coach Tommy Prothro signed him. In the 1973 season Harris played in eight games under a new head coach, Chuck Knox, who preferred to rotate his quarterbacks.

The Comeback Story of 1976

Going into the 1974 season Harris had played in the merged NFL for five seasons, but played starting quarterback in just three games. His breakout chance came in October of 1974 when the Rams traded John

Hadl to the Green Bay Packers and Coach Knox made Harris the regular starting quarterback. Harris had been nervous about the role, he admitted in the *Sports Illustrated* interview with Marshall later that season, but went on to reflect, "I decided just to do the best I could, and not compete. I had never relaxed in Buffalo, and it had hurt my performance." Though the quarterback's job is considered a leadership position on the team, Harris never called the plays—the plays had been called by the coaches from the sidelines.

Harris made NFL history that year when the Rams had a terrific finish and went on to meet the Minnesota Vikings for the National Football Conference (NFC) title on December 29. He was the first African-American quarterback to start in a conference championship game. The Rams lost to Minnesota by 14-10. At one point the Rams needed one touchdown to win, but repeated calls for timeouts seemed to rob them of momentum. Harris was blamed, as were two players who made more obvious missteps that let the Vikings gain the lead. "It's real tough," Harris told *New York Times* sportswriter Murray Chass in the locker room. "You work hard to get this far and then you have to start all over again. I know there are a lot of people who doubt what I can do, but all I can do is play the best I can. I'm not trying to satisfy any critics."

Harris had a solid season in 1976, even setting the NFC record for passing, 89.8 percent, but lost another shot at the Super Bowl to Minnesota that year. In early 1977 the Rams traded him to the San Diego Chargers in order to sign superstar Joe Namath, then at the tail end of his career. Harris was on the Chargers' roster for another five seasons but failed to play the last two seasons. By the end of the 1980s, he was working for the Tampa Bay Buccaneers as their West Coast college scout. In 1997 he became director of pro personnel for the Baltimore Ravens, and in 2002 he joined the Jacksonville Jaguars organization as personnel chief. At the close of the 2008 season, he resigned after the team finished 5–10. "To be fair, that's not entirely all on Harris because he doesn't have total autonomy over personnel," wrote Gene Frenette in the *Florida Times Union*. "'It's all our fault,' one Jaguars insider told me."

The Jaguars could take some consolation that they were not the worst finisher of the 2008 NFL season. That dubious honor went to the Detroit Lions, who reached a new low in season standings with a 0–16 record—a first in the League. The Lions' new general manager was Martin Mayhew, whom Harris had recommended as a Tampa Bay draft pick back in 1993. After Harris's resignation from the Jaguars, Mayhew hired him as the Lions' senior personnel executive. Harris, Mayhew said of his hiring decision according to an article on the Lions' official Web site, is "very well respected in the National Football League, he has a good eye—you ask any scout and they'll tell you James has a really good eye. I think it's important to have a guy like that."

Sources

Periodicals

Florida Times Union (Jacksonville, FL), December 14, 2008, p. C14.
Jet, March 24, 1977, pp. 50–52.
New York Times, December 30, 1974, p. 29; January 24, 1988; December 24, 2008.
Sports Illustrated, November 4, 1974.

Online

Rhoden, William C., "The James Harris Story: A Long, Painful Road," ESPN.com, February 12, 2007, http://sports.espn.go.com/espn/blackhistory2007/news/story?id=2762569 (accessed October 20, 2009).
Wywrot, Chrissie, "Adding More Experience," Detroit Lions, February 12, 2009, http://www.detroitlions.com/news/article-1/Adding-More-Experience/c95cb19c-0ba1-48a8-a2aa-d4be64e89aae (accessed October 20, 2009).

—Carol Brennan

Earle Hyman

1926—

Actor

Hyman, Earle, photograph. Astrid Stawiarz/Getty Images.

In the United States, Earle Hyman is probably best known for his role as Russell Huxtable, the tall, kindly, and often wise father of Bill Cosby's character on *The Cosby Show*. Among his fellow actors, however, his reputation rests upon an overwhelmingly long list of roles in classical theater, especially in the plays of William Shakespeare. Hyman is also a popular and highly regarded actor in Norway, where he has performed many roles speaking flawless Norwegian. Nominated for both Tony and Emmy Awards, Hyman was still amazing audiences with his performances into his 80s, and was presented with an Obie Lifetime Achievement Award in 2009 at the age of 82.

Developed Early Love of Shakespeare

Earle Hyman was born on October 11, 1926, in Rocky Mount, North Carolina. During the Great Depression, Hyman's family moved to Brooklyn so that he and his siblings could attend school there. However, like many African-American children who lived in the North, Hyman spent his summers in the South. In an interview with Tony Brown for the *Knight-Ridder/Tribune News Service*, Hyman recalled that in the summer of 1937, when he was eleven years old, the library in his parents' hometown of Warrenton, North Carolina, was opened to African Americans for the first time. When he went in and asked for the biggest book they had, the librarian gave him the complete works of Shakespeare. On summer afternoons, when there was nothing better to do, Hyman read Shakespeare. "I was too young to really understand it," he told Brown, "but it blew my mind."

Hyman's passion for the theater began only grew when he discovered the works of the nineteenth-century Norwegian playwright Henrik Ibsen. When he was thirteen, his mother gave him a choice of going to see *The Wizard of Oz* at a local movie theater or going to see his first play, a production of Ibsen's *The Ghosts*, at the Brighton Beach Theater. He chose the play. It was that experience that inspired Hyman to become an actor.

The teachers at Franklin K. Lane High School in Brooklyn encouraged Hyman's interest in the theatre. By the time he was fifteen, Hyman landed his first role when he performed in a radio series about African-

American history with actor Paul Robeson. When he graduated from high school, Hyman was offered an opportunity to attend the drama school at Columbia College. However, he decided to try acting on a full-time basis, and Robeson and others asked him to join the American Negro Theatre in Harlem. Early into this collaboration, Hyman took on the role of Rudolph in *Anna Lucasta*. The play was a hit and eventually moved from Harlem to Broadway. When the cast traveled to London to perform the play, Hyman—then only twenty-one—accompanied them. His role in *Anna Lucasta* firmly established his acting career.

Was Cast in First Shakespearean Role

In 1951 Hyman was cast in his first Shakespearean role by Owen Dodson, a playwright and chair of the drama department at Howard University in Washington, DC. Dodson was also a friend of Hyman's family. One day when Dodson was visiting, Hyman played him a recording of actors reading selections from *Hamlet*.

Three of the voices were of well-known Shakespearean actors; the fourth voice was Hyman's. Impressed, Dodson cast twenty-five-year-old Hyman in the title role of a production of *Hamlet* at Howard. The production was so well received that five hundred people had to be turned away on the last night of the show.

Two years later, Hyman was cast as the lead in a New York production of another Shakespearean tragedy, *Othello*. As a result of that performance, he was invited to join a Shakespeare repertory company that was just being formed, the American Shakespeare Festival in Stratford, Connecticut. During five seasons with the company, Hyman performed a wide variety of Shakespearean roles, which helped hone his acting skills and provide a strong foundation for his later work.

Hyman continued to be fascinated by the works of Ibsen, and he began studying Norwegian in order to read them in their original language. In 1957 he arranged a trip to Norway to learn more about his favorite playwright. He was able to visit Ibsen's grandson and his wife, who introduced him to many people in the Norwegian theatre world.

Enjoyed Performing in Scandinavian Theater

In 1962, when he was appearing in an American production of *Othello*, a friend contacted Hyman and asked him to consider playing Othello in a Norwegian production. He initially refused because he didn't feel that he had a command of the Norwegian language. However, he began reading the play in Norwegian during his tour, and, one day during rehearsal, his fellow actors fell silent. They told Hyman that he had just recited some of his lines in Norwegian. He contacted the Norwegian company and told them he would perform as Othello.

For Hyman, the Norwegian production of *Othello* was the beginning of a long association with Norway and with Scandinavian theater. During the play's run, he fell in love with the actress who played Desdemona and began a twenty-six-year romance with her. He also began to be invited to audition for other roles in the Norwegian theater. Soon Hyman had a thriving career on both sides of the Atlantic. He would often spend half the year performing in Norway, sometimes performing in English and sometimes in Norwegian, and then spend the rest of the year performing in the United States. In recognition of his distinguished acting career on the Norwegian stage, the king of Norway awarded Hyman the St. Olav's Medal, the highest civilian honor a foreigner can be awarded.

Starred as Russell Huxtable on Television

In the United States, Hyman was nominated for a Tony

Award for his performance in *The Lady from Dubuque* in 1980. While his most important roles have been on the stage, he has also worked in film and on television. He has appeared in hundreds of soap opera episodes, including *The Edge of Night* and *All My Children*. In 1983 Hyman won a CableACE Award for his performance in the Eugene O'Neil play *Long Day's Journey into Night*, which was broadcast on ABC. He played the role of Bill Cosby's father, Russell Huxtable, on *The Cosby Show* beginning in 1984 and was nominated for an Emmy for his performance. His television work did not preclude his working on stage. During one period, for example, he was filming *The Cosby Show* during the day and appearing in the two-person play *Driving Miss Daisy* in the evening.

In 1993, more than forty-five years after the summer he discovered Shakespeare, Hyman returned to North Carolina to play the role of King Lear at the age of 66. He was the first African-American actor to have played all four of the major Shakespearean tragic leads: Lear, Macbeth, Hamlet, and Othello. In expressing how he felt about his Shakespearean acting, he told the *Villager* "I'm so lucky. Twenty-nine Shakespeare roles in 20 Shakespeare plays. Only Ellis Raab and Bill Ball have done the complete canon. I'll never make it now. I'll be 80 in October."

Won Lifetime Achievement Award

In May of 2009, at the age of eighty-two and shortly after having performed in *Three Sisters* at the Classical Theater of Harlem, Hyman was awarded an Obie Lifetime Achievement Award. The Obies are given by the *Village Voice*, an arts-oriented newspaper in New York City, for excellence in Off-Broadway theatre. During Hyman's acceptance speech he proclaimed "To be an actor is the most glorious thing in the world!" In an interview with David Black at the New School in New York, Hyman elaborated on the passion he feels for the theater: "I cannot remember when I didn't want this life of illuminated emotion, this other world, this magic."

Selected performances

Theater

Three's a Family, American Negro Theater, 1943.
Run, Little Chillun, American Negro Theater, 1943.
Anna Lucasta, American Negro Theater, 1944; Mansfield Theater, 1944–46; His Majesty's Theatre, 1947.
Sister Oakes, Lenox Hill Playhouse, 1949.
Hamlet, Howard University, 1951.
The Climate of Eden, Martin Beck Theatre, 1952.
The Merchant of Venice, City Center Theater, 1953.
Othello, Jan Hus Auditorium, 1953 and 1955.
The Tempest, American Shakespeare Festival, 1955.

Mister Johnson, Martin Beck Theater, 1956.
King John, American Shakespeare Festival, 1956.
Waiting for Godot, Ethel Barrymore Theater, 1957.
The Duchess of Malfi, Phoenix Theater, 1957.
The Merchant of Venice, American Shakespeare Festival, 1957.
The Infernal Machine, Phoenix Theater, 1958.
Hamlet, American Shakespeare Festival, 1958.
A Raisin in the Sun, Adelphi Theatre, 1959
Antony and Cleopatra, American Shakespeare Festival, 1960.
Mister Roberts, Equity Library Theater, 1963.
St. Joan, Vivian Beaumont Theater, 1968.
Othello, Repertory Company of St. Louis, 1970.
Les Blancs, Longacre Theater, 1970.
The Life and Times of J. Walter Smitheus, Theater de Lys, 1970.
The Seagull, Center Stage, 1970.
Orrin, Theater de Lys, 1973.
The Cherry Orchard, Anspacher Theater, 1973.
Emperor Jones, Virginia Museum Theater, 1976.
Othello, Roundabout Theater, 1978.
Coriolanus, Public Theater then Delacorte Theater, 1979.
The Lady from Dubuque, Hartford Stage Company, 1980.
Long Day's Journey into Night, Theater at St. Peter's Church, 1981, then Public Theater, 1981–82.
A Doll's House, Yale Repertory Theater, 1982.
Richard II, Old Globe Theater, 1985.
Execution of Justice, Virginia Theater, 1986.
Driving Miss Daisy, John Houseman Theater, 1987.
Pygmalion, Roundabout Theatre, 1991.
The Master Builder, Belasco Theater, 1992.
The Play about the Baby, Alley Theatre, 2000.
A Last Dance for Sybil, New Federal Theatre, 2003.
The Cherry Orchard, Classic Theatre of Harlem, 2005.
Medea, Classic Theatre of Harlem, 2005.
The Room, Atlantic Theater, 2006.
The Lady from Dubuque, Seattle Repertory Theatre, 2007.
Three Sisters, Classical Theater of Harlem, 2009.

Film

The Bamboo Prison, Columbia Pictures, 1954.
The Possession of Joel Delaney, Haworth Productions, 1972.
Julius Caesar, New York Shakespeare Festival, 1979.
Coriolanus, New York Shakespeare Festival, 1979.
Fighting Back (Death Vengeance), Paramount Pictures, 1982.

Television

The Ivory Ape (Animal Attraction), ABC, 1980.
The Cosby Show, NBC, 1984–92.
Hijacked: Flight 285, ABC, 1996.
The Moving of Sophia Myles, CBS, 2000.

Sources

Periodicals

Back Stage, April 21, 2000, p. 2; May 12, 2000, p. 15.

Chicago Tribune, May 5, 1988, p. 17H; August 16, 1990, p. 15C.

Knight-Ridder/Tribune News Service, September 1, 1993, p. 1901K7115.

New York Times, March 24, 1991, sec. 2, p. 5.

Villager, January 11–17, 2006.

Village Voice, May 20, 2009.

Online

Buckley, Michael, "Stage to Screens: Stage and Screen Star Earle Hyman," Playbill.com, October 23, 2005, http://www.playbill.com/features/article/print/95808.html.html (accessed November 10, 2009).

Other

Additional information for this profile was obtained from Henderson Hogan Talent Agency.

—Rory Donnelly and Sandra Alters

Jermaine Jackson

1954—

Pop singer, entertainment producer

Jackson, Jermaine, photograph. Chris Jackson/Getty Images.

Singer Jermaine Jackson sprang into the national spotlight in 1968 with four of his brothers: Jackie, Tito, Marlon, and Michael. As The Jackson 5, they quickly became one of the most popular pop groups of the era. After leaving the band in the 1970s, Jermaine had a successful solo career and moved increasingly into television. His conversion to Islam in 1989 attracted considerable attention from the public, as did his activities in the weeks following his brother Michael's sudden death in 2009.

Jermaine LaJuane Jackson was born December 11, 1954, in Gary, Indiana, an industrial city just east of Chicago, Illinois. The fourth of nine children born to steelworker Joe Jackson and his wife Katherine, he gravitated toward music at an early age, as did his siblings. His father, who had once played in a rhythm-and-blues group called the Falcons, kept an old guitar that became the focus of the children's impromptu performances. By the mid-1960s, their talent was obvious, and Joe Jackson instituted a more systematic practice regimen for Jermaine and his older brothers, Jackie and Tito. After experimenting with a variety of combinations, the Jackson patriarch added younger brothers Marlon and Michael to the mix, and the Jackson 5 was born. The group's performances were well received, and in 1968 they signed a record contract with producer Berry Gordy's Motown Records, then a dominant force in popular music. Their first album, *Diana Ross Presents the Jackson 5,* appeared the following year.

When the group's first four singles ("I Want You Back," "ABC," "The Love You Save," and "I'll Be There") all reached number one on the *Billboard* singles chart, then an unprecedented feat, it became clear that the Jackson 5 had become a national phenomenon. Although Jermaine had initially been lead singer, that role was increasingly taken over by Michael. Jermaine's contributions, however, remained substantial, and his voice was unquestionably a major factor in the success of albums such as *ABC* (1970) and *Dancing Machine* (1974). As the decade wore on, however, tensions within the group grew, and both Michael and Jermaine left for a time to work on solo projects. The latter's first solo album, entitled simply *Jermaine,* was released by Motown in 1972. Though the album sold well, reaching number six on the *Billboard* R&B chart, it did not

At a Glance . . .

Born Jermaine LaJuane Jackson on December 11, 1954, in Gary, IN; also known as Jermaine Friday and Muhammed Abdul Aziz; son of Joe Jackson (a steelworker and music manager) and Katherine Jackson (a housewife and music manager); brother of noted pop stars Michael Jackson and Janet Jackson; married Hazel Gordy, 1973 (divorced, 1987?), Margaret Maldonado, late 1980s–early 1990s (common-law union); Alejandra Oaziaza, 1995 (divorced 2004); Halima Rashid, 2004; children: nine. *Religion:* Muslim.

Career: Singer and guitarist, The Jackson 5, 1968–76; independent recording artist, 1976—; television performer, 1970s—; entertainment producer, 1992—.

Addresses: *Office*—c/o World Awards Media GmbH Europe, Marc-Aurel-Strasse 10, A-1010 Vienna, Austria.

generate the level of excitement associated with a Jackson 5 release. A follow-up, *Come into My Life,* appeared the next year.

It was also in 1973 that Jackson married Berry Gordy's daughter Hazel. That union complicated Jackson's relationship with his brothers, who were increasingly unhappy with Gordy's management. In 1976, several months after the release of their last Motown album, *Moving Violation* (1975), the group split up. Jackie, Tito, Marlon, and Michael moved to Epic, where they became known as The Jacksons; another brother, Randy, joined them there as a replacement for Jermaine, who remained with Gordy and Motown.

For the next decade and a half, Jackson's solo career proceeded at a frenetic pace, with no fewer than eleven major albums between 1976 and 1992. One of his greatest hits in this period, "Do What You Do," from 1984's *Jermaine Jackson,* marked the beginning of his career with Arista, where he moved following the end of his contractual obligations to Motown. In addition to reaching number thirteen on *Billboard*'s pop chart, the song reached number one on the magazine's "adult contemporary" chart—a sign of the singer's maturing style and aging fan base.

As of 2009 Jackson had not had an album since *You Said,* released by the La Face label in 1992. While it won some strong reviews, its reception was marred by a controversy surrounding the track "Word to the Badd." Widely interpreted as a rebuke of his brother Michael, the song prompted an angry response from

the latter's fans. Public interest in the incident dissipated quickly, however, and it seemed to have little lasting effect, either on the brothers' relationship or on their respective careers.

In the 1990s and 2000s, Jackson moved increasingly into television. In 1992 he produced *The Jacksons: An American Dream,* a miniseries on ABC that proved popular with both fans and critics. His son Jermaine Jackson II was one of two actors to portray him in the film, a dramatic review of the family's rise to stardom. Jackson himself had a long history in front of the camera, though most of his appearances to that point had been in interviews or concert clips. The rise of reality television in the 2000s brought him new opportunities as an on-air personality. In 2007 he was a star on *Celebrity Big Brother,* then one of the highest-rated programs in the United Kingdom. That role was followed by another reality series, Country Music Television's *Gone Country,* several months later.

Jackson's religious life has been the subject of much discussion. He was raised, as were his siblings, in the Jehovah's Witnesses, a Christian denomination. After a 1989 trip to the Middle Eastern nation of Bahrain, however, Jackson converted to Islam. Coincident with that change was his adoption of the names Jermaine Friday and Muhammed Abdul Aziz. As of 2009, however, he continued to be known primarily as Jermaine Jackson.

Amid ongoing tensions between the West and much of the Muslim world, Jackson's conversion elicited some strong reactions. In an interview posted in 2006 on the Web site IslamReligion.com, he noted that he had the strong support of his family. The attitude of the American media, on the other hand, he found highly disrespectful. To counter what he termed anti-Islamic propaganda, he made a number of media appearances to talk about the charitable work his new faith had inspired him to undertake, including a trip to Bangladesh in 2007 to help orphans and other underprivileged children.

Michael Jackson's sudden death in June of 2009 brought Jermaine and the other family members back into the spotlight. After a very public mourning period that included a televised memorial service, plans were made for tribute concerts around the world. One of the most prominent of these, scheduled for September of 2009 at the Schönbrunn Palace in Vienna, Austria, was organized by Jackson in conjunction with the promoter Georg Kindel. Several weeks before it was to take place, however, the two abruptly canceled it. In its place, they announced, they would organize a concert at London's Wembley Stadium in June of 2010.

Jackson has had a complicated personal life. His marriage to Gordy ended in divorce in the 1980s. He was involved for several years in the late 1980s and early 1990s with Margaret Maldonado, generally spoken of as his common-law wife. Thereafter he married Alejandra Oaziaza. That union lasted for nine years, ending in 2004. He then married Halima Rashid. According to IslamReligion.com, he had a total of nine children as of 2006—seven sons and two daughters. As of the summer of 2009, Jackson and Rashid divided their time among Los Angeles, London, and Bahrain.

Selected works

With the Jackson 5

Diana Ross Presents the Jackson 5 (includes "I Want You Back"), Motown, 1969.
ABC (includes "ABC" and "The Love You Save"), Motown, 1970.
Third Album (includes "I'll Be There"), Motown, 1970.
Maybe Tomorrow, Motown, 1971.
Lookin' through the Windows, Motown, 1972.
Get It Together, Motown, 1973.
Skywriter, Motown, 1973.
Dancing Machine, Motown, 1974.
Moving Violation, Motown, 1975.

Solo Albums

Jermaine, Motown, 1972.
Come into My Life, Motown, 1973.
My Name Is Jermaine, Motown, 1976.
Feel the Fire, Motown, 1977.
Frontiers, Motown, 1978.
Let's Get Serious, Motown, 1979.
I Like Your Style, Motown, 1981.
Let Me Tickle Your Fancy, Motown, 1982.
Dynamite, Arista, 1984.

Jermaine Jackson (includes "Do What You Do"), Arista, 1984.
Precious Moments, Arista, 1986.
Don't Take It Personal, Arista, 1989.
You Said (includes "Word to the Badd"), La Face, 1992.

Television

(Producer) *The Jacksons: An American Dream,* ABC, 1992.
Celebrity Big Brother, Channel 4 (United Kingdom), 2007.
Gone Country, Country Music Television, 2008.

Sources

Online

Celizic, Mike, "Jermaine Jackson: 'I Wish It Was Me,'" MSN.com, July 2, 2009, http://www.msnbc.msn.com/id/31704337/ns/today-today_people/ (accessed November 12, 2009).

Itzkoff, David, "Jackson Tribute Concert Is Put Off until Next Year," ArtsBeat, NYTimes.com, September 11, 2009, http://artsbeat.blogs.nytimes.com/2009/09/11/jackson-tribute-concert-is-put-off-until-next-year/?scp=2&sq=%22jackson%20tribute%20in%20vienna%22&st=cse (accessed November 12, 2009).

"Jermaine Jackson, USA," IslamReligion.com, February 26, 2006, http://www.islamreligion.com/articles/90/viewall/ (accessed November 12, 2009).

Lowe, John, "Jermaine Jackson: Biography," AllMusic.com, http://allmusic.com/cg/amg.dll?p=amg&searchlink=JERMAINE|JACKSON&sql=11:gifuxqe5ldae (accessed November 12, 2009).

—R. Anthony Kugler

Mordecai Wyatt Johnson

1890–1976

Educator, minister

During his lifetime Mordecai Wyatt Johnson was one of the most prominent African Americans in the nation because of his role as the first black president of Howard University. The Baptist minister known for his fiery oratory was appointed to the post in 1926 and presided over the Washington, DC, institution for the next thirty-four years. Johnson is widely recognized for almost single-handedly turning Howard into an educational powerhouse by persuading federal officials, prominent philanthropists, and top-notch academics of the value of having a prestigious college for African-American achievers in the nation's capital. Half a century after his retirement in 1960, Howard University remained among the elite of the historically black colleges and universities (HBCUs).

The son of slaves, Johnson was born in 1890 in Paris, Tennessee. His father was both a minister and mill worker, while his mother worked as a domestic. As a young man, Johnson entered Atlanta Baptist College (later Morehouse College), where he excelled on both the debate team and the football field. Although he was expelled for taking part in a card game, he was later readmitted and graduated in 1911. Heading north to further his education, Johnson earned a second undergraduate degree from the prestigious University of Chicago in 1913 before moving to upstate New York to study toward his bachelor of divinity degree at Rochester Theological Seminary. During that period, he pastored a church in Mumford, New York.

Around 1917, after a stint as a national officer with the Young Men's Christian Association (YMCA), Johnson settled in Charleston, West Virginia, as pastor of the First Baptist Church. He also founded the city's chapter of the National Association for the Advancement of Colored People, or NAACP. In the early 1920s, he returned to school once again, this time at Harvard University Divinity School, which granted him a master's degree in sacred theology in 1922. He delivered the Divinity School's valedictory address, entitled "The Faith of the American Negro," and greatly impressed Julius Rosenwald, one of America's wealthiest moguls. Rosenwald was president of the Sears, Roebuck department store empire and a major philanthropist of the era. His Rosenwald Fund, established in 1917, donated heavily to African-American educational causes over the next thirty years, and Rosenwald became one of Johnson's influential allies.

Righted a Sinking Ship

In 1926 Johnson's name was mentioned at a meeting of the board of trustees of Howard University as a possible candidate for the newly vacant presidency. The District of Columbia school was founded just after the end of the U.S. Civil War. Like many other HBCUs, Howard had been founded by a religious group, and its presidents and senior administrators had been white. At the time of the 1926 meeting, the situation had improved to the point where seven blacks were among the eighteen trustees. There had been talk of finding a qualified African-American professional to lead the school, and Johnson's name was put forth after the former president of Wilberforce University in Ohio

At a Glance . . .

Born on January 12, 1890, in Paris, TN; died on September 10, 1976, in Washington, DC; son of Wyatt J. (a minister, mill worker, and former slave) and Carolyn (maiden name, Freeman; a domestic worker and former slave) Johnson; married Anna Ethelyn Gardner, December 25, 1916 (died, 1969); married Alice Clinton Woodson, 1970; children (with Gardner): Carolyn Elizabeth, Mordecai Wyatt Jr., Archer Clement, William Howard, Anna Faith. *Religion:* Baptist. *Education:* Morehouse College, BA, 1911; University of Chicago, AB, 1913; Rochester Theological Seminary, BD; Harvard University, master of sacred theology, 1922.

Career: Secretary for the Western U.S. region of the Student Young Men's Christian Association (YMCA); pastor of a Mumford, New York, Baptist church; First Baptist Church (Charleston, WV), pastor, 1917(?)–19; taught economics and history at Morehouse College; Howard University, president, 1926–60; member of the U.S. delegation to North Atlantic Treaty Organization (NATO) meetings, 1950s.

Memberships: National Association for the Advancement of Colored People (NAACP; founder of Charleston, WV, chapter).

declined the board's offer. There was some dispute over his qualifications—a few of the trustees felt that the new president should hold an advanced academic degree as well as possess some executive experience—but they voted to offer Johnson the job with a salary of $7,000 per year.

Johnson took on a job that few experienced administrators would have wanted. Howard had been poorly run in previous years, and its buildings were in terrible shape. In his first years on the job, Johnson rectified the financial mismanagement. Overcoming bitter opposition by white Southern members of Congress, Johnson and his allies won a boon for the university in the form of a record funding bill that gave the school what was then an enormous sum—$3 million—to improve its facilities. The funds were administered by the Department of the Interior, for a cabinet-level education department would not be created for another fifty years. Rosenwald was also a generous benefactor, donating $250,000 on the eve of the Great Depression for the construction of a new biological sciences building at Howard.

That new building was part of Johnson's plan to vastly improve the academic standing of the university's graduate schools. He began at the top, with the medical school. At the time, Howard and Meharry Medical College in Nashville, Tennessee, were the sole HBCUs training blacks to become board-certified physicians. Next, Johnson worked on enhancing the small law school at Howard, which at the time offered only night classes. For this project he enlisted the help of Louis D. Brandeis, who a decade earlier had become the first Jewish associate justice of the U.S. Supreme Court. Brandeis introduced Johnson to many law school deans across the United States who, in turn, helped him recruit talented black graduates to join Howard's law school faculty.

Aided Nascent Civil Rights Movement

One of Johnson's greatest achievements was securing the appointment of Harvard-educated Charles Hamilton Houston as the dean of the Howard law school. Houston, like Brandeis, believed that the laws already codified in the United States, particularly the Constitution, were the best tool for remedying inequality and achieving social justice. Thurgood Marshall, who later became the first black U.S. Supreme Court justice, graduated from Howard's law school during Houston's tenure. Nearly twenty years later Marshall's arguments as the lead NAACP lawyer in the landmark 1954 desegregation case *Brown v. Board of Education* drew on Houston's strategy. As president, Johnson helped the Howard University Law School secure an important accreditation from the American Bar Association, and the school was also admitted to the Association of American Law Schools. In 1938 Howard University Law School became the first law school in the United States to offer a course on civil rights.

Johnson found two other influential supporters in U.S. President Franklin D. Roosevelt and First Lady Eleanor Roosevelt. The president spoke in October of 1936 at the dedication of Howard University's new chemistry building, which was the largest of its kind at any U.S. university and had been built largely through Roosevelt's job-creation program, the Works Progress Administration. "So far as it was humanly possible, the government has followed the policy that among American citizens there should be no forgotten man and no forgotten races. It is a wise and truly American policy," Roosevelt asserted, according to the *New York Times.* Over the next quarter century Howard continued to grow under Johnson's leadership, with a greatly expanded campus and state-of-the-art library. Enrollment quintupled during his tenure: when Johnson took office in 1926, Howard was home to 2,000 students, but it boasted more than 10,000 students by the time of his retirement in 1960. He had also been instrumental in creating Howard's nursing program and College of

Dentistry and had greatly expanded graduate programs in the liberal arts.

Held Audiences Spellbound with Oratory

Johnson was not universally admired for his efforts. Many among the faculty bristled at his authoritarian managerial style and derided his lack of an advanced academic degree. It was unfitting, they argued, to have a Baptist preacher lead such a prestigious institution. Even an official centenary history of Howard University published in 1969 featured unflattering remarks about Johnson. The book, by Rayford W. Logan, did note by way of balance that while Johnson fought vigorously against any faculty input about how the university should be governed, "Faculty members could say and write and teach whatever they wanted to, within reason, because President Johnson was one of the most fearless critics of American democracy in modern times. There was, and still is, more unanimity on this point than on any other characteristic of the man who lifted Howard to greater heights than it had ever known."

Johnson was famous for his speeches at university commencements and other events. "The Lord told me to speak," Logan quoted one of his more frequent aphorisms, "but He did not tell me when to stop." Johnson delivered most of his riveting speeches with just an outline before him, and his style featured all the drama and eloquence of an orator trained for the Baptist pulpit. At a 1945 youth legislative conference of the NAACP held on Howard's campus, Johnson furnished an opening address whose message presaged the coming civil rights movement. It would be a period "of great social change," he asserted, according to a *New York Times* report by George Streator. Johnson further remarked that the delegates "must be aware by now that we are substantially unskilled in the methods of securing the redress available to us under the law."

Johnson was a member of the U.S. delegations to North Atlantic Treaty Organization (NATO) meetings. This joint military alliance between Western Europe and the United States was created to combat the threat of the Soviet Union, which had moved aggressively to install Communist regimes in Eastern Europe in the years just following World War II. In one 1959 speech he called upon member nations to work to eliminate bias in society and to help the underprivileged, no matter what their race. Johnson held that despite its flawed system the Soviet Union had made notable progress in eliminating racial bias from its society, and that other nations should follow suit. "Their slogan is workers of the world united—not just the white workers," he said, according to the *New York Times*. His commitment to democratic principles was unwavering. Earlier in the decade Johnson had vociferously defended Howard University faculty members targeted by the House Un-American Activities Committee for their suspected Communist sympathies.

In 1916 Johnson had married Anna Ethelyn Gardner, with whom he had five children. She died in 1969, and he was reunited with a college girlfriend, Alice Woodson, whom he wed in 1970. Johnson died in Washington, DC, at the age of 86 on September 10, 1976.

Sources

Books

Logan, Rayford W., *Howard University: The First Hundred Years 1867–1967,* New York University Press, 2005.

Periodicals

Journal of Negro Education, Summer 1998.
New York Times, October 27, 1936, p. 1; April 1, 1948, p. 15; June 7, 1959, p. 4.

—Carol Brennan

Tamara Johnson-George

1971—

Singer

Johnson-George, Tamara, photograph. Jemal Countess/Getty Images.

Tamara "Taj" Johnson-George first gained fame with the R&B act SWV, or Sisters With Voices, in the early 1990s. The singer went on to a respectable post-pop career, including a surprisingly strong finish on the reality television show *Survivor: Tocantins—The Brazilian Highlands* and as the subject of another reality show also featuring her husband, former Tennessee Titan Eddie George.

Born Tamara Antrice Johnson on April 29, 1971, Johnson-George was the youngest of six children in her family and was raised in the Bedford-Stuyvesant neighborhood of Brooklyn, in New York City. Her early years were bleak: she barely knew her father, who died of cancer the year she turned nine, and there were serious financial hardships. For a time the household included a stepfather who abused her mother. Then her mother was diagnosed with bone cancer, and the adolescent Johnson-George and her brothers cared for her at home until her death five years to the day after their father had died. Orphaned now, Johnson-George lived with various relatives, including an aunt who "was strict," Johnson-George recalled in a 1997 *Vibe* interview with Tonya Pendleton. "I was angry, very upset. I still go through my moments." She later said that as a

youth she had also been the victim of sexual abuse by male relatives.

In middle school Johnson-George found solace in singing with her best friend, Cheryl "Coko" Gamble, whose mother was the successful gospel artist Tibba Gamble. Intense fans of the singing group New Edition, the girls formed their own group, "Female Edition," with a third friend, Bronx native Leanne "Lelee" Lyons, and performed in local talent contests. The group split up in high school, when Gamble teamed up with Lyons as a gospel act. Johnson-George, meanwhile, earned top grades in high school and began accounting courses at Baruch College, part of the City University of New York system. The three friends decided to reunite professionally and in 1990 made some demo tapes, working with a producer who was a Lyons family acquaintance and who helped them find a manager and a label.

RCA Records signed the act, now dubbed SWV, and released their debut record, *It's about Time,* in 1992. Johnson-George co-wrote their first hit single, "Right Here." Two more hits—"I'm So into You" and "Weak"—helped the album sell more than two million

At a Glance . . .

Born Tamara Antrice Johnson on April 29, 1971; married Eddie George (business owner and former professional athlete), June 2004; children: Eriq Michael; stepson, Jaire David. *Education:* Belmont University, BBA, 2004.

Career: Singer and songwriter in the R&B group SWV, 1990–98; signed to RCA Records; cofounder of domestic-violence awareness group Visions with Infinite Possibilities (VIP).

Addresses: *Office*—c/o Visions with Infinite Possibilities, P.O. Box 150283, Nashville, TN 37215.

copies. The trio was initially compared to the quartet En Vogue, but SWV's lyrics were of a far franker nature and anticipated the racier women artists who came later, including Lil' Kim and Foxy Brown. "What distinguishes SWV is street-level imaging and aggressive, swing-style harmonies, which place them in the burgeoning 'ghetto soul' category," asserted Janine McAdams writing in *Billboard.* As their singles climbed the U.S. R&B charts, the first heady months of fame featured such memorable events as opening for Bobby Brown, one of the heartthrobs of the original New Edition, at Madison Square Garden. On the street, the singers were sometimes mobbed by male fans. "Sometimes it gets real bad, and we have to let security handle it," Johnson-George told writer Janice Min for *People.* "They mostly give us the usual 'we love you, I love you, I want to marry you.'"

SWV were contenders for the 1993 Grammy Award for Best New Artist of the Year, but lost out to Toni Braxton. They worked with the Wu-Tang Clan on the 1994 LP *The Remixes* before regrouping and heading back into the studio for *New Beginning,* which was released in 1996. It failed to perform as well as their debut, but the song "Can We?," written by a relatively unknown rapper and songwriter named Missy Elliott, appeared on the soundtrack of the 1997 comedy *Booty Call* and became a surprise hit for the group. Their 1997 LP, *Release Some Tension,* failed to garner any hits despite the magic touch of producer Sean "Diddy" Combs. By then it appeared that Coko Gamble had been pushed to the front role, and strains within the group began to tell. By the end of 1998 the group had disbanded.

Johnson-George proceeded to a modeling career with the Ford Modeling Agency and became romantically involved with 1995 Heisman Trophy winner Eddie George, who played for the National Football League's Tennessee Titans for several seasons. Seeking to complete her college degree, she enrolled at Belmont University in Nashville and graduated with a bachelor's degree in business administration in 2004. A month later she married George, who went on to have several successful business ventures in both Nashville and Columbus, Ohio. Their son, Eriq Michael, was born in 2005.

Johnson-George returned to the public spotlight in 2007 with two new projects. Her first book, *Player hateHER: How to Avoid the Beat Down and Live in a Drama-Free World,* was co-written with longtime friend Katrina Chambers and published by Amistad/HarperCollins. She and her husband also permitted a reality-television crew to follow them for *I Married a Baller,* which premiered on the TV One network in the spring of 2007. "The Georges are hardly a typical reality-TV couple," noted *Columbus Dispatch* writer Molly Willow. "They aren't coping with a drug addiction, working through a bubble-gum romance or dealing with any other made-for-TV weirdness. Instead, their nine-episode series depicts a happy, well-adjusted couple who get on each other's nerves occasionally, rely on family and friends, and come across as loving parents to their children."

Johnson-George's appeal prompted producers for the hit CBS television series *Survivor* to cast her for its eighteenth season. Johnson-George had never watched the series, and did not know how to swim, but gamely agreed to participate. She learned how to fish in order to catch her meals while camping out under grueling conditions in Jalapão, a Brazilian national park, for six weeks in late 2008. She "survived" several physical challenges as well as the usual interpersonal dramas that are a hallmark of each episode, and finished in fourth place.

Johnson-George and her husband founded a domestic-violence awareness group, Visions with Infinite Possibilities, or VIP, to aid women and children living in domestic-violence shelters in the United States. Johnson-George has spoken frankly of the traumas of her childhood, which included a stint in a Salvation Army hostel, and the boyfriend she had as a young adult who physically abused her. "I believe that people should know that every day is a new day to grow and heal for me," she explained on the organization's Web site. "The pain didn't happen over night and neither does the healing. Every day is a healing day for me and I want to help others see their way to and through this journey."

Selected works

LPs (with SWV on RCA Records)

It's About Time, 1992.
The Remixes, 1994.
New Beginning, 1996.
Release Some Tension, 1997.
A Special Christmas, 1999.

Books

(With Katrina Chambers) *Player hateHER: How to Avoid the Beat Down and Live in a Drama-Free World,* Amistad/HarperCollins, 2007.

Television

I Married a Baller, TV One, 2007.
Survivor: Tocantins—The Brazilian Highlands, CBS, 2009.

Sources

Periodicals

Billboard, March 13, 1993, p. 5.
Columbus Dispatch (Columbus, OH), April 18, 2007.

Ebony, June 1994, p. 52.
Essence, March 1994, p. 74.
In Style, January 4, 2005, p. 342.
People, September 6, 1993, p. 77.
Vibe, November 1997, pp. 109–110.

Online

"Melody Charles Interview with SWV's Taj," Soul Tracks, http://www.soultracks.com/story-taj (accessed October 20, 2009).
"Tamara's Story," Visions with Infinite Possibilities, http://visionswithinfinitepossibilities.org/index.php?option=com_content&task=view&id=5&Itemid=27 (accessed October 20, 2009).

—Carol Brennan

Eugene Kinckle Jones

1885–1954

Social worker, civil rights leader

Eugene Kinckle Jones is remembered as one of the seven founders—known as "Jewels"—of Alpha Phi Alpha, the first black fraternity in the United States, started at Cornell University in 1906. Jones went on to become one of the most important African-American social workers of the early twentieth century, serving as executive secretary of the National Urban League from 1918 to 1941, a period of tremendous social, cultural, and economic change for blacks in America. In his work with the league, he lobbied for better employment and educational opportunities for African Americans, as thousands were then migrating to the urban centers of the North and West, and fought against racial discrimination in America's cities. During the Great Depression years, as a member of President Franklin D. Roosevelt's so-called Black Cabinet, he provided a voice for African Americans in government and helped ensure that their concerns were addressed. Jones's efforts laid the groundwork for the civil rights movement, which would not begin in earnest until after his death.

Helped Found First Black Fraternity

Jones was born on July 30, 1885, in Richmond, Virginia, the son of Joseph and Rosa Jones, both of whom were educators. His father, who had been one of the first African Americans in Virginia to earn a college degree, was graduated from Madison University (now Colgate University) in 1876. For nearly fifty years, Joseph Jones taught at the Richmond Theological

Seminary (which became Virginia Union University in 1899). Eugene's mother, Rosa Jones, had attended Howard University and the New England Conservatory of Music, and taught music for more than forty years at Hartshorn Memorial College. Eugene Jones grew up among the black elite of Richmond, and as a young man, he observed how his parents socialized easily with their white colleagues. That experience would shape his approach to social work later in life.

Jones attended Virginia Union University, earning his bachelor's degree in 1906. That year, he enrolled in the master's degree program at Cornell University, initially studying civil engineering to demonstrate to university officials that he could perform at the level expected of Cornell's graduate students. Finding that employment opportunities for African Americans in the engineering field were limited, however, he switched to sociology, focusing in his thesis on the progress that African Americans had made since Reconstruction.

While at Cornell, Jones became the first initiate of Alpha Phi Alpha, the first intercollegiate black fraternity, which was formed in December of 1906 to bring African-American students together and provide mutual support to help them survive the racially hostile environment of the time. Jones served as the second president of the fraternity's original chapter, Alpha, and he organized three more chapters at other schools—Beta at Howard University, Gamma at Virginia Union University, and Delta at the University of Toronto—in 1907 and 1908. Jones also was a mem-

At a Glance . . .

Born on July 30, 1885, in Richmond, VA; died on January 11, 1954, in New York, NY; son of Joseph Endom Jones (an educator) and Rosa Daniel Kinckle Jones (an educator); married Blanche Ruby Watson, March 11, 1909; children: Eugene Kinckle Jr., Adele Rosa. *Education:* Virginia Union University, BA, 1906; Cornell University, sociology, MA, 1908.

Career: National Urban League, field secretary, 1911; associate chief executive, 1912–18, executive secretary, 1918–41, general secretary, 1941–50; U.S. Commerce Department, adviser on Negro affairs, 1933–37.

Memberships: National Conference of Social Workers.

ber of the fraternity's first Committees on Constitution and Organization and helped write the fraternity ritual. Despite his many contributions to the organization's growth and early development, Jones was not officially recognized as one of the fraternity's seven founders, known as "Jewels," until 1952.

Led the National Urban League

After completing his studies at Cornell in 1908, Jones taught high school for two years in Louisville, Kentucky. In 1911 he received an invitation from George Edmund Haynes, a professor of sociology at Fisk University, to join the Committee on Urban Conditions among Negroes. The committee had been formed a year earlier in New York by Haynes and Ruth Standish Baldwin, and it soon merged with the Committee for the Improvement of Industrial Conditions among Negroes and the National League for the Protection of Colored Women, calling itself the National League on Urban Conditions among Negroes. The organization was an outgrowth of the Great Migration, the movement of hundreds of thousands of African Americans out of the southern United States and into the urban centers of the North and West, in search of employment and educational opportunities. Haynes and Baldwin had formed the original committee in order to help these migrants adjust to urban life and combat the discrimination they faced.

Jones started out as a field secretary for the organization, which later shortened its name to the National Urban League. In 1918 he succeeded Haynes as executive secretary—and the only full-time employee—of the league, which then had an annual budget of $2,500. Under Jones's leadership, the league dramatically expanded its campaign against barriers to employment for blacks, targeting opportu-

nities for employment in the civil service and in national defense production, implementing programs for economic and social development, and even organizing boycotts of firms that refused to hire black workers. Jones was particularly eager for the league to work with organized labor: In 1913 he had arranged the first meeting of African-American leaders with the American Federation of Labor, headed by Samuel Gompers, and Jones was instrumental in persuading that union to end its exclusion of African Americans in 1929.

The league, as Jones conceived of it, was to be interracial in its approach to race relations in America. Although the organization's programs focused on bettering the lives of African Americans, the mission was broader, according to Jones. In a 1926 letter to the editor of the *New York Times,* he wrote, "The National Urban League ... has devoted itself to the welfare of Negroes in particular, but its work is designed to improve human relations in America—and thus our contribution to the cause of a better America."

In 1923 Jones helped found the monthly magazine *Opportunity: Journal of Negro Life* with Charles S. Johnson, who served as editor. As the flagship publication of the National Urban League, it aimed to provide a vehicle for African-American arts and culture, which most mainstream periodicals did not cover. Some of the most important writers of the Harlem Renaissance were published in its pages, including Countee Cullen, Langston Hughes, and Zora Neale Hurston. In 1926 Jones negotiated the purchase of a large collection of books and personal manuscripts from black scholar Arthur Alfonso Schomburg on behalf of the New York Public Library. Today, the Schomburg Center for Research in Black Culture is one of the leading research facilities devoted to the preservation of materials on African-American life.

Gave Blacks a Voice in Government

During the Great Depression of the 1930s, President Roosevelt appointed an informal group of African-American advisers to positions in federal departments and New Deal agencies to guide his administration on matters of concern to black Americans. Officially called the Federal Council of Negro Affairs, the group became informally known as the Black Cabinet or the Black Brain Trust. From 1933 to 1937, Jones took a leave of absence from the National Urban League to serve as adviser on Negro affairs in the U.S. Department of Commerce. He used his access to political leaders in Washington to push the league's agenda of economic empowerment for African Americans.

Jones returned to his post at the National Urban League in 1937 but was stricken with tuberculosis. He worked intermittently as executive secretary until he resigned in 1941. Jones then held the position of general secretary with the league until 1950, when he retired. By this time, the National Urban League had 58 affiliate organizations in 29 states, with a staff of nearly 400 and an annual budget of $1.5 million. Upon his retirement, Jones summarized the progress that African Americans had made during his lifetime: Much of it resulted not from mass pressure or political compromise but from logic, understanding, goodwill, and common sense. "I truly believe that it is economically and socially better to treat people fairly, and it is possible to convince others of that," he said, according to his obituary in the January of 1954 *New York Times.*

Selected writings

Letter to the editor, *New York Times,* May 18, 1926.

"Membership of Negro Fraternity," *New York Times,* December 10, 1948, Books sec., p. 24.

The First Forty Years of Service to the American People, National Urban League Fortieth Anniversary Yearbook, 1950, National Urban League, 1951.

Sources

Books

Mason, Herman, *The Talented Tenth: The Founders and Presidents of Alpha,* 2nd ed., Four-G, 1999.

Parks, Gregory S., ed., *Black Greek-Letter Organizations in the Twenty-First Century: Our Fight Has Just Begun,* University Press of Kentucky, 2008.

Periodicals

Afro-Americans in New York Life and History, January 2006.

New York Times, May 6, 1936, Books sec., p. 22; January 12, 1954.

Online

"Jewel Eugene Kinckle Jones," Omicron Delta Lambda Chapter of the Alpha Phi Alpha Fraternity, http://www.odlchapter.com/html/site_pages/jones.php (accessed October 14, 2009).

"Mission and History," National Urban League, http://www.nul.org/who-we-are/mission-and-history (accessed October 14, 2009).

—Deborah A. Ring

James Earl Jones

1931—

Actor

Jones, James Earl, photograph. Brian Ach/WireImage.

Some people know him as one of the nation's finest stage actors, an artist who tackles the works of such playwrights as William Shakespeare and Eugene O'Neill. Others know him as the deep bass voice of the network news channel CNN or the most menacing aspect of the evil Darth Vader in *Star Wars*. Still others recognize him as a television star who brings depths of humanity to clichéd character roles. James Earl Jones fits all these descriptions and more: for well over forty years he has been one of the most esteemed actors in the United States.

Grew up on Grandparents' Farm

The only child of Robert Earl and Ruth Connolly Jones, James Earl Jones was born on January 17, 1931, in Arkabutla, Mississippi, on his maternal grandfather's farm. Prior to his son's birth, James' father left the family to pursue a career as a prize fighter and later as an actor. Ruth Jones soon followed suit when she found tailoring work that kept her separated from her son for long periods of time. Jones remarked in *Newsweek* that he realizes that the economic circumstances of the

Great Depression forced his parents apart. Still, he said, the abandonment hurt him deeply. "No matter how old the character I play," he concluded, "those deep childhood memories, those furies, will come out. I understand this."

Living on his grandparents' farm, Jones was afforded a measure of security. As a youngster he hunted, fished, and performed farm chores. He also attended church, where he watched his grandmother's emotional displays of holy rapture. "There was a strong evangelistic aspect to her religion, and when she went to church and felt the spirit, she ended up behaving like a holy roller," Jones recalled in the *Saturday Review*. "There wasn't much touching in the family, but there was emotion."

Eventually Jones's grandparents formally adopted him and took him north to rural Michigan. Jones acknowledged in *Newsweek* that the move north helped him to escape "a certain self-castration" common among African Americans in the South at the time, but he did not adjust easily to his new surroundings. He developed a stutter and eventually found communication so difficult that at certain periods during grammar school he could talk only to himself or his immediate family. The

At a Glance . . .

Born James Earl Jones on January 17, 1931, in Arkabutla, MS; son of Robert Earl Jones (a prize-fighter and actor) and Ruth Williams (a tailor); married Julienne Marie (an actress), 1967 (divorced); married Cecilia Hart (an actress), March 15, 1982; children: (second marriage) Flynn Earl. *Military service:* U.S. Army, 1953–55; first lieutenant. *Education:* University of Michigan, 1949–53; American Theatre Wing, diploma, 1957.

Career: Actor, 1957—.

Memberships: Screen Actors Guild, member.

Awards: Obie Award, the *Village Voice,* 1962, 1965; Tony Award, American Theater Wing,1969, 1987; Honorary Doctorate (HDHL), University of Michigan, 1970; Golden Globe, Hollywood Foreign Press Association, 1971; Emmy Award, Academy of Television Arts and Sciences,1991, National Academy of Television Arts and Sciences, 2000; CableACE Award, National Cable Television Association, 1991; Common Wealth Award, PNC Bank and Common Wealth Trust, 1991; Image Award, American National Association for the Advancement of Colored People, 1993; Kennedy Center Honors, John F. Kennedy Center for the Performing Arts, 2002; DVDX Award, DVD Premier Awards Academy, 2003; CAMIE Award, CAMIE Awards, Inc., 2006; Life Achievement Award, Screen Actors Guild, 2009.

Addresses: *Agent*—c/o Horatio Productions Inc., PO Box 610, Pawling, NY 12564.

problem followed him to high school, where one of his English teachers discovered that he wrote poetry and, as Jones recalled in *Success* magazine, asked him to "recite the poem, by heart in front of the entire class. I did as he asked, got through it without stuttering, and from then on I had to write more, and speak more. This had a tremendous effect on me, and my confidence grew as I learned to express myself comfortably out loud."

Shifted from Medicine to Acting

Jones attended the University of Michigan on a scholarship, intending to study medicine. At first he took acting classes simply as an enjoyable sideline, but he soon switched his major to theater. When he was twenty-one years old and a college junior, he traveled to New York City to meet his father. They had only spoken briefly on the telephone several times. The relationship was strained by long years without communication, but Jones's father encouraged him to pursue a career in theater; Jones left Michigan after four years of schooling but without a degree. Years later the university awarded him an honorary doctorate.

During his years at Michigan, Jones joined the Army Reserve Officers' Training Corps (ROTC), performing well and enjoying the experience, and he spent much of his post-college service in a rigorous ranger-training program in the Colorado mountains. In 1955 he was set to reenlist when his commanding officer suggested that he taste civilian life before making a long-term commitment to the armed services. Taking his advice, Jones moved to New York City and enrolled in further acting classes. Two things helped ease his decision: he knew he could return to the army if he did not find success as an actor, and his tuition at the American Theater Wing was paid by the Army's G.I. Bill.

Jones lived with his father for a time, and the two supplemented their meager acting incomes by polishing floors in Off-Broadway theaters. In 1957 the younger Jones earned his first professional role as an understudy in an Off-Broadway production of *Wedding in Japan.* He was rarely out of work after that, but his salary during the last years of the 1950s averaged only $45 a week. He made ends meet by renting a cold-water flat on the Lower East Side. Jones tried any role, no matter how small. In 1959 he began a long tenure with the New York Shakespeare Festival, carrying a spear in *Henry V.* Before long he was given more prominent roles, culminating in his 1963–64 performance as the lead in *Othello*—one of a staggering thirteen plays he appeared in that year.

Worked on Stage, Screen, and Television

Othello ran for a year Off-Broadway with Jones in the lead. The actor also found time to do television spots and to make one film appearance—as the bombardier in Stanley Kubrick's dark comedy *Dr. Strangelove.* In the mid-1960s Jones began augmenting his theater work with television parts. He took cameo roles in shows such as *The Defenders* and *East Side/West Side,* and he became the first African-American man to take a continuing role on a daytime serial when he portrayed a doctor on *As the World Turns.* The big break for Jones, though, came during a period when he was touring Europe on stage as the lead in Eugene O'Neill's *The Emperor Jones.*

In 1967 Jones learned that the play *The Great White Hope,* which was a dramatization of the life of boxing champion Jack Johnson, was slated for a possible Broadway run. He wanted the part desperately. To build his muscles he began training, working with boxing managers and watching old footage of Johnson's fights. Jones was ultimately given the part, and the show opened on Broadway on October 3, 1968.

The Great White Hope was a success, and its reception propelled Jones to stardom. "Fourteen years of good hard acting work, including more Shakespeare than most British actors attempt, have gone into the making of James Earl Jones," wrote a *Newsweek* reviewer who also concluded that "only an actor with the bigness and power of Jones" could make such a play work. Jones won a Tony Award for his role in *The Great White Hope,* and he was nominated for an Academy Award in 1970 when the play was made into a motion picture.

Attained Celebrity Status

Instant celebrity status brought Jones a new awareness of his limitations. The actor told *TV Guide* that his work in *The Great White Hope* did not prove to be the career boost he thought it would. "I thought with the Oscar nomination that several projects would be waiting for me immediately," he said. "But then projects—very viable ones close to getting go-aheads—caved in under racism's insanity." One of those projects was a life story of civil rights activist Malcolm X, a version of which was finally directed by filmmaker Spike Lee, but not until many years later.

Jones returned to the stage, appearing in *Hamlet* in 1972, *King Lear* in 1973, and *Of Mice and Men* in 1974–75. He also performed in a series of minor films, including *The Man* and *The Bingo Long Traveling All-Stars and Motor Kings.* Jones's most notable movie role of the 1970s and early 1980s was one in which only his voice was used. He gave a memorable level of malevolence to the half-man, half-machine villain Darth Vader in all three *Star Wars* films.

In 1982 Jones appeared on Broadway as Othello to standing ovations. In sharp contrast, he also portrayed the villain in the film *Conan, the Barbarian.* To critics who faulted him for taking roles in substandard films and commercials, Jones had a simple reply: movies and television pay well; theater does not. "I can't afford to take a vacation unless I do some commercials when I'm in New York," he pointed out in the *Saturday Review.* "Money goes fast, and you can't get along doing only stage work. I've never minded doing commercials. ... Commercials can be very exciting." In 1991 Jones lent himself to a string of TV ads for the Bell Atlantic Yellow Pages, his first on-air product endorsement.

Played Varied Roles

Jones's work in the late 1980s and early 1990s was as varied as his early career. He played an enigmatic

writer in the 1989 hit film *Field of Dreams,* a CIA chief in the 1992 screen adaptation of Tom Clancy's novel *Patriot Games,* and an ex-convict private investigator in the award-winning television series *Gabriel's Fire.* Not neglecting his onstage work, he earned yet another Tony Award in 1988 for his portrayal of a disenchanted Negro League baseball player in August Wilson's play *Fences.* Jones explained the diversity of his work in the *Los Angeles Times*—he took so many minor film and television roles simply because he likes to work. "Just as, on stage, I waited years for a role like Jack [Johnson] in *Great White Hope,* or a role like Troy in *Fences,* you do the same thing in movies," he said. "Unless you are among that handful of exceptions, the stars who have projects lined up, you don't wait, at least I didn't want to wait. ... I don't think I've done many films that counted. What I'm getting at, rather than waiting for that wonderful role in a movie, I take 'off' jobs."

To quote *Los Angeles Times* correspondent David Wallace, those "off jobs" are often "memorable only for [Jones's] commanding presence [or] for the brevity of his appearance." That situation would change, however: in 1990 Jones announced that his age and health were forcing him to curtail his work in live theater. "After six months in a play, the fatigue factor begins to affect the quality of a performance," the actor conceded in the *Los Angeles Times.* "The audiences might not know it, but I do. My thing is serious drama, and usually the lead character has a heavy load to carry. I find that after six months, if you get four out of eight shows a week that work perfectly the way you want, you're lucky."

Received Lifetime Honors

As Jones was in the midst of his fifth decade of working in theater, film, and television, he was bestowed Kennedy Center Honors in 2002. The John F. Kennedy Center for the Performing Arts presents this award annually to performing artists for their lifetime contributions to American culture. President Bush attended the award presentation and joked about Jones' iconic voice: "People say that the voice of the President is the most easily recognized voice in America. Well, I'm not going to make that claim in the presence of James Earl Jones."

Jones might have slowed his pace a bit during his seventies, but he was still referred to as a "powerhouse" by *New York Times* theater critic Ben Brantley in his review of the 2005 production of "On Golden Pond." Jones played the lead role of Norman Thayer Jr. alongside lead actress Leslie Uggams, his onstage wife, Ethel. Although Brantley suggested that the "deep appeal" of this *On Golden Pond* "was not a one-man achievement," he did state that "it is hard to imagine the production working on the level that it does without Mr. Jones." Unfortunately for theater-goers, Jones contracted pneumonia while appearing in the production, missing many performances. Ultimately, the show had to close.

In the next year, Jones took on a the one-man show *Thurgood* at the quaint Westport Playhouse in Connecticut. Playing the first African-American Supreme Court justice, Jones performed so superbly that Thurgood Marshall's widow Cecilia commented to *New York Times* reporter Anita Gates that "I closed my eyes and I thought Thurgood was there."

In 2009, only days after his seventy-eighth birthday, Jones was honored with another lifetime achievement award—this time from the Screen Actors Guild (SAG). The headlines in *Variety* called Jones's range of performance "intergalactic." Kathy Connell, the SAG awards producer, characterized the actor as "An iconic figure." She continued that Jones has "appeared in film, TV, commercials, voiceovers, and animation. He's the Everyman actor." Paul Napier, an awards committee member added that Jones "has a long list of credits that makes an impressive cross section of work. He's represented the African-American artist as visibly as anyone. He's recognized everywhere."

Whatever Jones plays—villain or hero—he infuses each role with "enormous talent, range, courage, taste, [and] sensitivity," wrote a *Newsweek* correspondent. During a career that began in the late 1950s, James Earl Jones has struggled to define himself not as a black actor, but simply as an actor. He has opted for maximum variety, but each new part bears his particular, memorable stamp. In *Newsweek*, Jack Kroll called Jones "the embodiment of the living paradox that informs all great acting: his powerful persona is at once intimate and apart, friendly and heroic. He's right there in the room with you, but he's also in your mind, an electrifying double presence that only the strongest actors can create."

Selected works

Books

(With Penelope Niven) *James Earl Jones: Voices and Silences,* Scribner, 1993.

Films

Dr. Strangelove: Or, How I Learned to Stop Worrying and Love the Bomb, Columbia Pictures, 1964.
The Great White Hope, 20th Century Fox, 1970.
(Narrator), *Malcolm X,* Warner Bros., 1972.
Deadly Hero, AVCO Embassy Pictures, 1976.
The Bingo Long Traveling All-Stars and Motor Kings, Motown Productions, 1976.
(Voice) *Star Wars,* Lucasfilm, 1977.
The Greatest, British Lion Film Corp., 1977.
(Voice) *The Empire Strikes Back,* Lucasfilm, 1980.
Conan the Barbarian, Dino De Laurentiis Co., 1982.
(Voice) *Return of the Jedi,* Lucasfilm, 1983.

Gardens of Stone, ML Delphi Premier Productions, 1987.
Matewan, Cinecom Entertainment Group, 1987.
Field of Dreams, Gordon Co., 1989.
The Hunt for Red October, Paramount Pictures, 1990.
Sneakers, Universal Pictures, 1992.
Patriot Games, Mace Neufeld Productions, 1992.
(Voice) *The Lion King,* Walt Disney Feature Animation, 1994.
Clear and Present Danger, Mace Neufeld Productions, 1994.
Jefferson in Paris, Touchstone Pictures, 1995.
Cry, the Beloved Country, Alpine Pty Limited, 1995.
(Voice) *Primary Colors,* Award Entertainment, 1998.
The Annihilation of Fish, American Sterling Productions, 1999.
Finder's Fee, MysticArts Pictures, 2001.
(Voice) *Star Wars, Episode III: Revenge of the Sith,* Lucasfilm, 2005.
(Voice) *Robots,* 20th Century Fox Animation, 2005.
Welcome Home, Roscoe Jenkins, Universal Pictures, 2008.
(Voice) *Jack and the Beanstalk,* Avalon Family Entertainment, 2009.
(Voice) *Quantum Quest: A Cassini Space Odyssey,* Jupiter 9 Productions, 2009.

Plays

(Understudy) *Wedding in Japan,* Greystone Theater, 1957.
Sunrise at Campobello, Cort Theater, 1958–59.
The Blacks, 1961.
A Midsummer Night's Dream, 1961.
Othello, New York Shakespeare Festival, 1963–64.
The Emperor Jones, 1967.
The Great White Hope, Alvin Theater, 1968–70.
Hamlet, The Public Theater, 1972.
King Lear, 1973.
The Iceman Cometh, Circle in the Square Theater, 1973–74.
Of Mice and Men, Brooks Atkinson Theater, 1974–75.
Paul Robeson, Lunt-Fontanne Theater, Booth Theater, 1978.
A Lesson from Aloes, Playhouse Theater, 1980–81.
Othello, Winter Garden Theater, 1982.
Master Harold ... and the Boys, Lyceum Theater, 1982–83.
Fences, 46th Street Theater, 1987–88.
On Golden Pond, Cort Theater, 2005.
Cat on a Hot Tin Roof, Broadhurst Theater, 2008.

Television

The Defenders, CBS, 1962–64.
East Side/West Side, CBS, 1963.
Dr. Kildare, Arena Productions, 1966.
The Man, ABC Circle Films, 1972.
King Lear, New York Shakespeare Festival, 1974.

The Greatest Thing That Almost Happened, Charles Fries Production, 1977.

Paul Robeson, 1979.

Paris, MTM Enterprises, 1979.

Roots: The Next Generations, David L. Wolper Productions, 1979.

The Atlanta Child Murders, Finnegan/Pinchuk Productions, 1985.

Faerie Tale Theater, Lions Gate Films, 1986.

L.A. Law, 20th Century Fox Television, 1988, 1989.

Heat Wave, Avent/Kerner Productions, 1990.

Last Flight Out, The Manheim Company, 1990.

Gabriel's Fire, Lorimar Television, 1990, 1991.

(Narrator) *Lincoln,* Peter W. Konhardt Productions, 1992.

(Host) *Twilight Zone: Rod Serling's Lost Classics,* O'Hara-Horowitz Productions, 1994.

Merlin, Hallmark Entertainment, 1998.

Summer's End, Showtime Networks, 1999.

Feast of All Saints, Feast Productions Limited, 2001.

Everwood, Warner Bros. Television, 2003, 2004.

The Reading Room, Alpine Medien Productions, 2005.

House, M.D., Heel & Toe Films, 2009.

Sources

Periodicals

Back Stage, National ed., January 15, 2009, p. 10–11.

Chicago Tribune, May 26, 1990; May 5, 1991.

Ebony, April 1965; June 1969.

Hollywood Reporter, January 23, 2009, p. 22.

Jet, December 23–20, pp. 4–5.

Los Angeles Times, September 2, 1990; August 26, 1991; September 26, 1991.

Movieline, May 1999.

Newsweek, October 21, 1968; April 6, 1987.

New York Times, April 8, 2005, p. E1; May 21, 2006, Theater p. 13.

Saturday Review, February 1982.

Success, August 2009, p. 13.

Time, April 6, 1987.

TV Guide, October 27, 1990.

USA Today, January 23, 2009, p. 3D.

Variety, September 23, 1991; December 5, 2002; January 23, 2009, pp. A1, A8.

—Anne Janette Johnson,
Tom Pendergast, and Sandra Alters

Eric P. Lee

1958—

Pastor, civil rights leader

As the president and chief executive officer of the Los Angeles chapter of the Southern Christian Leadership Conference (SCLC), the civil rights group founded more than fifty years ago by Dr. Martin Luther King Jr., the Reverend Eric P. Lee believes that he has an obligation to speak out whenever he sees injustice and inequality in his community—even if that means butting heads with his own organization. In 2009 Lee found himself in hot water with the national board of directors of the SCLC for his outspoken opposition to California's Proposition 8, which banned same-sex marriage in the state, and threatened with removal from his post.

The battle, which had yet to be resolved by September 2009, revealed deep tensions within the SCLC and within the larger African-American community over the issue of same-sex marriage. Although many black clergy defended and even promoted Proposition 8, and 70 percent of African-American voters in California backed the measure, many others in the black community wondered how an organization dedicated to the preservation of civil rights could deny the rights of any group of people based on their identity. As Lee's future with the SCLC remained in question, members debated the contemporary meaning and implications of King's injunction from the Birmingham jail: "Injustice anywhere is a threat to justice everywhere."

Lee was born in 1958 in Oakland, California, and attended the University of California, Berkeley, as an undergraduate, earning a degree in political science and economics. He went on to earn a master's degree in pastoral studies from Azusa Pacific University, near

Los Angeles. Lee worked in the banking and finance industry for more than twenty years, opening a U.S. Bank branch in the Crenshaw district of Los Angeles and managing the flagship branch of OneUnited Bank, one of the largest African-American-owned banks in the United States. Before joining the SCLC, Lee founded In His Steps ministries, an African-American Wesleyan church in Los Angeles, and served as senior pastor there.

In 2007 Lee became the president and chief executive officer of the Los Angeles chapter of the SCLC, the organization that was founded in 1957 by King and other civil rights leaders to promote nonviolent social change. In the twenty-first century, the SCLC of Greater Los Angeles works to continue that mission by combating housing and employment discrimination, advocating quality integrated education, and lobbying for the economic rights of workers, among other goals. As the organization's head, Lee oversees a budget of approximately $2 million and a staff of twenty-five.

During the run-up to the November of 2008 general election in California, Lee was a vocal opponent of Proposition 8, the controversial ballot measure that banned same-sex marriage in the state, and he worked closely with the Courage Campaign, a political action group in Los Angeles that opposed the initiative. The measure passed with 52 percent of the vote, amending the state constitution to read, "Only marriage between a man and a woman is valid or recognized in California." According to the July 11, 2009, *New York Times,* exit polls in California showed that 70 percent

At a Glance . . .

Born in 1958 in Oakland, CA; married: Zena; children: three. *Education:* University of California, Berkeley, BS, political science and economics; Azusa Pacific University, master of pastoral studies.

Career: U.S. Bank, senior management; OneUnited Bank, senior management; In His Steps, senior pastor; Southern Christian Leadership Conference of Greater Los Angeles, chief operating officer/chief of staff, 2005–07, president and chief executive officer, 2007—.

Memberships: Alliance for Equal Opportunity in Education; Black Business Association; Kappa Alpha Psi; Los Angeles Urban League; National Association for the Advancement of Colored People; 100 Black Men of Los Angeles; Recycling Black Dollars; Stand for Security Coalition.

Addresses: *Office*—Southern Christian Leadership Conference of Greater Los Angeles, 4182 S. Western Ave., Los Angeles, CA 90062-1639.

of African-American voters supported the ban. Many black clergy actively campaigned for Proposition 8, appealing to their congregations to vote for the measure on moral and religious grounds. After the election, Lee and other opponents of Proposition 8 continued to fight the measure, seeking to have it overturned in the court system.

But Lee had not always been on the side of gay rights activists. At one time he believed that homosexuality was a sin. "I was very vicious. I was one of those Bible-toting Christians blinded by man's doctrine," he told the *Bay Area Reporter* in June of 2009. Later, however, he "had trouble reconciling condemning people with God's word ... to love people," and he changed his mind. As the debate over Proposition 8 heated up, Lee saw the issue as a matter of civil rights. "It was clear to me," he told the *New York Times,* "that any time you deny one group of people the same right that other groups have, that is a clear violation of civil rights and I have to speak up on that."

Within the SCLC, Lee was in the minority in his support for same-sex marriage. At a board meeting in Kansas City, Missouri, in April of 2009, he was informed by the SCLC's interim president, Byron C. Clay, that the organization publicly maintained a neutral position on the issue. The following month, Lee

received a letter from the SCLC's national board of directors that asked him to come to the organization's headquarters in Atlanta to explain why he had chosen to publicly take a position on same-sex marriage without the board's approval. Lee responded that he was unable to travel to Atlanta on such short notice but would agree to a telephone conference. He then received two more letters from the SCLC's attorney, threatening him with removal from office if he did not appear in Atlanta. As the dispute began to draw media attention, the national board refrained from comment, and as of September 2009, the board had taken no further action to remove Lee from his position.

Lee received the support of the Los Angeles chapter's board, which had earlier approved his stance on same-sex marriage and was responsible for hiring him, as well as the support of Los Angeles city councilman Eric Garcetti. In July of 2009, Sylvia Rhue, interim executive director of the National Black Justice Coalition, sent a letter to the national SCLC leadership denouncing its action, asking that the "SCLC reconsider, and support [Lee] as he continues to fight for equal rights for all," and that the organization demonstrate a commitment to gay and lesbian African Americans "as they pursue full civil rights that others would deny them."

The dispute between Lee and the SCLC leadership laid bare tensions in the organization—and among African Americans—over the issue of same-sex marriage and attitudes toward homosexuality more broadly. Supporters of marriage equality called the SCLC's refusal to take a stand on the issue hypocritical, wondering how an organization dedicated to fighting for civil rights could in good faith exclude same-sex couples from its mission. In Lee's view, the campaign for marriage equality is an extension of King's work—one in which he will persist regardless of the SCLC's ultimate decision. "I'm going to continue to fight for justice," he told *Our Weekly* in July of 2009. "As one of the bearers of the legacy of Dr. Martin Luther King, Jr., I follow the principles that injustice anywhere is a threat to justice everywhere. I have to fight against injustice wherever it appears."

Selected writings

Marriage Equality: Proposition 8: The California Divide, author, 2009.

Sources

Periodicals

Atlanta Journal-Constitution, July 30, 2009.
Bay Area Reporter, June 25, 2009.
Los Angeles Times, July 11, 2009.
New York Times, July 11, 2009, p. A11.
Our Weekly (Los Angeles), July 16, 2009.

Online

Harris-Lacewell, Melissa, "SCLC and Marriage Equality," *Nation* blog, July 13, 2009, http://www.thenation.com/blogs/notion/451285/sclc_and_marriage_equality (accessed October 14, 2009).

Powell, Tracie, "Gay Marriage: What Would King Do?" CQ Politics, July 16, 2009, http://www.cqpolitics.com/wmspage.cfm?docID=news-000003167460 (accessed October 14, 2009).

"Reverend Eric P. Lee," Southern Christian Leadership Conference of Greater Los Angeles, http://sclclosangeles.org/?page_id=74 (accessed October 14, 2009).

Rhue, Sylvia, interim executive director of the National Black Justice Coalition, letter to Dr. Byron C. Clay, president and chief executive officer of the Southern Christian Leadership Conference, July 24, 2009, http://www.pamshouseblend.com/upload/documents/FianlNBJCletteroSCLCJuly09.pdf (accessed October 14, 2009).

—Deborah A. Ring

Huey Long

1904–2009

Jazz guitarist, music educator

Long, Huey, photograph. AP Images.

Guitarist Huey Long spent eight decades at the forefront of popular music. His career spanned an enormous variety of styles, most of them associated with jazz. After beginning with a traditional Dixieland band in the 1920s, he moved on to swing and bebop, playing and recording with some of the nation's most popular ensembles. He is best known, however, for his short stint with the Ink Spots, one of the first African-American vocal groups to find "crossover" success among white listeners. Long also worked extensively as a music teacher, a role he relished until his death in 2009 at the age of one hundred and five.

Huey Long was born on April 25, 1904, in Sealy, Texas, a small farming community west of Houston. Few details are readily available regarding his parents or family background. It is clear, however, that he and his siblings were musically inclined from an early age. His brother Sam, a piano player, was a particularly strong influence, as were the traveling bands that dominated popular entertainment before the development of radio. By his teens Long was an accomplished player on a number of instruments. His favorites, however, were the ukulele and the banjo. His entry into the music business came in 1925, when he was working at a shoeshine stand in Houston. When the banjo player for a Dixieland group called Frank Davis's Louisiana Jazz Band failed to appear for a gig, Long stepped in. His performance pleased Davis, and he remained with the band for some time. Upon his return home, an aunt convinced him to move to Chicago, Illinois, where opportunities for jazz musicians were plentiful. One of his first major jobs there was with Texas Guinan's Cuban Orchestra, a group that achieved national attention for its performances during the Chicago World's Fair in 1933. During his time with Guinan, Long switched from banjo to guitar, a move that reflected his changing tastes as well as the orchestra's internal dynamics.

Long's success with Guinan drew the attention of other groups around Chicago. Among the band leaders for whom he played in this period were Richard M. Long and Zilner Rudolph; both played swing, which had succeeded Dixieland as the dominant style. In the intervals between concert appearances, Long worked as a session musician in recording studios, backing up artists such as the pianist Lil Armstrong. Then, around 1940, he joined Fletcher Henderson's orchestra.

Henderson soon moved the group to New York City, which became Long's home for the bulk of his remaining career. Long's time with Henderson was followed by a stint with Earl "Fatha" Hines, whose band was renowned as an incubator of jazz talent. Among the luminaries with whom Long played under Hines's direction were the vocalist Sarah Vaughn and the saxophonist Charlie Parker.

By the end of 1944 Long had formed his own trio and was spending most of his time with it. After a gig one night, however, he was offered the chance to join the Ink Spots, a vocal quartet whose smooth harmonies appealed to both white and African-American audiences. Long jumped at the opportunity. Though he was hired primarily for his guitar skills and not for his singing, his voice blended well in the background behind lead Bill Kenny's distinctive tenor. Among the songs the Ink Spots regularly performed in this period were the classics "If I Didn't Care," "When the Swallows Come Back to Capistrano," and "Street of Dreams." After roughly nine months of near-constant touring, Long lost his place when one of the original members returned suddenly from military service. Brief though it was, his tenure with the group shaped his public image for the remainder of his career, occasionally overshadowing his other contributions.

Following his departure from the Ink Spots, Long returned to bebop, a fast-moving style he had learned under Hines. After touring in the late 1940s with other bebop pioneers, including the trumpeter Fats Navarro and the saxophonist Eddie "Lockjaw" Davis, Long formed another trio and played a series of concerts for U.S. troops stationed overseas. He returned to the United States in about 1954, settling in California. He then entered Los Angeles City College to study music education, but after a few semesters he came to realize how much he missed the New York music scene. He moved back east shortly thereafter, though he would return temporarily to California in the early 1960s to tour with a new vocal group, also called the Ink Spots;

the original group had long since disbanded. According to Long's friend Bill "Porkchop" Proctor, the new group had a standing gig at a nightclub for nearly two years. "Needless to say," Proctor wrote on the Web site InkSpots.ca, "they must have had quite a following."

By 1965 Long had returned again to New York, where he began to shift his focus from performance to teaching. His efforts eventually resulted in the establishment of a small music school on Broadway, in the heart of the city's entertainment district. He taught classes in guitar, composition, and arranging there for the next thirty years. "I remember people from all over the world coming just to take lessons," his daughter, Anita Long, told Allan Turner of the *Houston Chronicle* in 2009. "He really enjoyed teaching. It was something he fully had control over. When he was with those other groups, he was just one of many musicians."

In the mid-1990s, Long moved to Houston to be close to family. Despite his advanced age, he pursued a variety of projects there, including the systematic collection and transcription of his own compositions. He also worked to raise public awareness of the contributions made by the Ink Spots and other African-American musicians in a period of pervasive racism. As late as 2008 he was a regular fixture at a Houston antiques center where he offered fans and passersby music, memorabilia, and his own recollections of a bygone era.

On June 10, 2009, Long died in Houston. Surviving him were two sons, Rene and Shiloh, as well as his daughter Anita; the latter is the founder and director of the Ink Spots Museum, a Houston institution dedicated to the preservation of her father's music and memory.

Sources

Periodicals

Houston Chronicle, June 11, 2009.
New York Times, June 13, 2009, p. A20.
Sealy News (Sealy, Texas), June 12, 2009.

Online

Chadbourne, Eugene, "Huey Long: Biography," AllMusic.com, http://allmusic.com/cg/amg.dll?p=amg&sql=11:gjfexq8jldse (accessed November 13, 2009).

"Huey 'Ink Spot' Long," InkSpotsMuseum.com, http://www.inkspotsmuseum.com/#/huey-long/4527926155 (accessed November 13, 2009).

Proctor, Bill "Porkchop," "Huey Long of the Ink Spots," InkSpots.ca, June 12, 2009, http://inkspots.ca/HUEY-LONG-PROCTOR.htm (accessed November 13, 2009).

—R. Anthony Kugler

Moses Malone

1955—

Professional basketball player, coach

Malone, Moses, photograph. AP Images.

Center Moses Malone was a dominant force in professional basketball for more than twenty years. Known for his quiet intensity on and off the court, the Virginia native sprang to national prominence in 1974 after a sterling high-school career. Though he played for a total of nine professional teams, he is most closely associated with the Houston Rockets and the Philadelphia 76ers.

Moses Eugene Malone was born March 23, 1955, in Petersburg, Virginia, a small town roughly twenty-five miles south of Richmond, the state capital. The only child of Mary Hudgins Malone, he was raised in considerable poverty. While his mother struggled to maintain the household on her meager salary as a nurses' aide and food-plant worker, Malone was often left to entertain himself. An indifferent student, he turned to the basketball court, where his height conferred an immediate advantage. Honing his skills with hours of practice every day, he was soon dominating playground games to such an extent that opponents often modified the rules to keep him far from the basket.

By the time he entered Petersburg High School, he was close to his adult height of six feet ten inches. His tenure there would later be remembered chiefly for his performance on the basketball team, which he guided to fifty straight wins and two state championships. By his senior year (1973–74), his achievements had drawn the attention of colleges nationwide. Of the several hundred scholarship offers he received, Malone chose the University of Maryland. Several days after entering that institution in August of 1974, however, he received word that he had been drafted by the Utah Stars of the American Basketball Association (ABA). Dropping out immediately, he signed a seven-year contract worth three million dollars. In doing so, he became the first prominent player in the history of professional basketball to begin his career straight out of high school. Dozens of players, most notably LeBron James in 2003, have followed his example in the years since.

Malone adjusted quickly to professional play, averaging nearly nineteen points and fifteen rebounds per game in his rookie season (1974–75). His team and his league, however, faced severe difficulties as they struggled to draw fans and media coverage away from an older, more established rival, the National Basketball Association (NBA). Those problems prompted the first two of the many moves Malone would make in the course of his career. The first came in December of 1975, when the Stars collapsed for financial reasons. Malone and several of his teammates were transferred to one of the remaining ABA franchises, the Spirits of St. Louis. Although the Spirits managed to finish the season, they too were essentially bankrupt, as was the league. In July of 1976, therefore, the ABA agreed to join the NBA. While several ABA teams were incorporated into the other league, the Spirits were not; its players were instead dispersed to NBA franchises in a special draft held in August of 1976. The Portland Trail Blazers selected Malone at that event but immediately traded him to the Buffalo Braves.

He did not remain long with the Braves, either. After only two games with the team at the beginning of the 1976–77 season, he was traded to the Houston Rockets. It proved a fortunate transaction, for it was in Houston that Malone finally found a stable franchise. He remained there for the next six seasons. His statistics, meanwhile, grew even more impressive, and he began to receive widespread recognition as one of the game's preeminent centers. At the end of the 1978–79 season he was named the league's Most Valuable Player (MVP) after averaging nearly twenty-five points and eighteen rebounds per game. Two years later, thanks in large part to Malone's efforts, Houston reached the NBA finals for the first time. Although the team did not return to the finals in 1981–82, that season brought his second MVP award. He received a third the following year.

By that time, however, he had moved from Houston, where his rapidly increasing salary was straining the budget, to the Philadelphia 76ers. His arrival helped send the team, already one of the league's strongest, to the 1982–83 NBA finals, which they won decisively, beating the Los Angeles Lakers in four straight games. Malone was named the MVP of the series.

Philadelphia remained Malone's home for three more seasons. While his role with the team continued to be a crucial one, particularly in terms of rebounding, he was increasingly hampered by injuries. At the end of the 1985–86 season, the 76ers traded him to the Washington Bullets, where he stayed for two seasons (1986–87 and 1987–88) before moving to the Atlanta Hawks (1988–89 through 1990–91), the Milwaukee Bucks (1991–92 and 1992–93), and back to Philadelphia (1993–94). His final season (1994–95) was spent with the San Antonio Spurs, for whom he played only seventeen games. Many of his contributions there took place in practice, where he served as an informal mentor to several of the squad's younger players.

In the course of his career Malone compiled some of the most impressive statistics in the history of professional basketball. At the time of his retirement, he was number three on the NBA's all-time rebounding list and number five on its scoring list. He also held the record for the most games played (1,212) without fouling out—a remarkable achievement for a center, given the highly aggressive style required in that position.

Malone's retirement was marked by several honors. In 1996 he was one of fifty players named to the NBA's 50th Anniversary All-Time Team. Five years later he was inducted into the Naismith Memorial Basketball Hall of Fame in Springfield, Massachusetts. These awards helped keep him in the public eye, even as he made the transition to private life. After several years of focusing on his family and his investments, he returned to the world of pro basketball in 2005, when he became a consultant for the 76ers. The following year he became an assistant coach for the same team. That position was not a good fit, however, and in 2007 he became a consultant once again.

Malone's marriage to Alfreda Gill ended in divorce in 1992. The couple had two sons, Michael and Moses Jr., both of whom participated in college athletics. In 2007 Michael Malone was signed as a free agent by the Miami Dolphins of the National Football League.

Sources

Periodicals

New York Times, October 6, 2001, p. D12.

Online

"Former Sixer Aaron McKie Officially Joins the Sixers as an Assistant Coach," Philadelphia76ersBlog.com, October 4, 2007, http://www.philadelphia76ers blog.com/index.php?itemid=123 (accessed November 13, 2009).

"Moses E. Malone," HoopHall.com, http://www. hoophall.com/hall-of-famers/tag/moses-e-malone (accessed November 13, 2009).

"Moses Eugene Malone," NBA.com, http://www.nba. com/history/players/malonem_bio.html (accessed November 13, 2009).

"Moses Malone," Basketball-Reference.com, http:// www.basketball-reference.com/players/m/malon mo01.html (accessed November 13, 2009).

—R. Anthony Kugler

Geraldine McCullough

1917–2008

Sculptor, educator

Geraldine McCullough is one of the most important African-American sculptors of the twentieth century. Her metallic sculptures combined abstract forms with identifiable representations to create a unique and powerful style informed by such wide-ranging influences as African ritual art, European expressionism, and modern American art. A resident of the Chicago area for most of her life, McCullough influenced subsequent generations of artists through her work as an art instructor at both the high school and college levels.

Geraldine McCullough was born on December 1, 1917, in Kingston, Arkansas. Her family moved to Chicago when she was three years old. Aspiring to an artistic career from an early age, McCullough enrolled in the School of the Art Institute of Chicago, graduating with a bachelor's degree in 1948. While studying at the Art Institute, she was awarded the John D. Steindecker Scholarship and the Memorial Scholarship, as well as a citation for her figure painting skill. After receiving her degree, McCullough accepted a job teaching art at Chicago's Wendell Phillips High School. She taught at Phillips for 14 years, from 1950 to 1964.

McCullough continued studying at the Art Institute through the first several years of her teaching career, earning a master's degree in arts education in 1955. Around this time she began to achieve recognition as an artist as well. By the late 1950s her paintings were being shown in national galleries around the country. In 1961 she was awarded first place at Atlanta University's Annual Art Exhibit.

McCullough took up sculpture in the early 1960s. She chose to focus on structures made out of bits of scrap metal fused together, with the help of her husband Lester, a journeyman welder who taught her how to weld and helped her lug heavy metal structures around. Her public debut as a sculptor came in 1963, when she participated in the Century of Negro Progress Exposition in Chicago. McCullough's breakthrough took place the following year when she entered her metal sculpture *Phoenix* in the 159th annual exhibition of the Pennsylvania Academy of Fine Arts. Artists usually entered this competition by invitation only, and typically only well-established artists were allowed to participate. Although uninvited, McCullough submitted her work anyway and was awarded the exhibition's top prize for sculpture (and the most prestigious prize for sculpture in America), the George D. Widener Memorial Gold Metal. Her upset victory transformed her into a widely acclaimed artist, placing her among the most prominent sculptors in the Untied States. A 1964 *Ebony* article described *Phoenix*—a 250-pound abstraction of welded steel and copper named for the mythological bird that burns to ashes and is then reborn—as "a rough, powerful work that suggests several views of a mutilated form struggling to free itself from its moorings ... against the force that tries to smother the fire out of which it is being re-born." To McCullough, the Phoenix was the perfect symbol of the struggle of African Americans to rise toward freedom from under the crushing weight of oppression.

As a rising star in the art world, MucCullough suddenly had opportunities for travel and media appearances.

At a Glance . . .

Born Geraldine Hamilton on December 1, 1917, in Kingston, AR; died on December 15, 2008, in Oak Park, IL; married Lester McCullough Sr., 1939 (died 1988); children: Lester Jr. *Education:* School of the Art Institute of Chicago, BA, 1948, MA, 1955.

Career: Wendell Phillips High School, Chicago, art teacher, 1950–64; Rosary College/Dominican University, art instructor, 1968–88, art department chair, 1976–88; working sculptor with numerous exhibitions and commissions, 1963–2008.

Memberships: The Links Inc.; Arts Club of Chicago; Delta Sigma Theta Sorority; Oak Park (IL) Area Arts council.

Awards: George D. Widener Gold Medal for Sculpture, Pennsylvania Academy of Fine Arts, 1965; Hard Hat Award, Monumental Sculpture, Illinois Arts Council, 1985; Osceola Award, Delta Black Arts Excellence, 1987; honorary doctorate, Dominican University, 1990; Joseph Randall Shapiro Award, Oak Park Area Arts Council, 2000.

She was written up in magazines including *Time, Ebony,* and *Chicago,* and she gave many interviews on radio and television. She even did a guest spot on the television game show *To Tell the Truth,* perhaps the most important hallmark of emerging celebrity in 1960s American pop culture. In 1966 the Russian government made her a distinguished guest artist, taking her on a tour of the Soviet Bloc that included stops in Moscow, Leningrad, Azerbaijan, and Prague. Returning home, McCullough presented a one-woman show of her work at the Ontario East Gallery in Chicago in March of 1967, where her sculptures received lavish praise from top art critics.

In 1968 McCullough joined the faculty of Rosary College (later renamed Dominican University) in River Forest, Illinois, a suburb of Chicago. She held that position through 1988, serving as chair of the Art Department for the last 12 years of that span. Ironically, McCullough taught painting and drawing at Rosary, but not her specialty, sculpture. As she explained in an article in *Ebony* in April of 1973, "From an educational standpoint, I am too close to sculptural forms, and I might have an unconscious tendency to impose my thinking." Upon her retirement in 1989,

the University awarded McCullough an honorary doctorate.

Following the assassination of Dr. Martin Luther King Jr. in 1968, the West Side Development Corporation commissioned McCullough to create a sculpture honoring King to be installed at one of its housing developments in Chicago's Lawndale neighborhood, on the site of a structure that had been burned during the rioting that followed King's death. As she prepared to work on the new piece, McCullough noticed that King's facial features bore a resemblance to pictures she had seen of ancient African kings. She decided to base the work on that idea. The resulting cast bronze sculpture, which McCullough called "Our King," presented King as a ruler of the West African kingdom of Benin. To emphasize King's philosophy of nonviolence, McCullough placed a broken sword in one hand and a Tibetan prayer wheel in the other. A dove of peace hovered above his head. Formally unveiled in 1972, *Our King* quickly became a West Side landmark.

McCullough continued to sculpt prolifically after retiring from her college teaching career. Her sculptures were exhibited in many important venues, including the Chicago International Art Expo in 1990 and the National Museum of Women in Washington, DC, in 2001. McCullough's art was also featured in the traveling exhibit *Three Generations of African American Women Sculptors,* which visited many of the nation's most prestigious museums in the late 1990s. Her sculptures are on permanent display in many museums and private collections. McCullough's commissioned sculptures also grace public areas in many locations, mostly in Illinois, including near the State Capitol in Springfield; the University of Illinois–Chicago; the Oak Park Village Hall; and the banks of the Fox River in Geneva.

In 2000 the arts council of Oak Park, where McCullough had made her home for many years, presented her with the Joseph Randall Shapiro Award in recognition of "exceptional contributions to the arts." When the Shapiro prize had been established four years earlier, McCullough had been commissioned to create the award sculpture itself. She stated, "To win it now, I feel as though I have come full circle." McCullough died in 2008 at the age of 91.

Sources

Books

Heller, Jules, and Nancy Heller, eds., *North American Women Artists of the Twentieth Century,* Garland, 1995.

Riedy, James L., *Chicago Sculpture,* University of Illinois Press, 1981.

Sanders, Charles L., ed., *Ebony Success Library, Vol.1: 1,000 Successful Blacks,* Johnson Publishing Co., 1973.

Periodicals

Chicago Tribune, December 24, 2008.

Ebony, June 1964, pp. 113–119; April 1973, pp. 95–102.

Jet, April 3, 2000, p. 6.

Wednesday Journal of Oak Park and River Forest, December 17, 2008.

Online

"Geraldine McCullough," ARTslant new york, http://www.artslant.com/global/artists/show/33644-geraldine-mccullough (accessed November 13, 2009).

"Geraldine McCullough," Woman Made Gallery, http://www.womanmade.org/biography.html?1 (accessed November 13, 2009).

"Geraldine McCullough (1922—) Painter, Sculptor," State of Florida's Task Force on African American History, http://afroamfl.com/blackhistory.aspx?artist=geraldinemccullough, (accessed November 13, 2009).

"Geraldine McCullough (1922–2008)," EbonyJet.com, http://www.ebonyjet.com/culture/index2.aspx?id=10948 (accessed November 13, 2009).

"Geraldine McCullough (1922–2008), Painter, Sculptor," Parish Gallery, http://www.parishgallery.com/ArtistPages/Geraldine%20McCullough/Geraldine%20McCullough.html.

"Geraldine McCullough Biography," History Makers, http://www.thehistorymakers.com/biography/biography.asp?bioindex=416&category=Artmakers&occupation=Sculptor%20and%20Painter&name=Geraldine%20McCullough (accessed November 13, 2009).

—Bob Jacobson

Ralph McDaniels

Media personality

A legendary New York City music figure, Ralph McDaniels was one of the earliest king-makers in rap music. Known as "Uncle Ralph" to artists and fans, McDaniels is host of *Video Music Box,* a locally produced show that was the first television showcase for rap and hip-hop videos. In 2008 the show celebrated its twenty-fifth year on the air. Another New York City icon, Fab Five Freddy, freely admitted modeling the ground-breaking MTV show *Yo! MTV Raps* on *Video Music Box,* which he hailed as "a cultural revolution leading us into this era where people of color could see images of them-selves not being negative," as he told Jason Newman for the *Village Voice.* "It was the guide for everybody in the culture."

McDaniels grew up in Brooklyn and Queens in a family of Trinidadian origins. After earning a television, com-munications, and film degree from the New York Institute of Technology in 1982, "I got a job at a public television station," he told *Vibe*'s Laura Checkoway, "and didn't see anything that looked like the public that I knew." That station was WNYC-TV on Channel 31, which was owned by the city of New York. His internship turned into an engineer's post, but McDaniels wanted to create and host a show for the city's burgeoning black music scene. Unsure about the

McDaniels, Ralph, photograph. Ray Tamarra/Getty Images.

format he proposed, the sta-tion's management offered him a show called *Studio 31 Dance Party.* He did voice-overs for that series until De-cember of 1983 when it mor-phed into *Video Music Box,* which soon became known by its shortened form, *VMB.*

Between introducing videos from the earliest rap artists, including Grandmaster Flash and the Furious Five, KRS-One, and Kool Moe Dee, McDaniels was out on the streets capturing the excite-ment of the growing scene. "The kids in the South Bronx and Bed-Stuy, all they knew was that they liked hip-hop," McDaniels told Newman in the *Village Voice* article. "They didn't realize that hip-hop was going out to all different arenas. If you never left your block, you didn't realize there were other people that didn't look like you that were into this. Even people in hip-hop didn't realize that white kids were going to the shows like that."

VMB aired six days a week at 3:30 p.m. McDaniels initially hosted the show with his childhood friend Lionel Martin, also known as the "Vid Kid." At a time when MTV's roster of African-American artists was essentially confined to Michael Jackson and the mega-seller *Thriller* LP, *VMB* introduced a generation of impressionable New Yorkers to artists like Run DMC, the Fat Boys, and LL Cool J. Segments on *VMB*

At a Glance . . .

Born on February 27, in Brooklyn, NY. *Education:* Earned degree from the New York Institute of Technology, 1982.

Career: Intern and studio engineer at WNYC-TV, 1982(?); host of *Studio 31 Dance Party,* WNYC-TV; host of *Video Music Box,* WNYC-TV, 1983—; Classic Concepts Productions (a video production company), founding partner, 1987; Uncle Ralph Productions, president; WQHT-FM (Hot 97), host and executive producer of *The Bridge*; Onfumes.com, founding partner, 2008—.

Addresses: *Office*—c/o Hot 97, 395 Hudson St., 7th Fl., New York, NY 10014.

featured McDaniels's interviews with artists, their fans, and frequent "shout outs" from anyone who spotted his camera equipment on the scene. In fact, the term "shout out" is said to have originated with *VMB.* Calling out one's neighborhood or friends "gave regular people a chance to represent who they were," McDaniels told Jesse Serwer in *Time Out New York* years later. "Some of these dudes became ghetto superstars in their 'hood—they were more popular than some of the artists we had on the show."

In 1985 McDaniels launched a concert series called the Fresh Fest. On the bill were Run DMC, LL Cool J, and Grandmaster Flash. Held at Nassau Coliseum on Long Island, it was the first live rap event to take place at a major sports arena. The tour's strong ticket sales in other cities caught the attention of industry decision-makers, and finally MTV—which wielded immense influence in the music industry during this era—launched *Yo! MTV Raps,* a two-hour weekly showcase of rap and hip-hop videos, in August of 1988.

In addition to hosting *VMB,* by this point McDaniels had also launched a video production company with Martin, the Vid Kid. In the late 1980s and early 1990s their company made more than 300 videos for emerging young artists, including "It Ain't Hard to Tell" by

Nas and "C.R.E.A.M." by the Wu-Tang Clan. McDaniels also made a documentary about the already well-known "Lifers' Group" at Rahway State Prison in New Jersey, who had launched an antiviolence outreach program in the 1970s that was the basis for the documentary *Scared Straight!* The Lifers continued their efforts with the help of McDaniels, who filmed them for another documentary, this one about their use of rap music to impart their message, which had its premier on *VMB.* He served as an associate producer on the 1992 Tupac Shakur film *Juice* and had a cameo in the 1993 comedy *Who's the Man?*

McDaniels also moved into other ventures, including a clothing store in the Crown Heights section of Brooklyn called Uncle Ralph's Urban Gear. The nickname "Uncle Ralph" dates back to 1995, when Kool DJ Red Alert bestowed the honorific on him because of the scores of younger artists whose careers he had aided. Red Alert went on to a career at WQHT-FM, one of New York's two main urban-music radio stations. McDaniels also appeared on the station as host of *The Bridge,* a weekly show tracing the history of hip-hop music. In 2008 he launched Onfumes.com, a video hosting and video-on-demand site.

Video Music Box was still on the air, though it had moved to WNYE-TV in 1996. In the summer of 2008 there was a twenty-fifth anniversary concert for the show in Central Park, which prompted a flood of media tributes. One of the many *VMB* co-hosts was Ray DeJon, who revealed that McDaniels had spurned many offers over the years to take his show to a national audience. "What stopped Ralph every time was that they wanted to take over the creative rights," DeJon told Serwer in the *Time Out New York* article. "Now, whenever BET, VH1 or any of those networks wants to do a behind-the-scenes bio on hip-hop, they've gotta come to Ralph because he's the only one with the original footage."

Sources

Periodicals

New York Times, February 4, 1985.
Time Out—New York, July 17–23, 2008.
Vibe, April 2003, p. 108; March 2006.
Village Voice, January 3, 2006; July 15, 2008.

—Carol Brennan

Steve McNair

1973–2009

Professional football player

McNair, Steve, photograph. AP Images.

A four-time Pro Bowl selection and co-winner of the 2003 National Football League Most Valuable Player (MVP) Award, Steve McNair was one of the great quarterbacks of the late 1990s and early 2000s. In a career that spanned thirteen seasons with two teams, the Tennessee Titans (which were still the Houston Oilers when McNair's career began) and the Baltimore Ravens, McNair completed 2,733 passes for 31,304 yards. He topped all quarterbacks in the history of the Titans/Oilers franchise, with 76 wins in the games he started and 3,439 yards rushed. He was also second in franchise history in passing yards and third in touchdowns thrown. McNair led his teams to the playoffs five times, including a trip to Super Bowl XXXIV.

McNair retired from football in April of 2008 and dedicated his time to holding football camps, working on his Mississippi farm and charitable foundation, and opening a restaurant in Nashville. His retirement did not last: in the early morning of July 4, 2009, McNair was found dead in a Nashville condominium, the victim of an apparent murder-suicide.

Showed Early Signs of Greatness

McNair's life was a classic American success story. He was born on Valentine's Day in 1973. His father, Selma McNair, left the family when Steve was young, leaving McNair and his four brothers to be raised by their single mother, Lucille, in a ramshackle house in rural Mount Olive, Mississippi. She toiled as a factory worker, and money was scarce. Despite material hardships, she instilled an unshakable set of values in her sons—including loyalty, fairness, an appreciation for education, and a strong work ethic. Fred, the oldest brother and a star athlete, served as the family's father figure, and he carefully instructed Steve in every aspect of sports. Quoted in *Sports Illustrated,* McNair said, "Fred has taught me absolutely everything I know. I can't thank him enough for giving me a map and then showing me how to take the short road when he's taken the longer one." In fact, Steve's nickname, "Air McNair," was borrowed from Fred, who was the original "Air" in the family.

In a family with deep athletic gifts, Steve McNair was especially blessed—and not only with extraordinary

At a Glance . . .

Born Steve LaTreal McNair on February 14, 1973, in Mount Olive, MS; died July 2009, in Nashville, TN; son of Selma McNair (an offshore oil rig worker) and Lucille McNair (a factory worker); married Mechelle Cartwright, June 21, 1997; children: Junior, Steven, Tyler, Trenton. *Religion:* Baptist. *Education:* Alcorn State University, BS, 1995.

Career: Tennessee Titans (formerly Houston, then Tennessee Oilers), professional football player, 1995—; created Steve McNair Foundation to support youth activities.

Memberships: Omega Psi Phi Fraternity, 1995.

Awards: SWAC Offensive Player of the Year, 1990–94; Nashville Sports Council, Sports Person of the Year, 2001–03; National Football League, Most Valuable Player (shared with Peyton Manning), 2003; Associated Press NFL Most Valuable Player Award, 2003.

talent (as well as huge hands), but also with the determination and discipline to cultivate it. He had multiple options for pursuing a professional sports career. He starred in three sports at Mount Olive High: baseball, as a shortstop and outfielder, where he was all-state four years running; basketball, at point guard; and football, in which he played both offense and defense. As a cornerback, McNair set a state record for single-season pass interceptions (15) and tied the career mark (30). In 1989, he quarterbacked Mount Olive to a small-school state title when he was a junior. A strapping 6' 2", 220-pounder who could run 40 yards in 4.6 seconds and hurl a baseball 90 miles per hour, McNair had both the strength and speed to play a multitude of positions. McNair was strongly tempted when he was drafted by the Seattle Mariners to play pro baseball, but with some guidance from Fred and Lucille he opted to pass up that opportunity, as well as several college basketball offers.

McNair's first pivotal decision in football concerned his choice of college. Many of the powerhouse schools courted McNair, including Louisiana State, Miami, Ohio State, Nebraska, and Mississippi State. But they all wanted him as a defensive back, whereas he was determined to be a quarterback. Again, Fred's counsel helped him set a course, this time to Alcorn State, in Lorman, Mississippi, where Fred had starred as a quarterback and where Steve was guaranteed a shot at the position.

Alcorn, a predominantly black school, was the country's first black land-grant institution, the first black state-supported school, and the first to provide the NFL with a black player—Jack Spinks, drafted in 1952 as a fullback by the Pittsburgh Steelers. It is a member of the Division I-AA Southwestern Athletic Conference (SWAC), which comprises other mostly black schools and has produced several football immortals, including all-time touchdown leader Jerry Rice (Mississippi Valley) and all-time rushing leader Walter Payton (Jackson State). It was virtually a foregone conclusion that attending a Division I-AA school, rather than an I-A, would seriously impair or even scuttle McNair's shot at a Heisman Trophy and potentially hurt his chances for the NFL. But the assurance of a quarterback role and the proximity to home were major pulls for him, and he decided to take the chance.

Glory Years at Alcorn State

McNair's college career became the stuff of legend. As a mere freshman, McNair set nine records and was named Southwestern Athletic Conference player of the year. In his sophomore year, he led the nation in total offense, averaging 405.7 yards per game. McNair racked up numerous 500-plus-passing-yard games, and many times he added another 100 or so yards rushing.

After his junior year, McNair again faced a choice—should he aim for an NFL contract or stay for his senior year of college? Experts projected McNair as a likely first- or second-round selection in the 1994 draft, and with top college quarterbacks signing contracts worth more than $15 million, the temptation was strong for McNair to forego his final year of college. Steve wanted to take care of his mother and family financially and to get on with his professional career. But both Lucille and Fred urged him to finish his education, as well as strengthen his hand even further with one more outstanding college season.

McNair opted to remain in school, as he was quoted in *Jet*: "I am an Alcornite and will continue to be an Alcornite. I want my degree." During his senior year several facets of his game improved. He learned how to hang in the pocket longer and find his receiver, while his rushing grew even more devastating. The result was statistically one of the best seasons in college football history: McNair averaged 527.2 total yards gained per game, a collegiate record. Among his other accomplishments that season, he finished with a phenomenal 44/17 touchdown/interception pass ratio.

Although McNair had a great year, his team fared poorly in post-season play. (Historically the SWAC champions had racked up an appalling 0–15 record in the I-AA playoffs.) In the first round of the playoffs, defending champion Youngstown (Ohio) State College destroyed Alcorn, 63–20. McNair showed great heart in playing with a badly pulled hamstring. His rushing ability crippled, he still achieved 514 passing yards and three touchdowns. The game did not hurt his standing as a potential NFL draft pick, but it did not enhance his shot at clinching the coveted Heisman Trophy, either. At season's end, McNair was third in voting for the prestigious award. However, over the course of his collegiate career McNair set five NCAA records, including becoming the first player to pass 16,000 total yards gained in his career; he also set 31 division I-AA records.

Signed with the Oilers

On April 22, 1995, following a successful showing at the Senior Bowl and at the NFL scouting combine, McNair was chosen as the third pick in the first round of the draft by the Houston Oilers. He was the highest-drafted black quarterback ever—displacing Andre Ware, who was chosen seventh in 1990 by the Detroit Lions. When negotiations were finalized in August of 1995, McNair signed a contract for $28.4 million over seven years. At twenty-two years old, he had become the Oilers' highest-paid player—not bad for a guy who had told *Jet,* "No matter what happens, I'm just Steve, the country boy from Mount Olive."

Quarterbacks usually develop more slowly than other players. It is not only the highest-profile position on the field, but also the most mentally challenging. NFL playbooks are vast, and reading the opposition's defense to make split-second play changes is incredibly complex. As ESPN draft analyst Mel Kiper, discussing the development curve, told *USA Today,* "With any quarterback, you really need to figure three years."

Oiler management made sure to cultivate McNair carefully; they did not want to rush him into play abruptly and expose him to damaging and unnecessary pressure. He was tutored intensively throughout the off-season by offensive coordinator Jerry Rhome, a premier quarterback teacher. Later, Les Steckel took on this role. During the 1995 and 1996 seasons, McNair's primary mission was to absorb knowledge and make the leap from the shotgun offense at Alcorn to the far more elaborate and turbo-charged conditions in the NFL.

Some of McNair's first games were rough initiations indeed, with the Arizona Cardinals blitzing him mercilessly in an exhibition game with as many as five pass rushers. But this merely fortified McNair's will; he knew this was part of his initiation. When starting quarterback Chris Chandler was injured late in McNair's first season, the rookie went into action. The results were impressive. On December 11, 1995, playing against the Detroit Lions, McNair entered after halftime with the Oilers down 17–7 and played the rest of the game. He completed 16 of 27 passes for 203 yards, including a touchdown. In fact, McNair nearly pulled off a come-from-behind upset. There was little question in anyone's mind as to whether he could make it as a pro. He started the next two games, helping the Oilers end the season with back-to-back victories over the New York Jets and the Buffalo Bills.

In the 1996 season McNair played in ten games (starting in four), and completed an impressive 88 of 103 pass attempts for 1197 yards and six touchdowns. The team went 8–8, missing the playoffs by one game. In his first six starts, McNair threw seven touchdown passes with only two interceptions. However, it was his leadership that impressed his coaches the most. In a *Sports Illustrated* piece Steckel said, "Even though he's the most humble athlete I've encountered in pro sports, he's also a leader who exudes extreme confidence." Head coach Jeff Fisher said in the same article, "If you were going to put together a list of all the things you can't coach—poise, ability to lead, competitiveness, responsibility—he has them all."

In February of 1997, the Oilers traded Chandler to the Atlanta Falcons, and McNair's career as a starter began in earnest. That same year, the franchise relocated to Tennessee. With big changes afoot, there was increased pressure on McNair.

Rose to NFL Elite

As the regular starter at quarterback, McNair steadily accrued impressive stats on third-down conversions and pass completions, touchdowns per starts, and rushing, among others. In the 1997 season, for example, his 674 yards rushing was the third-highest total for a quarterback in NFL history. By the end of that season, McNair had garnered the second-best overall rating of any quarterback drafted in the previous six years (trailing only the Jacksonville Jaguars' Mark Brunell). According to Bob Sherwin of the *Knight-Ridder/Tribune News Service,* McNair is "a quarterback on the cusp of greatness," one who "is beginning to make his impact on the NFL." In the article, McNair said: "The last part of the [1997] season it finally clicked for me."

From that point on, McNair steadily became one of the league's best quarterbacks. At the end of the 1998 season, the Titans—the Oilers' new name—had placed second in the AFC Central. In 1999 McNair led the Titans to an AFC championship. When he took the field as the starting quarterback against the St. Louis Rams, he became just the second black quarterback to start in the Super Bowl. Although the Titans lost the game to the Rams, McNair's strong performance did not go unnoticed around the league, where he was considered a rising star. The Titans signed McNair to a six-year, $47 million contract extension in July of 2001.

McNair's rise to prominence did not come without a great deal of pain. During the 1999 season, McNair had midseason surgery on a ruptured disk in his lower back, after which he shocked football fans by returning to lead his team through the playoffs. McNair's pain had been so severe that he could not sit for more than fifteen minutes at a time, yet he played like a champion. Coach Jeff Fisher told *Sports Illustrated for Kids* that during the 2001 season, "We literally had to help him off the plane when we landed because of his lower back and two or three other [injuries]. Twenty-four hours later, we're beating Oakland, with Steve running around making plays. That's how he is." McNair overcame great pain again in 2002, when turf toe, strained rib cartilage, and an injured thumb kept him from practicing throughout November and December, although he played in games. Michael Silver wrote in *Sports Illustrated* that "the mild-mannered Mississippian is becoming a mythical figure in a sport in which the athletes pride themselves on playing hurt." McNair's wife, Mechelle, offered a softer image when she explained, "he's a big baby at home. ... He'll be limping, grimacing, complaining all week, saying there's no way he'll play, and then I'll see him on Sunday running around like nothing's wrong." Coach Jeff Fisher told *Football Digest,* "Steve is the toughest player I have ever coached."

In 2002 the Titans rebounded from a 1–4 start by winning 10 of their last 11 games and taking the AFC Central championship. The *Football Digest* gave much of the credit for the turnaround to McNair, who inspired his teammates by overcoming a series of nagging injuries. Team owner Bud Adams told the magazine: "[McNair] doesn't know what pain is. He's a warrior." Ever humble, McNair explained: "We are professionals. We had to start playing like it. We had to look into ourselves and find a way to win. We couldn't allow things to keep going the way they started off." Their spectacular comeback season ended when they lost 41–24 to the high-powered Oakland Raiders in the AFC Championship game. McNair came in third in league MVP voting but was not named to the Pro Bowl.

McNair's sterling reputation was somewhat tarnished in the summer of 2003 when he was arrested on drunken driving charges and also found to be in illegal possession of a loaded handgun. McNair quickly acknowledged his fault in the incident. According to *Jet,* McNair announced: "It's something you don't usually see out of me. But I put myself in a situation. I've got to get out of it, and I will bounce back from it."

During the 2003 season, McNair put the troubles of the summer behind him and embarked on the most successful year of his career. Starting in 14 games, McNair piled up 3,215 passing yards while completing 62.5 percent of his passes. With 24 touchdowns and just seven interceptions, he led the NFL in quarterback ratings with a rating of 100.4. With running back Eddie George playing a smaller role in the team's offense, McNair was now clearly the star. The Titans finished the regular season 12–4 but were eliminated from the playoffs in a game played in frigid, snowy conditions against the New England Patriots.

In January of 2004 McNair was named the league's co-MVP, along with Indianapolis Colts quarterback Peyton Manning. McNair was the first black quarterback ever to win the NFL's highest honor. "I would like to thank the guys who paved the way for myself and a lot of other guys," McNair told *Jet,* naming quarterbacks Warren Moon, Doug Williams, and Randall Cunningham. "Those guys paved the way for us as Black quarterbacks to come into the league and be successful." Later McNair was named the league's MVP by the Associated Press. By the end of the 2003 season, he was one of just five quarterbacks to have passed for 20,000 yards and rushed for 3,000 yards. Reflecting on his successes in a 2003 interview with the *Sporting News,* McNair said: "This is all I've ever wanted to do, what I dreamed about in Mississippi, playing on Sundays in the NFL. I'm not surprised by what is happening to me now. I just want to enjoy it and have fun with it. The opportunity is here. I don't want to waste it."

Plagued by Injuries

Sadly, McNair did not have a strong follow-up to his MVP season. In the third game of the 2004 season, a fourth-quarter hit by Jacksonville Jaguars tackle Marcus Stroud aggravated a sternum injury McNair had suffered in 2000. Although he played eight more games that season, McNair was not the same player. The season's lowest point might have been when he threw four interceptions against the upstart Texans, the expansion franchise that in 2002 had replaced the Oilers in Houston. It was the first time the Texans had beaten the Titans in their history. The Titans fell to 5–11, dead last in the AFC South.

McNair considered retirement after the season. According to Jim Corbett of *USA Today,* the pain from the sternum injury was such that McNair feared he wouldn't be able to play catch with his kids ever again, much less throw a football in a professional game. "I haven't been able to sleep the last four years," he told Corbett. "I couldn't lay down because it hurt my chest. It was the most pain I've ever known. I had to sit in a recliner and sleep that way." On December 29, 2004, McNair underwent an innovative surgical procedure in which a piece of bone from his hip was grafted onto his sternum to protect the damaged area.

The surgery was a success. McNair was able to start 14 games in 2005. He once again exceeded 3,000 yards passing, had 16 touchdowns, and was invited to his third Pro Bowl. Although McNair was rejuvenated by the surgery, the team around him did not return to its 2003 form. The NFL's salary cap had forced the Titans to drop many of the team's well-paid veterans, including McNair's favorite receiver, Derrick Mason. The

Titans slid to 4–12, and for the first time in McNair's career, his team failed to score 300 points in a season.

Ended Career in Baltimore

Leading up to the 2006 season, it was clear that McNair would not be returning to the Titans. Once again, the team needed salary cap relief, and with the Titans in rebuilding mode, it was unlikely that the veteran McNair would be able to fulfill his dreams of winning a Super Bowl in Tennessee. Given the freedom to negotiate with other teams, McNair found a match with the Baltimore Ravens, the team where his longtime receiver, Mason, had settled. However, the Titans and the Ravens played a game of chicken over the rights to McNair—the Ravens waited for the Titans to cut their star player, making him a free agent, while the Titans waited for Baltimore to offer them fair return in a trade. Finally, Baltimore blinked, sending a fourth-round draft pick to Tennessee in return for their new starting quarterback.

The 2006 season would turn out to be the final hurrah of McNair's career. He led the Ravens to a 13–3 record and set a team record for highest pass completion percentage. On December 10, he completed the longest pass of his pro career, an 87-yard touchdown pass to Mark Clayton. However, the season ended in disappointment when the eventual Super Bowl champions, the Indianapolis Colts, beat the Ravens in the divisional round of the playoffs. After the season, McNair was selected for his fourth Pro Bowl, but he was unable to play due to injury.

Injuries plagued McNair's final season in the NFL. In the 2007 season's second game he injured his groin, and further injuries to his back and shoulder limited McNair to only six starts. Surgery on his left shoulder ended his season in December; for the Ravens, it was a lost season, and they finished at 5–11. The following April, after considering another comeback, Steve McNair decided to hang up his pads for good. In the end, he decided to put his team first. As he said in the press conference to announce his retirement, "All the things going through my mind, if I can't compete like I used to, with a healthy mind and body, I was not going to put this team in jeopardy."

Murdered in Nashville

McNair had numerous interests off the field to keep him occupied in retirement. He ran the Steve McNair Foundation, a charitable organization that had been active in providing relief to the victims of Hurricane Katrina in 2005. The foundation also funded summer football camps, which McNair often ran personally, in Mississippi and Tennessee, and raised money for local charities such as various Boys & Girls Clubs. He was also a mentor to Titans quarterback Vince Young, whom McNair had befriended prior to Young becoming

one of college football's biggest stars with the University of Texas Longhorns. Long an avid cook, McNair opened a restaurant in Nashville called Gridiron9 in 2009.

McNair would not live to enjoy the success of his various ventures. On the morning of July 4, 2009, he was found in a Nashville condominium he owned, dead of gunshot wounds. Also dead was a twenty-year-old woman later identified as Sahel Kazemi, McNair's mistress. A few days prior to McNair's death, she had been arrested for driving under the influence of alcohol—strangely, by the same police officer who had arrested McNair in 2003—while driving a luxury SUV registered to both herself and McNair, with McNair as her passenger. The Nashville police department's homicide investigation portrayed Kazemi as an unstable woman with money problems who was distraught that she was losing McNair to another lover and who had purchased a gun shortly before the killings. This, as well as the physical evidence at the scene, led the police to conclude that McNair had been the victim of a murder-suicide.

Thousands attended memorial services in the fallen quarterback's honor in Tennessee and Mississippi, as McNair's two hometowns grieved for their fallen hero. Cornerback Samari Rolle, who had played with McNair in Houston and in Baltimore, summed up his legacy: "Steve was the ultimate man. … If you were going to draw a football player, the physical part, the mental part, everything about being a professional, he is your guy. I can't even wrap my arms around it. It is a sad, sad day. The world lost a great man today."

Sources

Periodicals

Football Digest, April 2003, p. 52; February 2004, p. 48.

Jet, January 31, 1994, p. 50; September 26, 1994, p. 49; January 26, 2004, p. 46.

Knight-Ridder/Tribune News Service, November 27, 1998.

New York Times, September 28, 1994, p. B11; January 22, 1995, p. 2.

Sports Illustrated, August 30, 1993, p. 76; September 26, 1994, p. 40; December 5, 1994, p. 85; September 1, 1997, p. 188; November 17, 2003, p. 56; September 6, 2004.

Sports Illustrated for Kids, November 1, 2003, p. 58.

Sporting News, August 22, 1994, p. S8; November 28, 1994, p. 6; August 12, 1996, p. 42; January 3, 2000, p. 16; November 24, 2003, p. 14.

USA Today, April 12, 1995.

USA Today Sports Weekly, August 24, 2005.

Online

"Biography," *The Steve McNair Foundation,* http://www.officialstevemcnair.com/biography.php (accessed November 20, 2009).

"Case Summary," *Nashville.gov Police Department,* http://www.police.nashville.org/news/media/2009/10/McNairSummaryOct09.pdf (accessed November 20, 2009).

"A Look Back at the Career of Steve McNair," *Tennessee Titans Official Web Site,* http://www.titanson line.com/news/article-1/a-look-back-at-the-career-of-steve-mcnair/7bafa73a-0a67-4b0b-847d-c74e278737fb (accessed November 20, 2009).

"McNair Recalled Fondly in Baltimore," *NBC Sports Pro Football Talk,* http://profootballtalk.nbcsports.com/2009/07/04/mcnair-recalled-fondly-in-baltimore/ (accessed November 20, 2009).

—Mark Baven, Tom Pendergast,
and Derek Jacques

Harold D. Melton

1966—

Jurist

Harold D. Melton is an associate justice of the Supreme Court of Georgia. Appointed to the seven-member bench in 2005 by the state's Republican governor, Sonny Perdue, Melton is the third African American to serve on the state's high court. "I'm striving to be a justice who reads the law and applies it, and though that sometimes seems easier said than done, I'm bound by that," Melton told *Georgia Trend* journalist Jerry Grillo.

Melton was born in Washington, DC, in 1966. His father, Augustus Melton Jr., eventually became the manager of National Airport in Arlington County, Virginia, in the early 1980s, which was later renamed Ronald Reagan Washington National Airport. Melton grew up with his mother, Carole, near Atlanta, Georgia, in the communities of East Point and Marietta, and graduated from Marietta's Joseph Wheeler High School in 1984.

At Auburn University in Auburn, Alabama, Melton majored in international business and became so fluent in Spanish that he served as an interpreter for the Auburn basketball team when they traveled in South America. In 1987 he made Auburn history as the first African American to be elected president of the Stu-

Melton, Harold D., photograph. AP Images.

dent Government Association. The school had barred black students until 1964, when it complied with a federal desegregation order. Melton's achievement was noted by the Auburn University alumni magazine, and the wife of a judge in the Atlanta area read it and suggested to her husband that he contact the young man.

That woman was Helen Hines, who had family ties to Auburn. Her husband was Harris Hines, who was a judge on the Cobb County Superior Court bench at the time. Hines, knowing that Melton was about to enter law school at the University of Georgia, offered him a summer job at his private practice. Melton opted to take a post as an administrative aide for youth affairs to the governor of Alabama instead, but asked if he might reconsider at a later date. The following summer, he joined Hines's firm as a summer associate. It proved an excellent introduction into trial law, Melton told Michelle Hiskey in the *Atlanta Journal-Constitution*. "I learned how to read the law, what a solid judicial temperament was, and watching the whole judicial process," he said. "It took the gloss off. I wasn't afraid going into court."

After earning his law degree in 1991, Melton was hired by the Georgia Department of Law as an assistant attorney general in its Fiscal Affairs office. He spent four years there and then two with the Business Finance section of the agency. In 1997 he was recruited to serve as senior assistant to the state attorney general on the landmark tobacco settlement case. From 1998 to 2002 he was the section leader for the Consumer Interests division back at the Georgia Department of Law.

Georgia had been a Democratic stronghold dating back to the founding of the Republican Party in 1854 on an antislavery platform, but in 2002 the Republican candidate Sonny Perdue won a three-way gubernatorial race and ousted the Democratic incumbent. Upon taking office, Perdue appointed Melton to serve as his executive counsel. In the summer of 2005, Perdue appointed Melton to fill a vacancy on the Supreme Court of Georgia. It marked the first time that a Republican governor had filled a spot on that bench in 137 years.

Melton was a surprising choice for the state's Supreme Court. He had no judicial experience, and Perdue was criticized for not selecting a candidate from a list of state court judges. However, Melton had longstanding ties to the state's top Republican officials—although he never formally registered as a Republican—and was assumed to be a staunch conservative. This made him an especially attractive choice for supporters of capital punishment. As Governor Perdue said at the time, "the moral compass that Harold has is GPS-like in its accuracy: unwavering, unassailable and just the facts," he asserted, according to *Fulton County Daily Report* writers Jonathan Ringel and Meredith Hobbs. "I wanted someone who will respect and appreciate the constitutional separation of powers."

Prosecuting attorneys and other supporters of capital punishment in Georgia rejoiced at the news of Melton's appointment. Melton was also welcomed at the state high court by his longtime mentor, Harris Hines, who had been serving on the Supreme Court of Georgia since 1995. Just 38 years old at the time of his swearing in, Melton was the youngest on the bench and only the third African American to serve on it. His first case involved a death row inmate, Robert Dale Conklin, who the court declined to give a stay of execution by a vote of 5–2. Melton surprised many supporters of capital punishment with one of those two dissenting votes, and even wrote a separate opinion asserting that the inmate should be given a new trial. "A few months later, Melton authored a unanimous decision overturning an identity theft conviction, then criticized his colleagues for taking the easy way out when a majority reconsidered the case and reinstated the conviction," according to *Fulton County Daily Report* writer Alyson M. Palmer.

In other cases, Melton has sided with his conservative colleagues on the bench. As he told Palmer in the *Fulton County Daily Report* article, he considered himself bound only to the concept of law itself. "The laws of the state of Georgia declare that service on the court is a nonpartisan position, and I intend to uphold that," he said. Supreme Court of Georgia justices are elected to six-year terms, and in 2006 Melton ran unopposed to retain the seat to which Perdue had appointed him. He remained close to Hines, his longtime mentor. In late 2007 Hiskey, the *Atlanta Journal-Constitution* writer, accompanied the two on a quail hunt in Talladega County, Alabama. Hiskey characterized the outing as a mix of the old South and the new. "These 800 acres belong to Hines' wife's family; they are only the second owners since 1835," Hiskey wrote. "I don't know if Harold would be my oldest child or younger brother," the older judge said of his protégé. "But it's great to have him here either way."

Sources

Periodicals

Atlanta Journal-Constitution, June 13, 2005, p. A9; June 28, 2005, p. A11; December 16, 2007, p. M1.
Fulton County Daily Report (Fulton County, GA), June 9, 2005; March 23, 2007.
Georgia Trend, October 1, 2005, p. 22.
New York Times, March 18, 2008.

Online

"Governor Perdue Announces Appointment to Georgia Supreme Court," Governor Sonny Perdue, June 8, 2005, http://gov.georgia.gov/00/press_print/0 ,2669,78006749_79688147_93045038,00.html (accessed September 19, 2009).

"Justice Harold D. Melton," Supreme Court of Georgia, http://www.gasupreme.us/biographies/melton. php (accessed September 19, 2009).

—Carol Brennan

Festus Gontebanye Mogae

1939—

Head of State

Mogae, Festus Gontebanye, photograph. AP Images.

Festus Gontebanye Mogae became president of the Republic of Botswana on April 1, 1998, in a peaceful transfer of power that political analysts considered exceptional for southern Africa. Mogae was only the third president in Botswana's history since the country gained its independence from the United Kingdom in 1966. His resumé included decades of service in various governmental posts, most of them connected with finance and development. He also served as the alternate and then executive director for Africa of the International Monetary Fund. After decades of public service, Mogae retired in April of 2008. Both before and after retirement Mogae was been honored for the high quality of his governance of Botswana and for his work in helping to reduce the extent of his country's raging HIV/AIDS epidemic.

Trained in Economics

Mogae was born on August 21, 1939, in Serowe, Botswana, and was raised on a cattle farm. After completing his primary and secondary schooling in Botswana, Mogae traveled to England for his post-secondary education. He earned an undergraduate degree at North West London Polytechnic, an honors degree in economics at University College Oxford, and a graduate degree in developmental economics from Sussex University.

Intelligent and motivated, Mogae returned to his homeland and became a part of its vanguard of young, educated politicians and civil servants. Botswana had been a British crown colony until 1966. At the time that Mogae entered governmental work in the Republic of Botswana, just two years after the country gained independence, politics were dominated by the Botswana Democratic Party (BDP), which Mogae supported.

Botswana had been impoverished as a British Crown Colony. However, in the year after it achieved its independence, De Beers company geologists discovered diamonds in the northern part of the country. The discovery of these precious gems changed Botswana's economic landscape dramatically: the economy grew quickly, and the country achieved one of the highest per capita income growth rates in the world.

At a Glance . . .

Born Festus Gontebanye Mogae on August 21, 1939, in Serowe, Botswana; son of Dihabano and Dithunya Mogae (cattle farmers); married Barbara Gemma Modise, 1968; children: three daughters. *Politics:* Botswana Democratic Party. *Education:* North West London Polytechnic; University College Oxford, Economics (with honors); Sussex University, Development Economics.

Career: Botswana government, planning officer, 1968–70, senior planning officer, 1971, director of economic affairs, 1972–74, permanent secretary of the Ministry of Finance and Development Planning, 1975–76; International Monetary Fund, alternate and executive director for Africa, 1976–80; Bank of Botswana, governor, 1980–81; Botswana government, permanent secretary to the president, secretary to the cabinet, and supervisor of elections, 1982–89, minister of finance and development planning, 1989–98, vice president, 1992–98, president, 1998–2008.

Memberships: Botswana Society, president; Botswana Society of the Deaf, president; Kalahari Conservation Society; Commonwealth Parliamentary Association; Parliamentarians for Global Action; Global Coalition for Africa, National AIDS Council, chairman.

Awards: Officer of the National Order of Mali, government of Mali, 1977; Officer of the National Order of the Ivory Coast, government of the Ivory Coast, 1979; Presidential Order of Honour of Botswana, Botswana Confederation of Commerce, Industry and Manpower, 1989; Honorary Degree of Doctor of Laws, University of Botswana, 1998; Global Marketplace Award, Corporate Council on Africa, 1999; Distinguished Achievement Award for AIDS Leadership in Southern Africa, Medunsa Trust, 2000; AIDS Leadership Award, Harvard AIDS Institute, 2001; Honorary Fellow, University College Oxford, 2003; Naledi Ya Botswana–Gaborone, Republic of Botswana, 2003; Grand Croix, Government of Madagascar, 2006; Grand Cross of the Légion d'honneur, 2008; Ibrahim Prize for Achievement in African Leadership, 2008.

As Mogae began his civil service career in his homeland as a planning officer, the country was in need of intelligent leaders with backgrounds in economics. In Botswana, planning officers are economists who play important roles in the development of the country. Mogae kept this post from 1968 to 1970. In his first year as a planning officer, Mogae also married Barbara Modise and started a family; the couple went on to have three daughters.

Progressed Quickly in Development Planning Work

Young Mogae was quickly promoted. In 1971 he rose to senior planning officer and then to director of economic affairs, a position he held from 1972 to 1974. The following year, Mogae became permanent secretary of the Ministry of Finance and Development Planning, an important post that coordinates national development planning while managing economic resources.

Broadening his horizons to the international level, Mogae became an alternate and then executive director for Africa to the International Monetary Fund (IMF) from 1976 to 1980. The IMF is an organization of 186 countries that work together in matters of international trade, employment, and economic growth. During his tenure with the IMF, Mogae was given awards by the African governments of Mali and the Ivory Coast in recognition of his exceptional service.

After his tenure at the IMF, Mogae returned home to take over the position of governor of the Bank of Botswana from 1980 to 1981. A national bank, the Bank of Botswana was formed in 1975, and its governor holds a governmental cabinet post. Mogae stayed with the bank for a short time and then took the governmental posts of permanent secretary to president, secretary to the cabinet, and supervisor of elections from 1982 to 1989, serving under president Quett Ketumile Joni Masire, the second president of Botswana and co-founder of the BDP.

Became Third President of Botswana

In 1989 Masire named Mogae minister of finance and development planning, an office that is usually paired with the vice presidency in Botswana, and Mogae was appointed to the vice presidency in 1992. The vice presidency is usually considered a stepping stone to the presidency, but there were others within the BDP vying for power in the event of Masire's leaving office. Furthermore, in the 1994 elections, as a result of rising unemployment in the cities, Mogae's BDP had lost a number of seats in parliament to other parties.

Prior to stepping down in early 1998, Masire enacted a series of reforms that appeared to please both the BDP and its opposition in parliament, the Botswana National Front, and smoothed the way for Mogae's assumption of power. One reform was a constitutional amendment (which some called a constitutional manipulation) allowing the vice president to assume the presidency automatically when the president stepped down during his term of office. Despite the controversy, Mogae assumed the presidency and became the first president of Botswana to come to power through automatic succession.

Elections were not far away, however, being held every five years. Prior to the 1999 elections, a split occurred within the opposition party, which gave an advantage to Mogae in the election, and he won his own five-year term as president.

Established Prioriites of HIV/AIDS and Economy

As Mogae settled into the office of president, he became increasingly distressed by the HIV/AIDS epidemic overtaking his country. According to the World Health Organization, more than one-fourth of adults aged fifteen to forty-nine in Botswana were HIV positive at that time. Life expectancy in the country had declined to 55.6 years from 65 years between 1990 and 1995. Researchers estimated that half of all Botswana women in their twenties would die of the disease. To rally support for his country and its fight against HIV/AIDS, Mogae spoke to the U.N. General Assembly, telling them that his country was facing extinction. Not only was this disease debilitating and killing his people, but it was also resulting in a serious economic decline.

Mogae led a two-pronged attack on the disease by means of the Prevention of Mother to Child Transmission Program (PMTCT) and government-supplied antiretroviral drugs for those harboring the virus. By July of 2000, Mogae had partnered with the Bill and Melinda Gates Foundation and with Merck, one of the largest pharmaceutical companies in the world. The goal was to support and strengthen the health care infrastructure of Botswana as well as to provide free antiretroviral drugs to HIV/AIDS patients in need.

Mogae's other top priority as president was diversifying the economy so that the country was not exclusively dependent on diamonds. He worked to increase exports and manufacturing and to reduce poverty and unemployment. Mogae worked somewhat unsuccessfully to stimulate textile, ceramic, and craft production; he had more success with creating products from copper and nickel, metals that were mined in Botswana. As tourism expanded, the government upgraded airports to help support that industry.

Mogae and the BDP were victorious in the 2004 elections. While they certainly benefited from continu-ing discord and division among the opposition, Mogae was a strong candidate in his own right. Considered an outstanding leader who helped perpetuate Botswana's long history of political stability, he and his country both earned praise for the stable example they set for the country's African neighbors. Botswana has been called the continent's "showcase democracy."

Recognized with Prize at Retirement

In 2007 Mogae announced to the BDP that he would step down from the presidency in April of 2008, handing over the office to vice president Seretse Khama Ian Khama prior to the 2009 elections. Only a few months after leaving the presidency, in October of 2008, Mogae was honored with the Ibrahim Prize for Achievement in African Leadership. Described by BBC News as "the most valuable individual prize in the world," the prize was set up by Sudanese-born Mohamed "Mo" Ibrahim, a British mobile communications entrepreneur, to recognize excellence in African leadership and governance. The recipient of the prize receives $5 million over ten years, and beginning in year eleven receives $200,000 per year. He or she also receives $200,000 per year to use for good causes.

In response to winning the Ibrahim Prize, Mogae told BBC News, "One does one's work, one uses one's best endeavours to do a job as well as one could, and if other people then assess it and judge it to be meritorious and worth of recognition it's then honouring and humbling." As this modest statesman retired to his cattle ranch, he left behind a country that had "a vibrant, stable democracy with a relatively successful economy," in the words of *African Business* reporter Alfred Sayila. He was also successful in reducing the prevalence of adult HIV as well as dramatically reducing the number of deaths annually due to the disease. He was, as Alfred Sayila put it, a "pure diamond of a leader."

Sources

Periodicals

African Business, September 1995, p. 12; September 1996, p. 17; March 2009, pp. 54–55.
Independent (London), July 15, 2007.
Mail & Guardian (Johannesburg, South Africa), November 17, 1997; March 31, 1998; April 7, 1998.
Namibian, March 27, 1998; April 2, 1998; May 20, 1998; May 22, 1998.
New York Times, April 1, 1998.
Time, October 20, 2008.

Online

"Botswana: President Festus Gontebanye Mogae (1998–2008)," EISA, July 2009, http://www.eisa.org.za/WEP/botoverview7.htm (accessed November 15, 2009).

"Botswana's Mogae Wins $5M Prize," BBC News, October 20, 2008, http://news.bbc.co.uk/2/hi/africa/7679391.stm (accessed November 13, 2009).

"Festus Mogae," African Success, October 31, 2008, http://www.africansuccess.org/visuFiche.php?id=572&lang=en (accessed November 13, 2009).

Rose, Charlie, "A Conversation with the President of Botswana Festus Mogae," CharlieRose.com, December 6, 2006, http://www.charlierose.com/view/interview/100 (accessed November 13, 2009).

Other

Additional information for this profile was obtained from the African Presidential Archives and Research Center at Boston University, http://web.bu.edu/aparc/presidents/mogae/index.html.

—Carol Brennan and Sandra Alters

Tamera Mowry

1978—

Actor

Mowry, Tamera, photograph. Michael Buckner/Getty Images.

Tamera Mowry and her twin, Tia, literally grew up on camera as stars of the sitcom *Sister, Sister.* The series ran for six seasons in the 1990s, taking them from their teens into adulthood. Each has gone on to forge her own independent career, but the sisters still work together occasionally on projects such as the 2010 remake of the romantic-comedy classic *Double Wedding* for Lifetime Television.

Mowry was born two minutes before her sister Tia in Gelnhausen, Germany, on July 6, 1978. They were the first of four children born to an African-American mother and an Italian-American father who was stationed in West Germany with the U.S. military when the twins were born. Around 1980 their father was reassigned to Fort Hood, Texas, and a few years later the family moved once more, to Hawaii, before returning to Texas. "When you're an army brat, you move all the time," Tamera told *Ebony*'s Melissa Ewey. "I think Tia and I developed a closer bond because we were always leaving our friends. We had each other, so it wasn't a problem."

In 1986 the Mowrys were living in Killeen, Texas, where "Ti and I were really bored," Mowry recalled in

another interview, this one with *People*'s Mark Goodman. "My mom saw an ad in the newspaper for [beauty] pageants. And we won." After that, they signed with a modeling agency and appeared in catalogs and ads for Sears, J.C. Penney, and other retailers. They set their sights on Hollywood at an early age, begging their parents to move to southern California so they could be nearer to the entertainment industry. Their mother, Darlene, agreed to apply for a thirty-day leave from her Army job and took them to California one summer, telling them they had one month to find a job. After making the rounds of talent agencies, they were sent to audition for a Chrysler commercial which required them to show off their double-dutch jump rope skills. They claimed proficiency, but in reality had never mastered the complex dual-rope activity. "We were out in the middle of the street asking anybody to teach us," Mowry recalled in the *Ebony* interview. They faked it using one rope, the casting director liked their spirit anyway, and they won the job. With that, the family pulled up stakes and moved to the Los Angeles area.

The Mowrys settled in the San Fernando Valley area in 1989, and the twins attended school while continuing

At a Glance . . .

Born Tamera Darvette Mowry on July 6, 1978, in Gelnhausen, Germany; daughter of Timothy (a corrections officer) and Darlene Mowry. *Religion:* Christian. *Education:* Earned degree in psychology from Pepperdine University, 2001(?).

Career: Began professional career as an actor in a Chrysler television commercial, 1990(?); made television debut in *Flesh 'n' Blood*, NBC, 1991; made feature film debut in *The Hot Chick*, 2002; worked as a counselor at a women's center, 2001(?).

Addresses: *Agent*—Metropolitan Talent Agency, 204 N. Rossmore Ave., Los Angeles, CA 90004.

their modeling and acting careers. Tamera was cast in a 1990 project for ABC starring a then-unknown comedian, Tim Allen, which never aired. A year later she made her debut in an episode of a shortlived NBC sitcom *Flesh 'n' Blood*. That same year, her younger brother Tahj, known as the family clown, began appearing on the ABC sitcom *Full House* as Teddy. That led to the girls' first major break, when television executive Irene Dreayer met the five-year-old Tahj. As Dreayer recounted the episode to Mark Goodman, writing for *People,* she "fell in love and said to the mother, 'Anyone else at home?'" Dreayer then worked with others to create a sitcom project for the twins.

In *Sister, Sister* Mowry played Tamera Campbell, the adopted daughter of a widowed father portrayed by television veteran Tim Reid. One day at the mall, the character encounters her double—the identical twin from whom she was proverbially separated at birth. Her long-lost twin Tia (the producers used the Mowrys' real names for the characters to minimize confusion) is the daughter of a fashion designer played by Jackée Harry, and the two single parents agree to move in together so the girls can bond.

Sister, Sister debuted on ABC in the spring of 1994, but the network dropped the series after airing three episodes. The show was then picked up by the WB network, which ran nineteen more episodes in the 1994–95 season and regularly ordered twenty-two more in subsequent years. The twins' goal was to make it to the fifth year, or one-hundredth episode, which would make *Sister, Sister* a lucrative property on the syndication market. They met their goal in the spring of 1999 and ended the series as their fictional counterparts headed off to college. By that point, they were approaching their twenty-first birthday, and both were enrolled as psychology majors at Pepperdine Univer-

sity in Malibu. Mowry recalled in an interview with Charreah Jackson for Essence.com that for her, the transition from sitcom world to college "was humbling. Professors didn't care who you were, just get the work in on time."

For six years Mowry and her twin shared a house in the San Fernando Valley while they completed their degrees, explored various career options, and reaffirmed their commitment to acting. Mowry spent four months as a counselor at a women's center before deciding she was not suited for the job. Like her twin, she took acting classes and retooled her image in order to land a wider variety of roles. On *Sister, Sister,* Tamera had been the rowdier twin—the opposite of her role in real life, both say—and she had to convince casting agents to let her audition for more dramatic roles. Finally she landed a recurring role in *Strong Medicine,* a Lifetime series about doctors and their protégés at a Philadelphia hospital. Mowry was cast as Kayla Thornton, a medical student, in the series' last two seasons (2004–06).

Mowry continued to appear in the occasional project with her twin, including two Disney Channel movies, *Twitches* and *Twitches Too,* and their 2002 feature film debut *The Hot Chick.* In 2009 Tamera appeared in *Roommates,* an ABC Family sitcom featuring five young adults in the entertainment industry that aired for just one season. Mowry was cast as Hope Daniels, whose story involves the loss of her job in television production and her relationship with her father, again played by Tim Reid. "I hadn't shot in front of a live audience in ten years, so I am having all these thoughts of what if I'm not funny, but it's like riding a bike," Mowry confessed to Jackson in the Essence.com article. "This character was not originally written as a Black girl, so it's great to be able to represent for Black women, and for her to be the fashionista."

Selected works

Television

Sister, Sister, ABC, 1994–95, WB, 1995–99.
Strong Medicine, Lifetime Television, 2004–06.
Twitches (movie), Disney Channel, 2005.
Twitches Too (movie), Disney Channel, 2007.
Roommates, ABC Family, 2009.
Double Wedding (movie), Lifetime Television, 2010.

Film

The Hot Chick, Touchstone Pictures, 2002.

Sources

Periodicals

Ebony, November 1998, p. 166.
Fresno Bee (Fresno, CA), October 9, 2007.
Jet, November 12, 2007, p. 60.

People, May 9, 1994, p. 175.
Today's Christian, March/April 2005, p. 42.

Online

Jackson, Charreah, "Tamera Mowry Flies Solo in New Show," Essence.com, March 23, 2009, http://www.essence.com/news_entertainment/entertainment/articles/tamera_mowry_interview (accessed September 23, 2009).

—Carol Brennan

Youssou N'Dour

1959—

Musician

Senegalese singer Youssou N'Dour is the best-known African musician in the world. He works most often in a genre of African pop called "mbalax," a style of dance music that developed in Senegal in the 1970s. Mbalax combines traditional polyrhythmic drumming on the sabar, a drum used by the Wolof tribe, with electric instrumentation and Western musical forms.

N'Dour calls his music "African storytelling on the wings of 21st-century instrumentation," according to *Vanity Fair.* He is backed by a band consisting of as many as fourteen members, including multiple percussionists, guitarists, saxophonists, and backing vocalists. As N'Dour achieved greater recognition and acceptance among audiences in Europe and the United States during the late 1980s, he began to use more traditional African and Arabic sounds in his music. Although he is fluent in French, Arabic, and his native Wolof, his English is not very good. He is at his best when able to present an authentic brand of African pop, with its own unique rhythms and lyrics sung in Wolof, one of Senegal's major native languages.

N'Dour, Youssou, photograph. Matt Cardy/Getty Images.

Inspired by His Roots

N'Dour was born on October 1, 1959, in Dakar, the capital of Senegal, on the west coast of Africa. N'Dour grew up in a traditional African community within the Medina section of the city, a place that has continued to offer great inspiration for his music. He related to *Interview* that Dakar was to him "a living poem, a place of unbridled energy, remarkable ambition and legendary artistic flair. I know of no other city on earth where people do so much with so little."

N'Dour's father was a mechanic who discouraged him from a musical career. His mother, however, was a griot, or community historian and storyteller. A respected elder, she kept the community's past alive through oral history, traditional songs, and moral teachings.

With his mother's encouragement, N'Dour sang at kassaks, parties to celebrate circumcision. As N'Dour described his work then, "Sometimes on one street there would be four or five kassaks going on at the same time. They would start in the evening and I would go to one and sing two numbers, then on to the next.... Sometimes I used to sing at 10 kassaks a night. Gradually, my friends and others encouraged me and gave me confidence, because they liked my singing."

Success with the Super Etoile

By the age of fourteen, N'Dour was performing in front of large audiences and had earned the nickname, "Le Petit Prince de Dakar," or "The Little Prince of Dakar." As a teenager he joined the Star Band, the best-known Senegalese pop band of the time, recording with them and performing in clubs in Dakar. By the time he was twenty, he had left the Star Band to form his own group, Etoile de Dakar (Star of Dakar). They recorded three albums had a hit with their first single, "Xalis" (Money). Then they relocated to Paris and reformed as the Super Etoile de Dakar (Superstar of Dakar).

Living in Paris provided N'Dour with a array of new musical influences. In 1990 he stated: "When I started to play music, I was playing traditional music. But when I came to Europe to listen to the sounds around me, by 1984 I had a new attitude. I'm a new person now, opening fast. I like to change. I'm African, yes, but I like

to play music for everybody. But my identity is African. That will never change."

From his base in Paris, N'Dour and the Super Etoile began to win over Western audiences to the sound of mbalax. The Super Etoile, which consisted of fourteen members at that point, used traditional Wolof and African rhythms behind N'Dour's unique tenor.

Gained International Attention

By the mid-1980s, the group was ready for a major international breakthrough. They had toured the United States, Great Britain, and Holland, in addition to playing at N'Dour's nightclub in Dakar, the Thiosanne. Remembering his audiences in Dakar and his friends from the Medina, N'Dour made it a point to return there. A song he wrote, "Medina," celebrates his old neighborhood and his old friends, who "are still my friends today and are the people I have around me." As his career progressed, N'Dour remained in touch with his roots and made his home base in Dakar. He told *Time* in 2001 that living in Dakar "gives me a certain inspiration; it allows me to keep my passion for music alive."

N'Dour and Super Etoile released an album in 1985 that became an Afro-pop classic, *Immigres.* It was released in the United States three years later. N'Dour increased his exposure to Western audiences in 1986 by appearing as a drummer on Paul Simon's *Graceland* album. He recorded the *Nelson Mandela* album in Paris that year and toured the United States twice with Super Etoile, once on their own and once opening for Peter Gabriel. N'Dour sang backing vocals on Gabriel's *So* album, and it is Gabriel who is the Western musician most responsible for bringing Youssou N'Dour to the attention of audiences in the United States and other Western nations.

N'Dour continued to tour with Peter Gabriel in 1988, reducing the size of his band to six pieces and a dancer. In the summer of that year, N'Dour played New York's first International Festival of the Arts at the Beacon Theatre. The influence of American pop on N'Dour was revealed in his playing half a set's worth of American pop and soul, with Nona Hendryx joining him for a song in English and Wolof. *New York Times* writer Jon Pareles wrote of N'Dour, "What makes Mr. N'Dour an international sensation, along with the dance rhythms of mbalax, is his unforgettable voice, a pure, pealing tenor that melds pop sincerity with the nuances of Islamic singing." Noting that mbalax has always combined international influences with Senegalese traditions, Pareles expressed his concern that American pop was diluting the effect of N'Dour's singing and the band's rhythms. N'Dour would later echo this concern in *Rolling Stone,* when he said, "It's a very difficult balance to keep the roots and bring in a bit of the Western world."

Leveraged His Fame for the Needy

In the fall of 1988, N'Dour gained even greater international exposure as part of Amnesty International's "Human Rights Now!" world tour. At London's Wembley Stadium, N'Dour joined Bruce Springsteen, Sting, Peter Gabriel, and Tracy Chapman to sing Bob Marley's classic reggae song, "Get Up, Stand Up." It was the start of a forty-four-day tour of five continents, including stops in Hungary, India, Zimbabwe, Argentina, and Brazil. Only two U.S. dates were included, in Los Angeles and Philadelphia.

Over the years, N'Dour has tried to leverage his celebrity to benefit others. To create jobs in Senegal, he bought a newspaper, a nightclub, a radio station, and a recording studio. He has participated in several charity album recordings. He has campaigned for the debt relief of developing nations. He has served as Goodwill Ambassador to the United Nations, Goodwill Ambassador to UNICEF, and Ambassador to the International Bureau of Work. In 2001 he also started an Internet training company, called Joko, in order to introduce a greater number of Senegalese to the information age. N'Dour's original songs often include political and social commentary.

N'Dour also writes songs based on his own life: about his old neighborhood and childhood pals, about the youth of his country, and about roaming the countryside with a friend. In 1989 Virgin Records released a new N'Dour album, *The Lion (Gaiende).* It was recorded in Paris, England, and Dakar and was produced by George Acogny and David Sancious, whose backgrounds span jazz, pop, and rock. The Super Etoile, now in an eight-piece incarnation, was joined by some Western musicians, including pop-jazz saxophonist David Sanborn. Peter Gabriel and N'Dour sing a duet on one of the album's tracks, "Shaking the Tree." N'Dour sings in Wolof, but English translations of the lyrics are provided. In a review of the album, *New York Times* reviewer Jon Pareles again expressed his concern that too much Western influence was creeping into N'Dour's music, writing, "Despite an undercurrent of Senegalese drums, the rippling vocal lines and dizzying polyrhythms that made Western listeners notice him are usually truncated."

By the fall of 1989, Super Etoile was back to full strength with twelve pieces for N'Dour's club dates in the United States. The extra percussion and instrumentation helped restore the driving rhythm of N'Dour's music. Reviewing a performance at the Ritz in New York, Jon Pareles of the *New York Times* described the "two percussionists whose doubletime and tripletime rhythms restored mbalax's sense of swift, sprinting momentum." He noted that the intricate cross-rhythms combined well with a firm downbeat to provide a mix of Western and Senegalese styles. The show ended with a song about toxic waste that would be released in 1990 as a single from N'Dour's album *Set.*

N'Dour's songs on *Set* deal with personal emotions, social problems, and political issues. He says, "Most of the songs I heard in my youth were either love songs or traditional songs recounting the history of the people that I come from—praise songs, historical songs. The lyrics of my own works today I consider to be about the society in which I live, the world in which I live. I want my words to have an educational function."

Dubbed King of West African Music

The international success of *Set* set the stage for N'Dour to broaden his international fame. It inspired *Rolling Stone* contributor Brian Cullman to comment, "If any third-world performer has a real shot at the sort of universal popularity last enjoyed by Bob Marley, it's Youssou, a singer with a voice so extraordinary that the history of Africa seems locked inside it." Indeed, his star continued to rise. His 1994 album, *The Guide,* garnered two Grammy nominations. He wrote and performed, with Axelle Red, the anthem for the 1998 World Cup in France. By 2000 N'Dour was recognized as the "king of West African music," according to *Billboard.*

His greatest success came in 2004 when he released the album *Egypt.* N'Dour deftly combined Senegalese percussion traditions with Arabic instrumental arrangements in songs that explore his Islamic faith. N'Dour has said that the songs were so personal that he did not intend to release the album, which he recorded with both Egyptian and Senegalese musicians in 1999, but world events soon changed his mind. "My religion needs to be better known for its positive side," he told *Billboard.* "Maybe this music can move us toward a greater understanding of the peaceful message of Islam." Ironically, the record was extremely controversial in Senegal, where it was banned for a time as blasphemous. Nevertheless, the album was praised by critics worldwide. Reviewer Chris Nickson wrote in *Sing Out!* that *Egypt* is "one of those rare records that truly deserves to be called stunning, quite possibly the best thing N'Dour has ever achieved which is saying something indeed." His effort was honored in 2005 with a Grammy award.

N'Dour made his film debut in 2007, playing Oloudah Equiano in Michael Apted's historical drama *Amazing Grace.* The film depicts the battle to abolish slavery in the British Empire in the late eighteenth and early nineteenth centuries. N'Dour's character, Equiano, was a real-life freed slave who wrote a highly influential memoir detailing the horrors of his capture and passage to the New World. That same year N'Dour was named to the "Time 100," *Time* magazine's list of "the 100 men and women whose power, talent or moral example is transforming the world."

He also released *Rokku mi Rokka* (Give and Take). The album featured Bassekou Kouyate, a Malian player of the ngoni, an African stringed instrument. Departing to a large extent from N'Dour's well-known mbalax, *Rokku mi Rokka* was based on traditional music from the desert region of Senegal on the borders of Mali and Mauritania. The album received mixed reviews: while critics noted the sublime beauty of N'Dour's voice, his prodigious musical intelligence, and the talents of Kouyate, some considered it a lightweight and unsuccessful mixture of musical styles too heavily reliant on Western music. Particularly maligned were the opening and closing tracks, "4-4-44" and "Wake Up (It's Africa Calling)", the latter of which featured Neneh Cherry. Charlie Gillett of the *Observer* called the first "absurd" and the second "woeful." Tim Nelson of the BBC wrote: "It's when N'Dour is at his most adventurous and experimental that the album is most successful. ... On the evidence of this album, Youssou needs to stop trying to cross over and let us come to him."

Documentary Released

The year 2009 saw the release of a documentary on N'Dour entitled *Youssou N'Dour: I Bring What I Love*, by filmmaker Elizabeth Chai Vasarhelyi. "I moved to Africa," Vasarhelyi told *New York* magazine, "and have lived and breathed this film about Youssou for five years." The documentary covered a world tour, the period during which N'Dour released the album *Egypt*, and the controversy surrounding it in Senegal. Included was intimate footage of N'Dour with his grandmother and children. Critical reception was mixed: while the film was criticized for shapelessness and for treating complex subjects in a superficial fashion, reviewers were struck the beauty and joyfulness of his music, as well as by the visible humility and integrity of N'Dour himself. Ann Hornaday of the *Washington Post* reflected the view of many critics when she wrote: "By far the most powerful element is N'Dour's lone voice, a thing of high, pure beauty that feels at once ancient and new. When he sings, an otherwise earnestly conventional film becomes a vehicle of incantatory power."

Selected discography

Nelson Mandela, Polydor, 1986.
Immigres, Virgin, 1988.
The Lion (Gaiende), Virgin, 1989.
Set, Virgin, 1990.
Eyes Open, Columbia, 1992.
The Guide (Wommat), Chaos/Columbia, 1994.
Lii, Jololi, 1996.
St. Louis, Jololi, 1997.
Rewmi, 1999.

Joko, Wea/Atlantic/Nonesuch, 2000.
Batay, Jololi, 2001.
Le Grand Bal, 1 and 2, Jololi, 2001.
Et Ses Amis, Universal International, 2002.
Nothing's in Vain, Warner/Nonesuch, 2002.
Egypt, Nonesuch, 2004.
Rokku mi Rokka, Nonesuch, 2007.

Sources

Books

Graham, Ronnie, *Da Capo Guide to Contemporary African Music*, Da Capo Press, 1988.

Periodicals

Billboard, June 10, 2000; April 17, 2004.
Cape Times (South Africa), July 10, 2009, p. 2.
Detroit Free Press, October 5, 1990.
Detroit Metro Times, October 3–9, 1990.
Detroit News, October 5, 1990.
Down Beat, May 1987.
Guardian (London), October 26, 2007.
Houston Chronicle, August 28, 2009, p. 2.
Interview, May 2001, p. 76.
New York, May 10, 2009.
New Yorker, March 5, 2007, p. 94.
New York Post, June 12, 2009, p. 38.
New York Times, July 2, 1988; July 2, 1989; November 8, 1989; June 12, 2009.
Newsweek, September 12, 1988.
Observer (London), October 14, 2007.
People, October 10, 1988.
Rolling Stone, July 13–27, 1989; November 1, 2007.
Sing Out!, Fall 2004, p. 110.
Time, September 15, 2001, p. 66.
Vanity Fair, November 2004.
Washington Post, October 9, 2009.

Online

Nelson, Tim, "Youssou Gives Us a Needlessly Westernized Offering…," BBC, October 21, 2007, http://www.bbc.co.uk/music/reviews/gxgb (accessed November 27, 2009).
"Youssou N'Dour," *Nonesuch*, http://www.nonesuch.com/artists/youssou-n-dour (accessed November 14, 2009).
Youssou N'Dour, http://www.youssou.com (accessed November 14, 2009).

—David Bianco, Sara Pendergast,
and Paula Kepos

Johnnie B. Rawlinson

1952—

Jurist

Rawlinson, Johnnie B., photograph. AP Images.

In 2000 Johnnie B. Rawlinson became the first African-American woman to sit on the bench of the U.S. Court of Appeals for the Ninth Circuit in San Francisco, California. She was one of the last judicial appointments confirmed by the U.S. Senate in 2000 in the final months of President Bill Clinton's second term. Nine years later, Rawlinson's name appeared on the short list of possible U.S. Supreme Court nominations, but the new Democrat in the White House, Barack Obama, eventually selected New Yorker Sonia Sotomayor for the job.

Rawlinson was born in December of 1952 to parents who worked in the textile mills around Concord, North Carolina. In 1974 she earned a degree in psychology with top honors from North Carolina Agricultural and Technical (A&T) State University. Her choice of career was almost accidental. "No one in my family had been a lawyer," she was quoted as saying by the McGeorge School of Law Web site. "It wasn't until a friend of my husband's was studying for the LSAT that I thought about law as a career myself." Rawlinson scored well on the Law School Admission Test (LSAT) and was recruited by the McGeorge School of Law at the University of Pacific in Sacramento, California. By the time she finished her second year, she was married to an Air Force officer and had become a mother.

After Rawlinson graduated from law school in 1979, the young family moved to Nevada, where her husband had been posted at Nellis Air Force Base in Las Vegas. For a few months in 1980 she worked as a staff attorney with Nevada Legal Services. Thereafter she was hired as a deputy district attorney by the Clark County district attorney's office, which handled the area surrounding and including Las Vegas. By the end of the decade she had been promoted to chief deputy district attorney and had also served on the Nevada Gaming Commission, the state regulatory agency for casinos, after being appointed to that body by the Nevada governor. This was a part-time post but served to introduce Rawlinson to a future U.S. senator, Harry Reid, who chaired the commission from 1977 to 1981.

In 1995 Rawlinson became the assistant district attorney for Clark County in charge of the civil, family support, and administrative divisions. Two years later Reid submitted her name to President Bill Clinton to fill a vacancy on the bench of the U.S. District Court in

At a Glance . . .

Born on December 16, 1952, in Concord, NC; daughter of textile factory workers; married to Dwight (a municipal finance executive); children: Monica, Traci, David. *Education:* North Carolina A&T State University, BS (summa cum laude), 1974; University of Pacific, JD, 1979.

Career: Law clerk for a private practice in Las Vegas, 1979–80; Nevada Legal Services, staff attorney, 1980; Clark County District Attorney (Las Vegas, NV), began in 1980 as deputy district attorney; became chief deputy district attorney, 1989, and assistant district attorney, 1995; U.S. District Court of Nevada, judge, 1998–2000; U.S. Court of Appeals (Ninth Circuit), judge, 2000—.

Addresses: *Office*—U.S. Court of Appeals—Ninth Circuit, James R. Browning Courthouse, 95 7th St., San Francisco, CA 94103.

Nevada after his first choice for the job, Kathryn Landreth, bowed out. Rawlinson's appointment would make her both the first African American and the first woman on the federal bench in Nevada. "She's the most capable person around, no matter the sex, no matter the person," Reid was quoted as saying by Jane Ann Morrison in the *Las Vegas Review-Journal.* "I feel I have the best person for the job." Rawlinson's boss, Clark County District Attorney Stewart Bell, agreed, telling Morrison, "she probably has the best judgment of any lawyer I've ever met."

The process of becoming a federal judge requires a background check by the Federal Bureau of Investigation and the Internal Revenue Service, followed by a vote of the Senate Judiciary Committee. After that, the Senate confirms the appointment by vote. During the administration of Democratic president Bill Clinton, a Republican-controlled Senate intentionally delayed the process for several Clinton nominees. A report in the *Las Vegas Sun* in September of 1997 about Rawlinson's nomination and the delayed confirmation process noted that the U.S. "Attorney General Janet Reno has accused Senate Republicans of an unprecedented slowdown that has led to a vacancy crisis, with 43 nominations pending in the committee."

In March of 1998 Rawlinson finally went to Washington for her Senate confirmation hearing. She was questioned for a half hour by the chair of the Senate Judiciary Committee, Utah Republican Orrin Hatch, and by a future U.S. vice president, Democrat Joe Biden of Delaware. They posed questions about her positions on sensitive topics that federal judges are often asked to consider on the job, including affirmative action. "The Supreme Court has said that race-based programs are subject to the strictest scrutiny," was Rawlinson's reply, according to a report in the *Las Vegas Review-Journal* by Steve Tetreault. "It's abundantly clear that programs of that nature have to be carefully examined." She also affirmed that she had no reservations about the proper application of the death penalty for certain capital crimes. For Republican lawmakers in the Senate, this issue was critical when considering a federal judicial nominee.

Rawlinson was confirmed by Senate vote and sworn into office in June of 1998. Two years later, Clinton submitted Rawlinson's name to the Senate once again to fill a vacancy on the U.S. Court of Appeals for the Ninth Circuit. She was formally nominated in February of 2000, and this time a delay in the confirmation process actually prompted a statement from the Congressional Black Caucus rebuking the Republican-controlled Senate for dallying on Rawlinson's name and those of several other federal court judicial appointments who were female, African American, or Hispanic. The rebuke seemed to hasten the process, and she was confirmed on July 21, 2000.

Rawlinson was the first African-American woman to sit on the Ninth Circuit bench. The court is headquartered in San Francisco, and its jurisdiction encompasses Arizona, California, Idaho, Nevada, Montana, Oregon, and Washington, as well as Alaska and Hawaii. The judges meet in several cities, including Seattle, Washington, and Pasadena, California. Rawlinson has three children with her husband Dwight, the purchasing and risk manager for the city of North Las Vegas.

Sources

Periodicals

Las Vegas Review-Journal, August 26, 1997; March 19, 1998.
Las Vegas Sun, September 2, 1997.

Online

"Judge Johnnie Rawlinson '79," University of the Pacific—McGeorge School of Law, http://www.mcgeorge.edu/x2032.xml (accessed September 19, 2009).

—Carol Brennan

Reverend Ike

1935–2009

Evangelist

Reverend Ike, photograph. Thos Robinson/Getty Images.

The Right Reverend Dr. Frederick J. Eikerenkoetter II, or Rev. Ike, was a multi-media evangelist. The flamboyant minister came from a Baptist background but did not remain with his religious roots. Instead he developed a non-denominational church founded on his "Science of Living" doctrine. "Thinkonomics," as the doctrine was also called, emphasized prosperity and self-empowerment, but critics maintained that he was simply swindling his followers to support his extravagant lifestyle. At the peak of his career in the 1970s and 1980s, Rev. Ike had about three million followers who attended his church and listened to him on radio and television. He retired in 2005, handing over the ministry to his son Xavier. Rev. Ike suffered a serious stroke in 2007, which may have led to his death in 2009.

Heard "the Call" Early in Life

Rev. Ike was born Frederick J. Eikerenkoetter II on June 1, 1935, in Ridgeland, South Carolina, to a Dutch Indonesian father and an African-American mother. As a young boy, Eikerenkoetter attended the one-room schoolhouse in which his mother taught. By the age of fourteen he realized that he had "the calling" and entered the ministry, becoming an associate pastor at his father's congregation, the Bible Way Baptist Church. When it was time for his college education, Eikerenkoetter traveled to Chicago to attend the American Bible College. In 1956 he graduated with a bachelor's degree in theology as the valedictorian of his class.

After college, Eikerenkoetter enlisted in the U.S. Air Force and became a chaplain service specialist, a noncommissioned officer who assists military chaplains. After serving two years in the chaplains' corps, Eikerenkoetter returned to South Carolina and founded the United Church of Christ for All People in Beaufort. Many of Eikerenkoetter's parishioners were poor, which led the pastor to think about what he could do to help people in this world, rather than focusing on the traditional Christian view of rewards in the afterlife.

In 1964 Eikerenkoetter moved from South Carolina to Boston. There he founded the United Christian Evangelistic Association, which was known as the Miracle Temple, because Eikerenkoetter made faith healing a focus of his ministry. He later told Clayton Riley, the

At a Glance . . .

Born Frederick J. Eikerenkoetter II on June 1, 1935, in Ridgeland, SC; died July 28, 2009, in Los Angeles, CA; son of a Baptist minister and a teacher; married Eula May Dent (a pastor), 1962; children: Xavier Frederick Eikerenkoetter. *Military service:* U.S. Air Force, chaplain service specialist. *Religion:* Nondenominational church; founded the doctrine "Science of Living." *Education:* American Bible College, bachelor of theology, 1956; Science of Living Institute, PhD ,1969; Science of Living Institute, doctor of science of living degree, 1971.

Career: Bible Way Baptist Church, assistant pastor, 1949–52; U.S. Air Force, chaplain service specialist, 1956–58; United Church of Jesus Christ for All People, founder and pastor, 1958–64; United Christian Evangelistic Association (Miracle Temple), founder, 1964–66; Christ Community United Church (Palace Cathedral from 1969), founder and senior pastor, 1966–2005; United Church Schools, founder and chancellor, 1966–2005.

Awards: Lifetime Achievement Award in Mentoring, Zoe Ministries, 2004.

author of *The Golden Gospel of Reverend Ike,* that faith healing "was big at the time, and I was just about the best in Boston, snatching people out of wheelchairs and off their crutches, pouring some oil over them while I commanded them to walk or see or hear." He also told Riley "It's a wonder I didn't kill anybody," an admission that his obituary in the London *Independent* called "remarkably frank."

Despite his belief that he was "just about the best in Boston," Eikerenkoetter was dissatisfied with his ministry and in 1966 moved it to New York City, where he bought a run-down movie theater in Harlem and turned it into a church. The marquee was so small that he had to shorten his name to fit, and the moniker "Rev. Ike" was born. While in this location, Rev. Ike honed his preaching skills and began radio broadcasts.

Preached a Doctrine of Prosperity

After a few years at the Harlem location, Eikerenkoetter began to focus less on the poor and more on the middle class—"people who wanted to hear that their hard work should be rewarded here and now," as Christopher Lehmann-Haupt described it in the *New*

York Times in 2009. To that end, Rev. Ike moved his ministry out of Harlem to the old Loew's movie theater in Manhattan's Washington Heights neighborhood, paying more than a half million dollars for the building in 1969 and then totally renovating it. He called his new church the "Palace Cathedral." With the new church came a new doctrine developed by Eikerenkoetter: "The Science of Living: Prosperity Now!" Eikerenkoetter added an educational arm to his church, the United Church Schools, of which he was chancellor. The schools were The Science of Living Institute and Seminary, The Business of Living Institute, The Health Education Institute, and the Youth Ministries. The Science of Living Institute and Seminary granted Eikerenkoetter a PhD degree in 1969 and a doctor of science of living degree in 1971.

Rev. Ike's new doctrine characterized God as an entity that existed within every person and called this concept the "God in me." This holy force, preached Rev. Ike, could empower the individual to achieve whatever he or she aspired to, resulting in prosperity, good health, and peace of mind. Commenting on his new approach, Eikerenkoetter told Clayton Riley that he was "the first black man in America to preach positive self-image psychology to the black masses within a church setting."

By the 1970s, Rev. Ike was not only preaching in the Palace Cathedral, but he was also seen on syndicated television and heard on 1,770 radio stations by more than 2.5 million followers. Additionally, Rev. Ike took his ministry on the road, conducting live services in his characteristically flamboyant manner at various locales across the nation.

Generated Controversy

In 1972 *Time* correspondent Timothy Tyler visited one of Rev. Ike's services and reported on Eikerenkoetter's invention of the money rake. As Rev. Ike explained it, "The money rake is your good, positive belief about money. If on the inside you have a right, positive feeling about money, this feeling will rake money to you." Rev. Ike appeared to be following his own philosophy and raking in money. As *Time* reported, his "Blessing Plan" urged his parishioners to "Pledge at least $100!" And during the service, as the red donation buckets were passed, Ike would say "I don't want to hear change rattling; it makes me nervous in the service." Tyler concluded his article by noting that Eikerenkoetter waits "only long enough to hear the rustle of the bills, grins and makes for the airport."

According to Dennis McLellan writing the *Los Angeles Times* in 2009, in 1976 Eikerenkoetter's church owned six residences and sixteen Rolls-Royces, as well as other high-end vehicles. (Rev. Ike stated: "My garages runneth over.") He was investigated by the Internal Revneue Service, and, as his television appeal waned and he turned to direct mail solicitations, by the U.S. Postal Service. Direct mail donations to Rev. Ike were estimated at $1 million per month.

Eikerenkoetter's critics saw him as preying on the poor and the middle class, duping them into donating money that he used to sustain his extravagant lifestyle. Many traditional Christian ministers were opposed to Eikerenkoetter's approach because of its materialistic nature and the false hopes it would likely engender. Nonetheless, his followers loved him. Rev. Ike had the ability to inspire, and many believers subscribed to his philosophy of mind over matter.

Retired and Suffered a Stroke

Eikerenkoetter ended his television show, "The Joy of Living," and retired from his ministry in 2005, leaving his son Xavier to handle the day-to-operations of the Palace Cathedral, the direct mail ministry, and the Web site www.revike.org. During his retirement Rev. Ike and his wife remained out of the spotlight in their oceanfront mansion near Los Angeles.

Eikerenkoetter suffered a stroke in 2007 from which he never fully recovered. He died on July 28, 2009, in a Los Angeles–area hospital at the age of 74. Bishop E. Bernard Jordan, the family spokesperson, told *Jet* magazine that Rev. Ike had lost the will to live: "He willed himself out of here. He felt like his work was over, so the body took that as a command and began to shut itself down." In a tribute to his colleague, Jordan said, "Rev. Ike is a pioneer. He should be hailed as the grandfather of prosperity gospel. He was a man who loved God and a teacher who was about empowering mankind and would only give wisdom to those willing to listen."

Selected works

Books

Rev. Ike's Secrets for Health, Joy, and Prosperity— For You!, Science of Living Books, 1982.
Rev. Ike's Secrets for Health, Joy, and Prosperity— For You! A Science of Living Study Guide, Science of Living Books, 1982.

Music Singles

(Guest appearance with Hank Williams Jr., Reba McEntire, Willie Nelson, and Tom Petty) *Montana Cafe* (includes "Mind Your Own Business"), WB Records, 1986.

Sources

Books

Riley, Clayton, *The Golden Gospel of Reverend Ike,* 1975.

Periodicals

Independent (London), August 10, 2009.
Jet, July 12, 2004, p. 64; September 10, 2007, p. 64; August 24–31, 2009, p. 26.
Los Angeles Times, July 31, 2009, p. A26.
New York Times, July 30, 2009, p. A28; August 3, 2009, p. A19.
Time, December 11, 1972, p. 121.

—Sandra Alters

Wilson C. Riles

1917–1999

Educational administrator

Riles, Wilson C., photograph. AP Images.

Wilson C. Riles became the first African American to hold statewide office in California when he won an upset election in 1970 against conservative incumbent Max Rafferty for the job of state superintendent of schools. Riles held the job for three terms, from 1971 to 1983, and served on the education task forces of three U.S. presidents. As superintendent, Riles was an advocate for disadvantaged children in California's public schools, and he worked to secure legislation and funding for special education and early childhood education. Born into a poor family in backwoods Louisiana and orphaned at the age of eleven, Riles overcame great obstacles in his own life; as a public servant, he considered it his duty to ensure that all children had fair and equal access to education and a chance to succeed, as he had.

Determined to Get an Education

Riles was born on June 27, 1917, in the Louisiana parish of Rapides, near Alexandria, the only child of Wilson Roy and Susie Anna Jefferson Riles. Alexandria was a remote sawmill town in which the chief industry was the distillation of turpentine from the resin of pine trees. Riles's father worked as a foreman in an itinerant turpentine camp, where the younger Wilson was born and raised. Although his family was poor, Riles did not want for love and affection. When he was nine years old, Riles's mother died, and his father followed two years later; the orphan was taken in by a childless couple, Leon and Narvia Bryant, who had been friends of his parents.

Riles was determined to get an education so that he could have a better life than his parents. Parishioners at the local African Methodist Episcopal church collected money to send him to one of the best high schools in the state, in New Orleans. He worked his way through school by delivering milk for a dairy and caddying on weekends at the New Orleans Country Club, returning each summer to stay with the Bryants. When the couple decided to move to Flagstaff, Arizona, after Riles had been graduated from high school, they invited him to come along.

In September of 1936, Riles enrolled in Arizona State Teachers College (now Northern Arizona University), where he was the only black student. He soon found a

At a Glance . . .

Born Wilson Camanza Riles on June 27, 1917, in Rapides Parish, LA; died on April 1, 1999, in Sacramento, CA; son of Wilson Roy Riles and Susie Anna Jefferson Riles; married Mary Louise Phillips (a teacher), November 13, 1941; children: Michael, Narvia, Wilson Jr., Phillip. *Military service:* U.S. Army Air Corps, 1944–46. *Politics:* Democrat. *Education:* Arizona State Teachers College (now Northern Arizona University), BA, education, 1940, MA, school administration, 1947.

Career: Dunbar School for Blacks, Flagstaff, AZ, teacher, 1941–44, teacher/principal, 1947–54; Fellowship of Reconciliation, executive secretary of the Pacific Coast region, 1954–58; California Department of Education, chief of Bureau of Intergroup Relations, 1958–65, associate superintendent of public instruction, 1965–69, deputy superintendent, 1969–71, superintendent, 1971–83; Wilson Riles and Associates, consultant, 1983–99.

Memberships: Association of California School Administrators; National Academy of Public Administration; Phi Beta Kappa.

Awards: Alumni Achievement Award, Northern Arizona University, 1968; Spingarn Medal, National Association for the Advancement of Colored People, 1973; Distinguished Alumni Honoree, Northern Arizona University, 1975; Distinguished Service Award, Harvard Club of San Francisco, 1978; Robert M. Hutchins Award, *Encyclopedia Britannica*, 1978; Distinguished Alumni Award, American Association of State Colleges and Universities, 1979.

job on campus through the National Youth Administration that paid fifteen dollars a month, enough to cover his books and fees, and hosted a late-night jazz program on a local radio station, calling himself "Doctor Rhythm the Educated DJ." Riles completed his undergraduate degree in education in 1940 and took his first teaching job that year, working in a one-room schoolhouse on an Apache reservation near Pistol Creek, Arizona, where his students were black children of sawmill workers in the area. The following year, he met and married Mary Louise Phillips, a teacher at a school for black students in Phoenix.

Began a Career in Education

The couple began teaching in 1941 at the all-black Dunbar School in Flagstaff, which had been established in 1926 when the state mandated the segregation of black and white students. Wilson continued his studies at Arizona State Teachers College, working toward a master's degree in school administration. During World War II, he entered the U.S. Army Air Corps, serving from 1944 to 1946. When he returned home, he went back to the Dunbar School as a teacher-principal and finished his graduate work in 1947. After the U.S. Supreme Court issued its landmark ruling in *Brown v. Board of Education of Topeka, Kansas* in 1954, ending legal school segregation, the Dunbar School closed and its students were integrated into other schools in Flagstaff.

Riles moved his family to Los Angeles, where he took a job as executive secretary of the Pacific Coast region for the Fellowship for Reconciliation, a pacifist organization run by Quakers. In this capacity, he worked with the staff at the California Department of Education on equal opportunity initiatives for school personnel. He joined the Department of Education in 1958, initially heading up its Bureau of Intergroup Relations.

Riles compiled an impressive résumé of accomplishments at the department, and in 1965 he became associate superintendent of public instruction, responsible for the $100 million federal Compensatory Education Program, which aimed to improve educational outcomes for low-income children. Four years later, state school chief Rafferty promoted Riles to deputy superintendent—a position that proved to be less responsibility and more "window-dressing," as Riles told *Ebony* magazine in 1971.

Won an Upset Election

In October of 1969, Riles began to consider running for superintendent himself. Rafferty, who had served two terms, was an ultraconservative who had tried to cut state spending on public education and made no bones about his opposition to busing to effect school desegregation. Riles viewed him as a poor administrator who was more interested in seeking higher office than in improving the state's school system. But Riles was a virtual unknown, with no political base, no money, no organizational ties—and seemingly no chance to win. Despite these obstacles, Riles decided to throw his hat in the ring. "Win, lose or draw, I wouldn't have it on my conscience five years from now—knowing all I knew about the condition of the system—that I didn't try," he told *Ebony.*

In the primary in June of 1970, Riles was one of nine candidates in the race. He placed second, garnering 25.2 percent of the vote to Rafferty's 48.6 percent, setting the stage for a showdown between the two in the general election. At first, Riles's prospects seemed dim. Rafferty accused him of hiding his race—although Riles's photo appeared in all campaign ads—and called him a communist sympathizer; early polls showed that Riles was supported by only 7 percent of those polled. In November, however, Riles managed an upset, winning the election by a margin of nearly half a million votes to become the first African American elected to statewide office in California., He received more than 3 million votes, more than any other black man in any election in the United States at the time.

As superintendent of California's public school system—the largest in the country—Riles oversaw 4.5 million students in 1,100 school districts, and was responsible for an annual budget of $2.5 billion and an administrative staff of more than 2,300. In addition, he served as an ex-officio regent of the University of California and as a trustee of the California State University and Colleges. During his tenure, Riles sponsored legislation to emphasize early childhood education; advocated the adoption of computers in the classroom; and established school councils to bring parents, teachers, and administrators together to evaluate school performance. He worked to expand federal programs for disadvantaged students, and developed a special education plan for disabled students in the state. Riles was reelected to his post two more times, serving until he lost the 1982 election to challenger Bill Honig.

In 1983 Riles founded the firm Wilson Riles and Associates, an education consulting group, which he headed for the remainder of his career. He suffered a series of heart attacks and strokes, and died on April 1, 1999, in a hospital in Sacramento, California, at the age of eighty-one.

Riles earned many accolades for his work in education. He served on the U.S. Office of Education's Task Force on Urban Education under three presidents. In 1973 the National Association for the Advancement of Colored People awarded him the Spingarn Medal, its highest honor. He also received the Robert M. Hutchins Award from the *Encyclopedia Britannica* in 1978 and the Distinguished Alumni Award from the American Association of State Colleges and Universities in 1979.

Selected writings

(With Jessie Heinzman) *Countdown to Retirement for Educators,* BoothMark Books, 1988.
"'No Adversary Situations': Public School Education in California and Wilson C. Riles, Superintendent of Public Instruction, 1970–1982," oral history conducted by Sarah Sharp, Regional Oral History Office, Bancroft Library, University of California, 1981–82, http://ia331333.us.archive.org/0/items/noadversarysit00rilerich/noadversarysit00rilerich.pdf (accessed October 1, 2009).

Sources

Periodicals

Ebony, May 1971.
New York Times, November 8, 1970.
San Francisco Chronicle, April 13, 1999, p. A17.
Time, November 16, 1970, p. 69.

Online

"Wilson and Louise Riles Collection," Northern Arizona University, Cline Library, http://www.nau.edu/library/speccoll/guide/r/riles.html (accessed October 1, 2009).

—Deborah A. Ring

Sylvia Robinson

1936—

Musician

Sylvia Robinson holds a legendary place in the history of American music as the godmother of rap. In the summer of 1979, the songwriter and producer brought together three novice rappers at her New Jersey recording studio to make "Rapper's Delight," the first commercially successful rap single. Robinson dubbed the group the "Sugar Hill Gang" as a promotional tie-in to the label she and her husband had recently created, Sugar Hill Records. "Having begun the 1970s with a bang of Afro-conscious funk and mean-streets social conscience, soul music ended the decade with a disco whimper," wrote *Vanity Fair*'s Steven Daly in 2005 in a nine-thousand-word article on the making of the song, its importance to urban music, and the role Robinson played in the birth of a multimillion-dollar industry. "Against that grim backdrop, 'Rapper's Delight' was a futuristic re-assertion of black pride, combining as it did the culture's oral traditions with its eternal drive to modernism."

Robinson was born Sylvia Vanderpool on March 6, 1936, and grew up in Harlem. As a teenager, she recorded a few singles under the name "Little Sylvia" that failed to garner much airplay. Giving up on a career in the music business, she enrolled in nursing school but was lured back into the studio by the man who became her husband, a Navy veteran named Joe Robinson. A native of Englewood, New Jersey, Joe was already known in New York City's nightlife scene as a bar owner and concert promoter. They wed in 1956, and that same year Robinson entered the studio again, this time with guitarist Mickey Baker, to record the song "Love Is Strange." The single went to No. 11

on the Billboard pop charts and No. 2 on the R&B charts and is often cited as an important release in the timeline of early rock 'n' roll music. Their song was borrowed from Bo Diddley's stage act, but songwriting credits went to Diddley's wife, Ethel Smith, along with Baker and Robinson. Baker eventually moved to France, and Robinson attempted to retire from the music business once again.

Raised Three Sons

Robinson spent most of the 1960s as a New Jersey housewife and mother of three boys, but she also worked alongside her husband in his various enterprises. These included the Blue Morocco, a Bronx nightclub patronized by Motown acts and sports figures like Muhammad Ali, and an Englewood recording studio they opened in 1968 called All Platinum. This was also the name of their independent record label, which had several offshoots. In the era before major labels dominated the music business, the deal making involved in creating and distributing a single was cutthroat and rife with unsavory characters. Robinson's husband, who died in 2000, was a formidable figure, both physically and at the negotiating table. He was said to have been on good terms with figures ranging from civil rights hero Malcolm X to alleged Harlem underworld figure Nicky Barnes. "I was clearly told that if Joe Robinson came in the room you stopped talking," a *Billboard* writer from this era, Robert Ford, told *Vanity Fair*'s Daly. "Everyone knew that this was not a man to be messed with."

At a Glance . . .

Born Sylvia Vanderpool on March 6, 1936, in New York; married Joseph Robinson (a bar owner and record producer), 1956; children: sons Joseph Jr., Rondo, Leland. *Education:* Attended nursing school, mid-1950s.

Career: Recorded under the name "Little Sylvia," early 1950s; recorded with guitarist Mickey Baker as "Mickey and Sylvia," late 1950s–1962; recorded under the name "Sylvia," 1970s; All Platinum Records, co-founder, 1968, and songwriter and producer for several acts signed to the label and recorded at the All Platinum/Sugar Hill studio.

Addresses: *Office*—Sugar Hill Records Ltd., 96 West St., Englewood, NJ 07631.

At the studio, Robinson began writing songs for other artists to record. One of them was "Love on a Two-Way Street," a minor hit single for an R&B group called the Moments. In 1973 she tried to convince soul crooner Al Green to record a song she had written called "Pillow Talk," but the singer thought its lyrics a little too racy. Robinson recorded it on her own as just "Sylvia," and it was issued by her and her husband's Vibration imprint. Its closing lines were famously explicit, and the song went to number one on Billboard's Black Singles chart in the spring of 1973. "Pillow Talk" became part of a wave of sexual empowerment songs recorded by female singers in this era, including Diana Ross, Millie Jackson, Patti Labelle, and Donna Summer.

Robinson had other hits that decade, including "Shame, Shame, Shame," an early disco hit for an act called Shirley & Company, but the family business endured financial and legal troubles for many years, including a lawsuit with the giant PolyGram. All Platinum filed for bankruptcy, but Joe Robinson borrowed some money from a reputed underworld figure to launch a new label, Sugar Hill Records. In June of 1979, his wife went to a party at Harlem World, a nightclub on Lenox Avenue, and on that night first encountered the phenomenon that would become known as rap. It had emerged a few years earlier in the dance music scene at discotheques and private parties in Harlem, Brooklyn, and Queens and owed some of its birthright to the Jamaican practice of "toasting," in which emcees talked over the beats of records played by disc jockeys. At Harlem World, Robinson witnessed a disc jockey who billed himself as "Lovebug Starski" playing records and rapping over them. "I saw him talking to the kids and saw how they'd answer back,"

she told Daly in the *Vanity Fair* article. "He would say something every now and then, like 'Throw your hands in the air,' and they'd do it. If he'd said, 'Jump in the river,' they'd have done it."

Found Three Rappers

Robinson thought this style of music—a perfect dovetailing of disco's heady beats and black-consciousness-era spoken-word recordings pioneered by Gil Scott-Heron and others—was going to be the next big thing. Among those in the music industry she apparently was alone in this conviction, and few of the actual artists believed that the energy of the scene could be effectively captured in the recording studio anyway. Robinson recruited her teenage son Joey Jr. to help her find a few rappers to put out a single.

On a Friday in August of 1979, Robinson and her son drove around Englewood looking for rappers with Joey's friend Warren Moore, who suggested a pizzeria employee he knew. This was Henry (Big Bank Hank) Jackson, a Bronx native who had ties to the music scene and was actually working as manager of Crispy Crust Pizza in order to pay off the $2,000 his parents had loaned him to buy a sound system for the act he managed, the Cold Crush Brothers. Still wearing his apron, Jackson auditioned for them in the parking lot, rapping along to an instrumental track Robinson had already laid down in the studio that borrowed heavily from one of the biggest hits of 1979, Chic's "Good Times." At that point, another Englewood figure came up to the car and said he had a better rapper than Jackson. This was Guy O'Brien, who was active with a local DJ crew called One on One. He, too, auditioned on the spot, followed by a third would-be rapper, Mike Wright.

Robinson took the trio back to the studio, signed them to a contract as Big Bank Hank, Master Gee, and Wonder Mike, and told the newly christened "Sugar Hill Gang" to come back on Monday for the recording session. She produced the single, pointing at them to deliver their tradeoffs, and the trio delivered an impressive single-take record despite the fact they had never worked together before. The twelve-inch, released on Sugar Hill Records as "Rapper's Delight," clocked in at fourteen minutes and thirty-seven seconds. She later said that his had been a source of friction with her opinionated business partner. "My husband said, 'We can't put out a record that long,'" she told Daly. "I said, 'What do you mean?! We're independent people. I don't care how long it is—we're gonna put every word in it. We don't have to go according to what the industry says.'" Robinson was convinced that if just one disc jockey gave "Rapper's Delight" airplay, the song would generate instant buzz. "All the record needed was one play," she said in the *Vanity Fair* interview. "Once it had one play it was broken. That's the kind of record it was."

One of 1980's Top-Selling Records

It fell to Robinson to find the disc jockey who would agree to play a fourteen-minute-long song that sounded like a novelty record to listeners outside of the urban music scene in New York. The process involved shipping out the twelve-inch to radio stations, then following it up with phone calls to the stations' music programmers. The first to agree was Jim Gates, a disc jockey on an AM urban radio station in St. Louis, followed by influential New York City disc jockey Frankie Crocker on WBLS-FM. Robinson had been right about the appeal of the song, for shortly afterward orders started flooding in. The New York–area vinyl factory that the Robinsons used was reportedly pressing fifty thousand copies a day of a record that had cost the Sugar Hill label just $750 to make.

"Rapper's Delight" reached number four on the Billboard R&B charts and ignited a frenzy for rap. Robinson quickly signed other artists to the Sugar Hill label and released a few more decisively influential records in the early 1980s at the Englewood studio, including "The Message" from Grandmaster Flash and the Furious Five in 1982. Unfortunately, the Robinsons' financial troubles did not end with the massive breakthrough of "Rapper's Delight." They entered into a deal with MCA Records that quickly soured and spawned a rash of lawsuits and countersuits. The couple divorced in 1989, reportedly as a business move, but stayed together until Joe Robinson's death from cancer eleven years later. The famed Englewood studio was destroyed in a 2002 fire. "I made a lot of people a lot of millions," the matriarch of the Robinson clan and of rap and hip-hop told Daly in the 2005 *Vanity Fair* article. "And

I got jerked. I didn't get nothing. I never got one cent of royalties from any of this. If you're working with your husband, he thinks you're working for him."

Selected discography

LPs

(With Mickey Baker as "Mickey and Sylvia") *Love Is Strange,* RCA Camden, 1965.
(As Sylvia) *Lay It on Me,* Vibration, 1978.

Singles

(With Mickey Baker as "Mickey and Sylvia") "Love Is Strange," Groove, 1956.
(As Sylvia) "Pillow Talk," Vibration, 1973.

Sources

Books

"Robinson, Sylvia," in Hoffmann, Frank W., and Howard Ferstler, *Encyclopedia of Recorded Sound,* Vol. 1, CRC Press, 2004, p. 935.
Watkins, S. Craig, *Hip Hop Matters: Politics, Pop Culture, and the Struggle for the Soul of a Movement,* Beacon Press, 2006, pp. 12–20.

Periodicals

New York Times, June 15, 1997, October 12, 2002.
Vanity Fair, November 1, 2005, p. 250.

—Carol Brennan

Rick Ross

1976—

Musician

Ross, Rick, photograph. AP Images.

Rapper Rick Ross put his hometown on the music map with his 2006 debut LP, *Port of Miami.* Boosted by the catchy single "Hustlin'," *Port of Miami* reached the number one spot on the Billboard 200 chart in August of 2006 and made Ross the most successful urban music artist to emerge from South Florida since 2 Live Crew. Ross's second album, *Trilla,* appeared in 2008 and his third, *Deeper Than Rap,* in 2009. Writing in the *New York Times,* Jon Caramanica called the latter "unexpectedly fantastic, by far his best. ... It's a throwback to a time of sonic and attitudinal ambition in hip-hop— the Bad Boy era of the mid- to late '90s. ... Few rap albums have sounded this assured, this sumptuous, in years."

Ross was born William Leonard Roberts II in Coahoma County, Mississippi, in 1976. His mother was from Coahoma County, but she eventually moved to the South Florida area to be nearer to Ross's father. They settled in Carol City, Florida, a relatively rough suburb of Miami. "It's a real hardcore place," Ross told *Houston Chronicle* journalist Brett Johnson. "And at the same time, you got to see some of the finer things being near Miami. That made me a big dreamer."

Ross's father left the family when Ross was around ten. In his teens, Ross grew to refrigerator-like proportions, with a six-foot, two-inch frame supporting three hundred pounds. He played football at Carol City High School and even won a football scholarship to Albany State University in Georgia, a historically black college, but dropped out. "I said to myself, 'I can't waste these people's time. I can't even do my times tables'," he recalled in the *Houston Chronicle* interview.

Ross had been writing rhymes since his teens. Returning to Miami, he immersed himself in the local music scene and began making his first mixtape recordings under the name "Teflon Don." He teamed with two old friends from the Carol City neighborhood, Elric "E-Class" Prince and Alex "Gucci Pucci" Bethune, who had started their own entertainment management company. A connection to an influential local emcee and radio personality, DJ Khaled, opened more doors, and after signing with Miami-based Slip-n-Slide Records, Ross was a featured guest on records by two local artists, Trick Daddy and Trina.

Slip-n-Slide released Ross's debut single, "Hustlin'," in March of 2006. The song caught on outside of Miami

At a Glance . . .

Born William Leonard Roberts II on January 28, 1976, in Coahoma County, MS; father of two. *Education:* Attended Albany State University, 1994(?).

Career: Corrections officer, Florida Department of Corrections, December 1995–June 1997; signed to Suave House Records; appeared on the 2002 Trina song "Told Y'All"; signed to Slip-n-Slide Records; released debut LP, *Port of Miami,* on Def Jam, 2006.

Addresses: *Home*—Davie, FL. *Office*—c/o Def Jam Group, 825 8th Ave., 28th Fl., New York, NY 10019.

as part of a wave of so-called "cocaine rap." "Hustlin'" also paid homage to the real Rick Ross, a convicted drug trafficker from the Los Angeles area known as "Freeway" Ricky Ross for the real estate he owned along Southern California's Harbor Freeway. "Although 'Hustlin'' has a bull of a beat that might have trampled a lesser personality, Ross managed to harness it, overshadow it, turn it into an instant star-making platform," wrote Will Welch in the *Fader.* The song made the top twenty on Billboard's Hot R&B/Hip Hop chart and generated buzz for the forthcoming LP. A bidding war between major labels ensued, with the Def Jam/Atlantic empire winning out. A video portraying the two distinctive sides of Miami—the glossy one known to tourists and gritty neighborhoods like Carol City—introduced Ross to a national audience. *Port of Miami* was released in early August and reached the number one spot on the Billboard 200 chart two weeks later.

"Everyday I'm huss-a-lin," Ross's catchy refrain on "Hustlin'," propelled the song to the top of another chart, too, as his debut single set a ringtone sales record of one million downloads. Ross spent much of 2007 enjoying the financial rewards that his success brought and appearing as a guest artist on singles by other musicians. His follow-up, *Trilla,* was released in February of 2008 and debuted at number one on the Billboard 200 chart. Its first single, "Speedin'," featured R. Kelly. A second single, "The Boss," recruited rapper T-Pain for a guest performance.

Ross's public image and street credibility were heavily based on a past that, he hinted, included illegal activities. There were rumors in South Florida, however, that Ross may have actually served time as a law enforcement authority instead. In the summer of 2008 a gossip Web site, the Smoking Gun, published a report that William Leonard Roberts II had indeed spent eighteen months as a prison guard with the Florida Department of Corrections. Initially he denied the charge, but the Smoking Gun then found documents linking him to a stint from 1995 and 1997 as a $25,000-a-year guard. There was even a graduation photo of the immense Ross in his guard's uniform. Finally, Ross conceded that it was indeed him, but as he told Caramanica about his past in the *New York Times* article, "the truth is more sinister than the obvious."

Ross formed his own record label, Maybach Music Group, which released this third LP, *Deeper Than Rap,* in the spring of 2009. Its first single, "Magnificent," featured John Legend, while the second, "Usual Suspects," showcased rapper Nas. In the weeks prior to the LP's release, Ross had been engaged in a particularly brutal war of words and lyrics with Queens native 50 Cent that even drew in family members of Ross and his entourage. The battle seemed to have been sparked by a disrespectful look at an awards event and escalated into special YouTube videos and hastily released tracks.

In 2009 Ross lived in the exclusive Miami suburb of Davie, where his home featured a pool deck made out of marble that could be mechanically cooled on particularly hot South Florida afternoons. The property also housed a few of his beloved luxury Maybach automobiles, made by Mercedes-Benz. On 2008's *Thrilla,* Ross sang "Some things money can't buy" on the track "Maybach Music." When *Vibe*'s Pete L'Official asked him to clarify those lyrics, he said, "You can't buy happiness. You can't buy love, you can't buy life. My father dead, I got a slew of homeys that dead and gone; I just wish I could see their expression at seeing where I'm at today.'

Selected discography

LPs

Port of Miami, Def Jam, 2006.
Trilla, Def Jam, 2008.
Deeper Than Rap, Maybach, 2009.

Singles

"Hustlin'," Slip-n-Slide, 2006.
"Push It," Def Jam, 2006.
"Speedin'" (featuring R. Kelly), Slip-n-Slide, 2007.
"The Boss" (featuring T-Pain), Slip-n-Slide, 2008.
"Magnificent" (featuring John Legend), Def Jam, 2009.
"Maybach Music 2" (featuring Kanye West, T-Pain, and Lil Wayne), Maybach Music Group, 2009.

Sources

Periodicals

Fader, July–August 2006, p. 99.
Houston Chronicle, August 10, 2006, p. 1.
Miami New Times, January 10, 2008.

New York Times, April 23, 2009.

Vibe, August 2008, p. 63.

Online

Hoard, Christian, "Rick Ross, Miami's Latest Hip-Hop Phenom," RollingStone.com, June 1, 2006, http://www.rollingstone.com/news/story/10464338/a_primer_on_rick_ross_miamis_latest_hiphop_phenom (accessed October 11, 2009).

Reid, Shaheem, "Rick Ross Reaffirms Gangster Past in New Freestyle, Despite Report That He Worked as Prison Guard," July 22, 2008, http://www.mtv.com/news/articles/1591284/20080722/ross__rick__rap_.jhtml (accessed October 11, 2009).

—Carol Brennan

David Rudder

1953—

Singer, songwriter

David Rudder is a Trinidad-born singer and songwriter in the musical traditions of calypso and soca. Both a major star in his native country and appreciated worldwide, he has won numerous awards as a singer, songwriter, arranger, and producer.

Began Singing at Age Eleven

David Michael Rudder was born on May 6, 1953, in the Belmont section of Port of Spain, the capital city of the Republic of Trinidad and To-

Rudder, David, photograph. AP Images.

bago. One of nine children, Rudder spent much of his time as a young boy with his grandmother, who lived near a pan yard (where a steel band practices) and a Shango yard (a place of worship for the Shango religion), and the melodies of steel drums and Shango chanting filled the air. The melodies and rhythms of both would influence Rudder's music later in his life.

Rudder aspired early to become an entertainer. In school he leaned toward the arts, and in 1964 at the age of eleven first began to realize his ambition by becoming a singer with a local calypso group, The Solutions. During Carnival season, Rudder also sang

backup vocals in calypso tents, venues where calypso musicians performed during the festive season before Lent. Throughout his teens he supplemented his music income by working as an accountant for the Trinidad Bus Company.

In 1977, thirteen years after joining The Solutions, Rudder was asked to substitute for the lead singer of a popular brass band called Charlie's Roots. When the singer returned to the band after recovering from an illness, the band asked Rudder to stay—an important break in Rudder's career.

As Rudder's career was on the rise in the 1970s, so was the musical form known as soca, an offshoot of calypso. Soca was described as " an updated, sped-up variety of calypso—a kind of disco calypso" by Jon Pareles in the *New York Times* in 1986. The lyrics of both soca and calypso often contain political and social commentary. As Rudder explained to Daisann Mc-Clane of the *New York Times in 1991,* "Calypso is an art form that laughs at pain. That's the way we deal with our blues. We begin to heal ourselves immediately, through our culture and our music."

Success Struck in the Mid-1980s

Although Rudder became popular as part of Charlie's Roots and made a few singles in the late 1970s and early 1980s, it was not until 1986 at the age of thirty-two that he gained widespread success. Entering the Calypso Monarch competition, he won awards with the singles "The Hammer" and "Bahia Girl." He was signed by London Records and toured England and North America. His relationship with London Records did not last long, however, and Rudder continued to record on his own label, Lypsoland.

In 1988 Joe Brown of the *Washington Post* recognized Rudder's work, saying that he "means to raise spirits with his soca." Brown noted that in Rudder's album *Haiti,* which had just been released, "Rudder cloaks his concerns for his politically and economically anguished homeland with deceptively exuberant music." Brown added that Rudder's songs "refuse to accept a troubled situation as a lost cause" and characterized Rudder as "a marvelously nimble singer."

In 1990 Rudder's album *1990* was named Album of the Year at the Caribbean Music Awards in New York,

and the title song won Song of the Year at the Nefeita Awards. During the rest of that decade and into the next, Rudder's music won many awards in the Caribbean, most notably numerous Caribbean Sunshine Awards, and he became one of the most successful performers in the history of Trinidad. However, international renown remained elusive. Rudder explained to Campbell "There is a form of calypso that can do that (break into major markets), but it's never going to be easy. Calypso is a personal Caribbean music where people sing about our politics and what's going on in our societies. It can go beyond Caribbean boundaries but don't look for it on the Billboard charts." Dermot Hussey, a Jamaican musicologist acquaintance of Rudder's, expressed his view that Rudder could become popular beyond the Caribbean and told Campbell: "He would have to make adjustments for the American market but he has the writing skills to make adjustments. I don't think he wants to be a pop star, but he is definitely the one to take calypso further."

Became Trinidad's Biggest International Music Star

Jim Beckerman, writing for the Bergen County New Jersey *Record,* expressed the view that Rudder had taken calypso further already and "broke through to international fame with his 1986 album *The Hammer.*" Covering Rudder's performance at Prudential Hall in the New Jersey Performing Arts Center in December of 2000, Beckerman referred to Rudder as "Trinidad's biggest international music star who has sometimes been compared to Paul Simon or Springsteen for his topical, socially conscious music." At the New Jersey venue, Rudder was still performing with Charlie's Roots, but the group had become a twelve-piece band and Rudder was at the helm.

In May of 2001 Rudder married, and in 2002 he and his wife Christine moved to her hometown of Toronto, Canada. By 2004 Rudder was not only performing internationally, but he was also gracing the covers of magazines all over the world. One of his albums had even been translated into Japanese. At his home base in Toronto, he enjoyed living in the relative anonymity that is impossible when he is in Trinidad. At the same time, Rudder told Nicholas Davis of the *Toronto Sun,* "I can't see myself shoveling snow when I'm old and grey. Trinidad is my heart and soul, and I feel I will go back to Trinidad to live one day. But right now I'm happy, my children are thriving and my music has taken on another perspective." Rudder explained: "It's nice to see how my "Canadian" neighbors react to my music. I used to wonder if they would get it, but now I realize how universal music is."

Selected discography

Albums

This Is Soca, Vol. 1, Sire, 1987.
Haiti, Sire, 1988.

Here Comes the West, Lypsoland, 1988.
Ministry of Rhythm, Lypsoland, 1988.
New Day Dawning, Lypsoland, 1988.
1990, Sire, 1990.
Frenzy, 1992.
Tales from a Strange Land, Alex, 1996.
Lyrics Man, Lypsoland, 1996.
No Restriction: The Concert [live], Lypsoland, 1997.
Beloved, JWP, 1998.
International Chantuelle, JWP, 1999.
Zero, Lypsoland, 2000.
The Autobiography of the Now, JWP, 2001.

Sources

Periodicals

Jouvert: A Journal of Postcolonial Studies, Spring 2002.
New York Times, May 26, 1986; September 13, 1987; March 31, 1991, Section 2, p. 22.

Record (Kitchener-Waterloo, Ontario), July 14, 2004, p. C4.
Record (Bergen County, NJ), December 15, 2000, p. 14.
Toronto Sun, July 18, 2005, p. 26.
Washington Post, August 26, 1988, p. N21.

Online

"David Rudder: Biography," Caribbean Hall of Fame, http://caribbean.halloffame.tripod.com/David_Rudder.html (accessed November 21, 2009).
Funk, Ray, "David Rudder," National Geographic Music, http://worldmusic.nationalgeographic.com/view/page.basic/artist/content.artist/david_rudder/en_US#contents_top (accessed November 22, 2009).
Trotz, Maya, "Interview with Trinidadian David Rudder," Jouvay.com, January 2, 2004, http://jouvay.com/interviews/davidrudder.html (accessed November 21, 2009).

—Sandra Alters

Leah Ward Sears

1955—

Attorney

Leah Ward Sears was the first woman justice to serve on the Supreme Court of Georgia, and she later became the first African-American woman to serve as chief justice of any state supreme court. At the time of her initial appointment by Governor Zell Miller, which came when she was just thirty-six years old, she was also one of the youngest high court jurists in the nation. In a seventeen-year career on the supreme court, Sears authored important decisions and guided the court on issues ranging from capital punishment and mandatory life sentences to Georgia's controversial sodomy laws.

Sears, Leah Ward, photograph. AP Images.

Sears retired from the Georgia Supreme Court in June 2009, at the age of fifty-four. She was rumored to be on President Barack Obama's short list to replace Justice David Souter on the U.S. Supreme Court, as well as on the short list to serve as dean of the University of Maryland Law School. However, Sears elected to return to private practice as a partner with the law firm Schiff Hardin LLP, while also pursuing scholarship in the area of family law.

Wanted to Be a Judge from an Early Age

Sears was born June 13, 1955, in Heidelberg, Germany. Her father was a U.S. Army colonel whose work took the family all over the world; she had circled the globe twice before she turned sixteen. Throughout her academic career, Sears strove to do well in her schoolwork. Both of her parents stressed the importance of education, but the youngster seemed highly self-motivated as well. "She was a very studious child," Sears's mother told the *Atlanta Constitution*. "Many nights I'd go into her room and find her asleep and take the glasses off her face and the book off her chest. I used to have to insist she go outside and play sometimes."

As a child, Sears had a burning ambition: she wanted to be a judge. When she was only eight years old, she began ordering law school catalogues from prestigious institutions like Yale and Harvard universities. Paging through them, Sears wondered why all of the law students pictured in the catalogues were white men. Even then, she knew she would have to overcome the

At a Glance . . .

Born June 13, 1955, in Heidelberg, Germany; daughter of Thomas J. (a U.S. army officer) and Onnye Jean (Rountree) Sears; married Love Collins III (a business executive), July 3, 1976 (divorced, 1995); married Haskell Ward (a business executive), 1999; children: Addison, Brennan. *Politics:* Democrat. *Education:* Cornell University, BS (with honors), 1976; Emory University, JD, 1980; University of Virginia School of Law, LLM, 1995.

Career: Columbus (Georgia) *Ledger,* reporter, 1976–77; Alston & Bird Attorneys at Law, Atlanta, GA, lawyer, 1980–85; City Court of Atlanta, traffic court judge, 1985–88; Fulton Superior Court, Atlanta, judge, 1988–92; Supreme Court of Georgia, justice, 1992–2005, chief justice, 2005–09; Schiff Hardin LLP, partner, 2009—; Institute for American Values, fellow, 2009—; University of Georgia School of Law, visiting professor, 2009—.

Memberships: Alpha Kappa Alpha Sorority; American Bar Association; Atlanta Bar Association; National Association of Women Judges; Georgia Association of Black Women Attorneys (founding president); National Association of Alcoholism and Drug Abuse Counselors; Georgia Chapter of Links, Inc.

Awards: American Bar Association, Margaret Brent Women Lawyers of Achievement Award, 1992; *Georgia Trend,* 100 Most Influential People in Georgia, 1992, 2004–08; Morehouse College Honorary Doctor of Laws, 1993; Georgia Commission of Women, Georgia Woman of the Year, 1999; Emory University, Emory Medal for Outstanding Young Alumna, 2001; National Bar Association, Legal Trailblazers Award, 2007; Emory University, Rosalyn Carter Fellow in Public Policy, 2007–09.

Addresses: *Office*—Schiff Hardin LLP, One Atlantic Center, Suite 2300, 1201 West Peachtree Street, Atlanta, GA 30309.

era. Both of her brothers graduated from the U.S. Naval Academy, became pilots, and earned law degrees.

Sears feels that she benefited from the rootless upbringing she experienced as a military officer's child. "When you grow up around people of all different nationalities, you learn to feel at ease with people of every kind," she said in the *Atlanta Constitution.* "You really have to learn to live, work and play with people who aren't like yourself."

When Sears was in her teens, her family settled in Savannah, Georgia. She attended Savannah High School, where she was the first black student to make the cheerleading squad. The justice remembered that she tried out for cheerleading because she saw the color barrier as a challenge and wanted to be the first to break it. After high school Sears entered the Ivy League as a student at Cornell University. She graduated from Cornell in 1976 with honors and was accepted to law school at Atlanta's Emory University.

"Leah has always recognized that the civil rights movement opened doors that we, as the next generation, can charge through," Sears's first husband, Love Collins III, told the *Atlanta Constitution.* "Doing that, she has often been first." Sears earned her law degree in 1980 and took a position with the Atlanta law firm of Alston & Bird. For five years she worked there as a trial lawyer. Then, at the tender age of thirty, she achieved the dream she had held since childhood. She became a judge.

Rose through the Judicial Ranks

Her first judicial appointment was to the Atlanta Traffic Court, a position that might seem tedious and far removed from the high-stake cases of a state supreme court. But her days in traffic court gave her considerable experience in courtroom administration. She then moved on, in 1988, to Fulton County Superior Court. At thirty-two, she was the first black woman and the youngest person ever elected to a superior court seat in the state of Georgia. There, Sears established herself as "a magistrate of special distinction," according to an unsigned editorial in the *Atlanta Constitution.* The editorial went on to note that lawyers who pleaded cases before Sears praised "her preparation, her grasp of the law and her practical sense of how to apply it." Sears often worked ten-hour days and right through the weekend to keep abreast of the cases before the court.

One of the highly publicized cases Sears decided for the Fulton County Superior Court concerned the removal of life support for a terminally ill child. When the child's parents objected to the proposed termination of the support system on religious grounds, the judge—in a well balanced and skillfully written decision—denied the Scottish Rite Hospital the right to withhold life support.

Early in 1992, Governor Zell Miller began interviewing candidates for a position on the Georgia Supreme

hurdles of gender and color in order to achieve her goals. Times changed as Sears grew up, and she and her siblings were afforded educational opportunities that might well have been denied them in a previous

Court. Several women were called to interview for the position, as were a few men, and Sears was among them. She was thirty-six at the time and felt that her chances of winning the seat were slim. Still, she made a convincing argument that diversity on the high court bench should include age as a criterion. She also could point to her service as a judge on two quite different Georgia courts. "Many people thought I was appointed by Governor Miller only because I'm black or a woman," she told the *Atlanta Constitution*. "But Robert Benham (the first African American to serve on the Georgia Supreme Court) was already on the court and there were four other women that the governor could have chosen. I think the high ratings I am getting from my peers tells me I have overcome that hurdle."

Won Statewide Election to Remain on Supreme Court

In order to retain her seat, Sears had to win a July election against a popular challenger, Clayton County Superior Court judge Stephen Boswell. At that time, no woman had won a contested statewide election in Georgia's history. Sears crossed the state to win voters and was a lightning rod everywhere she went. Speaking to *Emory Magazine*, Sears recalled the introduction she was given by a friendly attorney before speaking to a South Georgia Rotary Club chapter on the campaign trail: "Look, y'all, this is the governor's choice. I know y'all may not like it, but things are changing, and if we don't vote for her, there's gonna be somebody else after her. So you're just gonna have to suck it up and take it."

Despite such chilly receptions, Sears continued to campaign, and slowly won people over. *Atlanta Journal* columnist Jim Wooten's endorsement was much more heartfelt. Wooten called her a "refreshing change" and "wonderfully different," a high court judge who is "not afraid to lead." On July 23, 1992, Sears won the close race to retain her position. Almost immediately thereafter, *Ebony* magazine named her one of the fifty black women of highest achievement in the nation.

Despite being half the age of many of her colleagues on the supreme court, Sears quickly earned their respect through her intelligence and hard work. "I've worked my butt off," she told the *Atlanta Constitution*. "I come in at 7 or 7:30 every morning, and I work late whenever I have to. I don't shy from the difficult cases; those are the ones I love."

There were plenty of difficult cases for Sears in her first two terms in the supreme court. In 1996 Sears dissented in the case of *Greene v. State*, arguing that it was improper for a judge to exclude jurors in a capital murder case because they had reservations about the death penalty. The U.S. Supreme Court later agreed with Sears and reversed the majority opinion. In 1998

she was in the majority in the case of *Powell v. State*, which struck down Georgia's controversial statute criminalizing sodomy. In her concurring opinion to *Powell*, Sears wrote, "To allow the moral indignation of a majority (or, even worse, a loud and/or radical minority) to justify criminalizing private consensual conduct would be a strike against freedoms paid for and preserved by our forefathers."

Sears long opposed Georgia's use of the electric chair for executions, despite not objecting to capital punishment itself. As she explained in her 1999 dissent in the case of *Wilson v. State*, it was her belief that the electric chair violated the Eighth Amendment's protection against "cruel and unusual" punishment, noting that "both the American Veterinarian Medical Association and the Humane Society of the United States prohibit electrocution as a means of euthanatizing animals." The Georgia Supreme Court eventually came around to her point of view in the 2001 case of *Dawson v. State*, which outlawed the electric chair as a means of executing prisoners.

Became First Black Female Chief Justice

Sears's views on the death penalty—supporting its existence, but insisting that it be applied fairly and humanely—were consistent with her political inclinations, which she repeatedly described as "moderate, with a progressive streak." However, to Georgia's Republicans, Sears remained a lightning rod, someone who, according to *Athens Banner-Herald* columnist Bill Shipp, conservatives referred to as simply "that activist judge." When Republican Sonny Perdue became governor in 2003, he specifically targeted Sears, who was up for re-election the following year.

Sears's opponent, former Superior Court Judge Grant Brantley, would have an advantage Sears's previous opponents had lacked. In Sears's successful 1998 re-election campaign, her opponent George Weaver had been cited by Georgia's Judicial Qualifications Commission (JQC) for running false and misleading negative ads against her. Until that time, Georgia's rules for judicial elections basically forbade candidates from disparaging or distorting each other's judicial records. Weaver later challenged the JQC's ruling in federal court and won. In Sears's 2004 re-election campaign, the rules of civility that had for decades governed Georgia's judicial elections would be out the window.

Despite the governor campaigning against her and Brantley's attacks under the new rules, Sears won re-election handily, with more than 62 percent of the statewide vote. The victory was particularly momentous for Sears because by 2004, even though she was still the court's youngest member, she had risen in seniority to become next in line to serve as the court's chief justice when Chief Justice Norman Fletcher's term expired in 2005. She would be the first African-American woman to serve as the chief justice of any high court in the United States.

Sears's induction as Chief Justice took place on June 28, 2005. The event was marked by controversy, as some of the state's top African-American leaders refused to attend when they learned that conservative U.S. Supreme Court Justice Clarence Thomas would be at the swearing-in ceremony. Thomas, a personal friend of Sears's since the early 1990s, was a pariah to Georgia's civil rights community, who felt that he had failed to protect African-American interests as Thurgood Marshall's successor to the country's highest court. Sears defended her friendship with Thomas, a fellow Georgian who grew up a near Sears's childhood home in Savannah, telling NPR's Ed Gordon, "We need ... to raise civil discourse to another level. ... [Y]ou can disagree very much with the next guy and still be friends and acquaintances."

As chief justice, she would be administratively responsible for the entire judiciary of the state of Georgia. She would also be in position to lead such efforts as the supreme court's Committee on Civil Justice—a group dedicated to ensuring access to legal services for all Georgians—and her own initiative, the Commission on Children, Marriage, and Family Law, a commission dedicated, in large part, to decreasing Georgia's divorce rate. During her tenure as chief justice, the Georgia Supreme Court was ranked the most productive high court in the nation by a University of Chicago Law School study.

Perhaps the best-known decision during her tenure as Chief Justice came in the Genarlow Wilson case. Wilson was an honors student and top high school athlete who was convicted of receiving oral sex from a willing fifteen-year-old when he was seventeen. Due to an oddity of Georgia law, intercourse between teenagers was a misdemeanor punishable by a maximum of one year in jail, while oral sex was a felony—called aggravated child molestation—with a mandatory ten-year sentence and lifetime registration as a sex offender.

The case generated international attention. Georgia's legislature re-wrote the statute to make oral sex between teens who were close in age a misdemeanor, but they refused to apply the change in the law retroactively to Wilson. Finally, on Wilson's third attempt to get the case before the Georgia Supreme Court, he was freed from prison. Writing for the majority, Sears found that the rewriting the statute represented a "seismic shift in the legislature's view of the gravity of oral sex between two willing teenage participants" sufficient to make Wilson's sentence under the old law unconstitutional cruel and unusual punishment.

Considered for U.S. Supreme Court

In October 2008 Sears decided that she would retire from the Georgia Supreme Court at the end of her term as chief justice in June 2009, rather than remain on the court and run for re-election in 2010. The move was unpopular in Democratic circles, because it would allow her nemesis, Governor Perdue, to appoint an interim replacement. But for Sears, it was simply time to move on. "I'm interested in exploring another chapter in my life," Sears told Bill Rankin of the *Atlanta Journal-Constitution.* "I want to see whatever else is out there."

One option that seemed to be out there was a nomination to the U.S. Supreme Court. Even before Justice David Souter announced his retirement in May 2009, Sears was rumored to be on President Obama's list of candidates for a spot on the Supreme Court should one become available. Sears was frequently mentioned as a candidate alongside such luminaries as solicitor general Elena Kagan, Michigan governor Jennifer Granholm, Homeland Security secretary Janet Napolitano, and federal appellate judges Diane Wood, Merrick Garland, and Sonia Sotomayor, who was ultimately selected to replace Souter.

Sears had also indicated that she was open to becoming a college dean or president. In January of 2009 the University of Maryland named her as one of five finalists to be dean of its law school, but a month later, Sears withdrew her name from consideration for that position.

At the time she left the bench, Sears had made two choices for her next adventure. The first was a partner position with the law firm of Schiff Hardin LLP. A national law firm with offices in Atlanta, Schiff Hardin announced that it would put Sears's skills to use in "high stakes" litigation and appellate practice. The firm also agreed to allow Sears to work part time in her first year with the practice so that she could pursue another post-judicial opportunity—teaching and studying matrimony and family law and policy as a fellow with the Institute for American Values (IAV) and lecturer at the University of Georgia School of Law.

Sears's choice to join the IAV, a think tank dedicated to "strengthening families and civil society" through research and scholarship, followed from her deep interest in combating high rates of divorce and fatherlessness in America. Sears's experiences as a judge, along with her own divorce and experiences as a single mother in the late 1990s, left an indelible impression on the jurist regarding the importance of marriage to America's social fabric. That view took on added urgency for Sears in November of 2007 when her brother Tommy, who was in the midst of a contentious divorce, took his own life. Indeed, Sears's position with the IAV was named the "William Thomas Sears Distinguished Fellow in Family Law," in honor of her brother. As Sears wrote at CNN.com shortly after her retirement from the Georgia Supreme Court, when dealing with the problems of "disposable" marriages, "answers must be found. The coupling and uncoupling we've become accustomed to undermines our democracy, destroys our families and devastates the lives of our children, who are not as resilient as we may wish to think. The one-parent norm, which is necessary and successful in many cases, nevertheless often creates a host of other problems, from poverty to crime, teen pregnancy and drug abuse."

Sources

Periodicals

Atlanta Constitution, February 18, 1992, pp. A1, D1, D4; February 24, 1992, p. A12; March 6, 1992, p. A1; July 6, 1992, p. C3; July 22, 1992, p. C3.

Atlanta Journal, July 8, 1992, p. A10.

Atlanta Journal-Constitution, October 28, 2008.

Athens Banner-Herald, May 9, 2004; February 13, 2009.

Ebony, October 1992, p. 118.

Emerge, June 1992, p. 18.

Emory Magazine, Summer 2006.

Georgia Trend, June 2005.

Jet, March 9, 1992, p. 24.

New York Times, May 22, 2009, p. A12.

Washington Post, May 10, 2009.

Working Woman, November 1992, p. 20.

Online

"Commentary: Let's End Disposable Marriage," *CNN.com,* July 2, 2009, http://www.cnn.com/2009/LIVING/07/02/sears.family.divorce/index.html (accessed November 22, 2009).

"Georgia High Court Chief Justice Leah Ward Sears," *National Public Radio,* August 2, 2005, http://www.npr.org/templates/story/story.php?storyId=4781681 (accessed November 22, 2009).

"Leah Ward Sears," *Schiff Hardin LLP,* http://www.schiffhardin.com/LeahWardSears.htm (accessed November 22, 2009).

—Anne Janette Johnson
and Derek Jacques

Columbus Short

1982—

Actor, dancer, choreographer

Short, Columbus, photograph. Jesse Grant/WireImage.

American actor, dancer, and choreographer Columbus Short has appeared in a Broadway show, choreographed a national concert tour, and acted with Oscar winners—all before the age of thirty. With no formal training in theater or dance, Short broke into show business while a teenager as part of the national tour of the hit Broadway show *Stomp,* and before long, he was dancing and then choreographing for pop singer Britney Spears. Buoyed by this early success, Short made the jump to film, appearing in a trio of dance-related films: *You Got Served, Save the Last Dance 2,* and *Stomp the Yard.* But Short was not content to be pigeonholed as only a dancer. As he has accumulated more film roles, he has demonstrated that he can take on dramatic and even comedy roles as well. Short is among Hollywood's hottest young stars.

Short was born on September 19, 1982, in Kansas City, Missouri, the oldest of three sons of Columbus Keith Short Sr. and his wife Janette. The younger Columbus began entertaining as early as age three, when he would perform for his family, dancing and doing impressions, and learned to play the drums and keyboard. At age five, Short's family relocated to Los

Angeles—a fortuitous move for the budding performer—and he soon began acting in youth theater. By his early teens, he was appearing in commercials for products such as Mountain Dew, Denny's, Nike, and Pizza Hut, and he landed his first leading role in a junior high school production of *Bus Stop* by William Inge. The experience convinced Short that he wanted to pursue acting as a career.

Short attended Orange County High School of the Arts in Santa Ana, California, and continued to go on auditions. In his senior year, he was graduated two months early in order to join the cast of the Broadway show *Stomp,* a rhythmic stage performance that combines percussion and dance using found objects such as brooms, trash cans, drumsticks, and even bananas. Although he had no formal training in dance, the rhythm and movements came naturally to Short, thanks to his experience playing music: "Because I was a musician, I understood the language," he told the *Washington Post* in 2007. After touring with *Stomp* for two years, Short returned to Los Angeles but found little theatrical work. Instead, he threw himself into dancing, aiming to make up for his lack of training. He "went headfirst into dance lessons. I mean three classes

At a Glance . . .

Born Columbus Keith Short Jr. on September 19, 1982, in Kansas City, MO; son of Columbus Keith Short Sr. and Janette Short. Married Brandi (divorced); children: one son.

Career: *Stomp,* national touring production, 1999–2001; dancer, choreographer, and creative director for Britney Spears, 2002–04; film and television actor, 2004—.

Awards: NAACP Image Award for Outstanding Supporting Actor in a Motion Picture, 2009, for *Cadillac Records;* Young Hollywood Award for Action Star, 2009.

Addresses: *Agent*—Osbrink Agency, 4343 Lankershim Blvd., Ste. 100, North Hollywood, CA 91602-2705. *Management*—Brillstein-Grey Entertainment, 9150 Wilshire Blvd., Suite 350, Beverly Hills, CA 90212-3453.

a day, seven days a week. Any kind of classes going on, I was there," he explained to the *Washington Post.*

All of that hard work paid off, and in 2002 Short was hired as a backup dancer for pop singer Spears. The next year he became her choreographer, and in 2004 Spears enlisted him as the creative director for her "Onyx Hotel" concert tour. During this time, he got his first taste of celebrity scandal when photos of Short and Spears kissing appeared in the tabloids, linking them romantically. Although the two denied the rumors—unconvincingly, to many fans—the affair earned Spears the label "home wrecker," as Short had a young wife at home who was then eight months pregnant. His marriage ended shortly in divorce, and he was fired from the tour. For Short, the tabloid treatment was a valuable lesson in the pitfalls of stardom: "Getting chased around by cameras and paparazzi is not fun at all. I really saw that. I saw the glitz and glamour that to other people might look like it's fun, and it's cool, and it's all that, but it's really hellish," he told the *Washington Post.*

After Short left the Spears tour, he decided to refocus his career on acting. He made his big-screen debut in 2004, playing a dancer in the movie *You Got Served* opposite Marques Houston and Omarion Grandberry. The following year, he had a minor role in the Tom Cruise film *War of the Worlds,* and then appeared in *Accepted* and *Save the Last Dance 2,* both released in

2006. On television, Short made two guest appearances on Disney's *That's So Raven* (2005–06), and played writer Darius Hawthorne on the short-lived NBC series *Studio 60 on the Sunset Strip* (2006–07).

In 2007 Short used his connections in the dance world to land a breakout role in the motion picture *Stomp the Yard,* directed by Sylvain White. The choreographer for the film, Dave Scott, had trained Short a few years earlier, and he put in a call to the head of Sony Pictures to recommend the young actor and dancer. Short was cast in the lead role of DJ Williams, a street dancer from inner-city Los Angeles who leaves the ghetto behind and heads to college at a historically black university, where he pledges a fraternity and joins its stepping team. The plot of *Stomp the Yard* centers on a series of step competitions between two rival fraternities on campus, providing an opportunity for Short to showcase his dance skills.

Stepping, a form of percussive dance that combines clapping, marching, and chanting, is a tradition among African-American fraternities and sororities. Although Short had seen stepping before at African-American celebrations, during the film he came to "understand the rhythmic language of stepping... . Dancing is the visual personification of music, but stepping is the rhythmic personification of music and dance," he explained to the *Washington Post.* Critics gave the film tepid reviews, praising the dance sequences but noting the weak and clichéd plot. Audiences, however, were more receptive: The film grossed $22 million on its opening weekend, and went on to earn $75 million worldwide.

With three dance-themed movies under his belt, Short feared being typecast as a dancer, so he began to seek out more dramatic roles that would draw attention to his acting abilities. "All I want to do is focus on doing quality work and solidifying myself as a credible actor and not just that kid who was in dance movies," he told Julie Bloom of *Interview* magazine in 2007. That year Short appeared in the family drama *This Christmas,* and in 2008 he had roles in the thriller *Quarantine* and the musical biopic *Cadillac Records.* In the latter film, Short portrayed blues musician Little Walter, learning to play the harmonica and speak in a Cajun dialect from coach Laurence Fishburne. The film, which costarred Oscar winner Adrien Brody and Beyoncé, was named one of the top-ten films of 2008 by the *New York Times* film critic A. O. Scott. Short won an NAACP Image Award in 2009 for his performance.

In 2009 Short had major roles in the motion pictures *Whiteout,* with Kate Beckinsale, and *Armored,* with Matt Dillon and Fishburne. In films scheduled for release in 2010, he was slated to appear in the American remake of *Death at a Funeral,* an ensemble comedy cowritten by Chris Rock and directed by Neil LaBute, and *The Losers,* based on the graphic novel by Andy Diggle and directed, once again, by White.

Selected works

Films

You Got Served, Screen Gems, 2004.
War of the Worlds, Paramount Pictures, 2005.
Accepted, Universal Pictures, 2006.
Save the Last Dance 2, Paramount Home Entertainment/MTV, 2006.
Stomp the Yard, Rainforest Films, 2007.
This Christmas, Facilitator Films, 2007.
Quarantine, Andale Pictures, 2008.
Cadillac Records, Parkwood Pictures, 2008.
Whiteout, Warner Bros., 2009.
Armored, Buckaroo Entertainment, 2009.

Television

Studio 60 on the Sunset Strip, NBC, 2006–07.

Sources

Periodicals

Interview, February 2007, p. 68.
New York Times, December 5, 2008; December 18, 2008.
Washington Post, January 12, 2007.

Online

Nichole, Arlice, "Columbus Short: Renaissance Man," Clutch, March 1, 2009, http://clutchmagonline.com/lifeculture/feature/columbus-short-renaissance-man/#2 (accessed September 30, 2009).
Williams, Kam, Interview with Columbus Short, NewsBlaze, September 18, 2007, http://newsblaze.com/story/20070918101509tsop.nb/topstory.html (accessed September 30, 2009).

—Deborah A. Ring

E. Denise Simmons

19(?)—

Politician

E. Denise Simmons is the first openly gay black woman to serve as mayor of a U.S. city. Simmons was chosen by her colleagues on the City Council of Cambridge, Massachusetts, in January of 2008 to lead the famous city, home to both Harvard University and the Massachusetts Institute of Technology. "I am serving as a woman, as a lesbian, as a parent, as a business woman," she told Alison Lapp in *Passport* magazine. "I remember being a young mother applying for housing, and watching the owner walk by me when he realized who I was. I've been through all that, and I know what it was like."

Simmons is a native of Cambridge, a 6.5-square-mile city with a population of 101,000. She attended its public schools and graduated from the University of Massachusetts in Boston with a degree in sociology. From there, she went on to Antioch College in Ohio, which granted her a master's degree in psychotherapy. Although she has never been a practicing therapist, she has said that the training was invaluable for a future public servant.

In 1980 Simmons was hired by the Cambridge Civic Unity Committee, a city-funded citizens' rights group. She spent the next dozen years with the organization, including ten of them as executive director. Her work with the Civic Unity Committee was not a full-time job, and around this same time she opened an insurance agency with a business partner.

Cambridge is one of the oldest cities in North America. Founded by Puritan colonists in the early 1630s, it was incorporated in 1636, the same year that Harvard College opened its doors. Citizens elect their municipal leadership by a complex system known as single-transferable vote, or STV, which is unusual in the United States but seen more often in British Commonwealth nations. The nine members of the City Council and six who serve on the school board, which is known as the School Committee, are elected to their jobs every two years via the STV method.

Simmons was first elected to the School Committee in 1991 and served on it for the next decade. In 2001 she ran for and won a seat on the City Council. The Council, in turn, elects a mayor from among their nine members. The Council also hires a city manager, who wields much of the power in Cambridge.

Simmons was elected mayor by unanimous vote of her fellow council members on January 14, 2008. She was thrilled, she told Matt Dunning, a journalist whose work appears on the Web site Wicked Local: Cambridge. "It feels really great. When I first came to the School Committee, one of the things I always said was that I wanted to be mayor." She was neither the first black nor first openly gay person to serve as Cambridge's mayor—both of those firsts went to her predecessor, attorney Kenneth Reeves, who served from 1992 to 1995 and again from 2006 to 2008.

Simmons began her term with plans to usher in a new era for Cambridge. She made her inauguration a public event, which was a first, and announced that she would hold open office hours on Friday mornings for citizens

At a Glance . . .

Born in Cambridge, MA; married Mattie B. Hayes, August 2009; children: Jada, Nadine, Atieno. *Education:* Earned BS from the University of Massachusetts; master's degree in psychotherapy from Antioch College.

Career: Cambridgeport Insurance Agency, co-founder, 1982; Cambridge Civic Unity Committee, 1980–82, executive director, 1982–92; elected to the Cambridge School Committee, 1991, 1993, 1995, 1997, 1999; elected to the Cambridge City Council, 2001, 2003, 2005, 2007; elected mayor of Cambridge by the Cambridge City Council January 14, 2008.

Memberships: Massachusetts Municipal Association; Massachusetts Democratic State Committee; Baystate Stonewall Democrats.

Addresses: *Office*—Cambridge City Hall, 795 Massachusetts Ave., Cambridge, MA 02139.

to meet with her and voice their concerns. One of her goals was to improve Cambridge's underperforming public schools, which have a higher percentage of minorities than the city as a whole because many white residents with high incomes send their children to private schools. Simmons also sought to develop green jobs and more affordable housing in the city.

Cambridge and its police force came under national scrutiny in the second year of Simmons's two-year term when one of its most prominent citizens was arrested. In July of 2009, Harvard professor Henry Louis Gates Jr., who is widely considered America's foremost scholar on African-American issues, was returning from a trip and was unable to unlock the front door of his house, which had jammed. A neighbor, not recognizing him, called the police, the encounter between Gates and the police officer became heated, and Gates was arrested for disorderly conduct. Although the Middlesex County prosecutor dropped the charges five days later, the incident prompted a national debate on racial profiling. By the end of the following week, Gates and the Cambridge police officer had been invited to the White House by President Barack Obama to for an informal conversation on the matter, in a meeting that came to be known as the "Beer Summit."

Simmons appeared at a press conference two days before that White House meeting, alongside Robert Healy, the city manager. Both assured residents that the city government was handling the matter respon-

sibly, noting that the police commissioner was forming a panel to issue recommendations for officers. "One thing that I love about the city of Cambridge is that we've never been afraid to look at the hard issues," she told Wendy L. Wilson in *Essence,* noting that her administration had already held a town meeting on race a few months before the Gates arrest. "We always want to strive to be the best that we can be as individuals so that we can have an even better city. Cambridge is going to be America's classroom. Those looking from outside in will see how we'll handle this. We can discuss these delicate matters respectfully, calmly and productively."

Raised a Roman Catholic, Simmons attends church services throughout Cambridge in order to meet her constituents. A mother of four, she is raising three of her grandchildren. In August of 2009 she married her longtime partner, Mattie B. Hayes, at St. Bartholomew's Episcopal Church. Massachusetts became the first U.S. state to grant marriage licenses to same-sex couples in 2004.

Simmons once told a reporter from the *Crimson,* the student newspaper of Harvard, that she was pleased that her career had taken her to the mayor's office of one of the oldest communities in the United States. "I think there's no better calling than public service," she told *Crimson* writer Hyung W. Kim, saying that in her college years she had considered a more business-oriented career path. "But I chose public service because it gave me a direct opportunity to have direct impact. This may sound silly, but I take pleasure in seeing that the streets are well paved, that we're educating our kids—those things you don't get on Wall Street."

Sources

Periodicals

Harvard Crimson, October 29, 2008.
Passport, November 2008.

Online

Dunning, Matt, "Simmons Is New Mayor of Cambridge," Wicked Local: Cambridge, January 14, 2008, http://www.wickedlocal.com/cambridge/homepage/x1925662189 (accessed September 20, 2009).

Fennimore, Jillian, "Cambridge Mayor Marries Longtime Partner," Wicked Local: Cambridge, August 31, 2009, http://www.blogcatalog.com/search.frame.php?term=denise+simmons&id=bc60819b9e6a2ca51dfd68f1c957c25e (accessed September 21, 2009).

Wilson, Wendy L., "Cambridge Mayor E. Denise Simmons Uses Her City to Teach America a Lesson on

Race," Essence.com, July 29, 2009, http://www.
essence.com/news_entertainment/news/articles/
mayor_e_denise_simmons_cambridge_ma/
(accessed September 20, 2009).

—Carol Brennan

Naomi Sims

1948–2009

Fashion model, entrepreneur

Sims, Naomi, photograph. Yale Joel/Time & Life Pictures/Getty Images.

Naomi Sims began her career as the first black supermodel and went on to become one of the top African-American businesswomen in the United States. According to *Essence* magazine, "Never had a model so dark-skinned received so much exposure, praise, and professional prestige." After just five years, however, Sims decided to give up modeling to start her own wig business. Sims continued to expand her business interests in the 1980s, launching her own perfume and a line of high-end cosmetics. As founder and CEO of the Naomi Sims Collection, she oversaw a multimillion-dollar range of wigs, skin care products, and cosmetics specifically designed for black women.

Struggled to Begin Modeling Career

Naomi Sims was born on March 30, 1948, in Oxford, Mississippi. Her parents divorced shortly thereafter, and the family moved to Pittsburgh. When her mother became ill, Sims was placed in foster care but remained close to her two older sisters. After graduating from Westinghouse High School, Sims moved to New York to live with her sister Betty, a flight attendant who later also became a model. Sims had won a small scholarship to the Fashion Institute of Technology, where she studied merchandising and textile design. At the same time, she earned another small scholarship to study psychology at New York University, where she took classes in the evening. Despite the scholarships and her sister's help, Sims soon realized that she needed a job, and a counselor at the Fashion Institute suggested that she try modeling.

At 5'10" tall, with dark skin, Sims had not been considered particularly attractive as a teenager. "Black *wasn't* beautiful then," she said in *Black Enterprise*. "The darker your skin, the less good-looking you were considered; and I was too tall, and too skinny." In the wake of the civil rights movement and the Black Power movement, however, the idea that only light-skinned women were attractive was ready to be challenged.

Still, when Sims approached modeling agencies in New York, she was told outright that there was no work for African-American models. Alternatively, Sims told *Mademoiselle* that the agencies made "very insipid excuses—'too many of my type'—and there were no other black women and certainly not anybody of *my* type!"

Undeterred, Sims tried a different approach. She contacted a well-known fashion photographer, persuading him to meet with her; to her surprise, he agreed. Immediately spotting Sims's potential, the photographer sent her to meet his wife, a fashion editor at the *New York Times.* In 1967, after her first modeling session, Sims found herself on the cover of the *New York Times Magazine.*

It was a huge break, but when Sims returned to the modeling agencies, she found that nothing had changed; they still insisted there was no work for black models. Finally, she approached former top model Wilhelmina Cooper, who was starting her own agency. A born businesswoman, Sims made Cooper an offer she could not refuse: Sims would mail out copies of the *Times* layout to 100 different advertising agencies, along with Cooper's telephone number. If anyone was interested, Cooper had just earned a modeling commission; if not, she had wasted neither time nor energy on the project. To Cooper's amazement, the response to the mailing was immediate and overwhelming, and a few days later, Sims was officially on her books.

Became First Black Supermodel

After that brief period of discouragement, Sims saw her modeling career take off at blinding speed. Within a week of joining Wilhelmina Cooper, she was hired for a national television commercial for AT&T. Later that year she appeared on the cover of *Life* magazine, which ran an article about new black models. She also appeared on the cover of *Ladies' Home Journal* in 1968 and became the icon for the "Black Is Beautiful" movement. In 1969 and 1970, Sims was voted top model of the year by International Mannequins.

Just two years after beginning her modeling career, Sims had appeared in virtually every fashion magazine in the world. Her success was setting the stage for the emergence of other African-American models and supermodels in the 1970s. Audrey Smaltz, fashion editor at *Ebony* magazine and a friend of Sims, told CNN on her death, "They had so many fabulous black models in the '70s. It was our heyday, and Naomi made that way for the rest of the girls to come along."

While Sims's skin color was newsworthy, her walk received just as much attention. According to the *Kansas City Star,* "Her walk became her hallmark. It wasn't like the glide or bounce of many models. Her serpentine movements of the arms, torso, and legs were beautiful to watch and as subtly controlled as a dancer's."

"When she put on a garment, something just m-a-arvelous happened," fashion designer Halston, one of the first to hire Sims, was quoted as saying in *Black Enterprise.* Even Cooper, who had been slow to see Sims's potential, was quoted in *Black Enterprise*: "She could make any garment—even a sackcloth—look like sensational haute couture."

Gave up Modeling for Business

In 1973 Sims married Michael Alistair Findlay, a Scot who ran an art gallery in New York; the couple later had one son, Robert. The same year, Sims decided to give up modeling, although she was just twenty-four and potentially had a long career in front of her. "Modeling was never my ultimate goal," she was quoted as saying in *African American Business Leaders.* "I started to model to supplement my income to go to college. ... But the idea of starting my own business had always appealed to me, and I was fortunate that my first career led to my second."

As her second career, Sims developed a business selling wigs designed for black women. The idea came directly out of Sims's struggle with her own hair while she was modeling, when she was under pressure to look different in every picture. "I was sort of driven to distraction in terms of how to vary my hairstyle," she told *Black Enterprise.*

One easy solution would be to wear a wig, but Sims was dissatisfied with the wigs available at the time, which had smooth, straight fibers that looked nothing like African-American hair, so she started experimenting in her kitchen. "I got hold of a current best-selling fiber for white women, wet the fiber down, put it in my oven at a very low temperature, and baked it for maybe five or ten minutes," she explained in *Black Enterprise*. The result was a curlier, coarser fiber—and a new business idea. "I thought it might be possible to market this type of product."

After approaching several wig manufacturers, she finally signed a deal with Metropa Company, a small import-export firm that sold a line of wigs for black women. The company agreed to provide some financing and make its research laboratories available to Sims. "Those were scary days in the beginning," Sims was quoted as saying in *Black Enterprise*. "It had to be a fiber that wouldn't get too frizzy, wouldn't get too straight, and wouldn't lose its curl."

Company Developed New Wig Fiber

After experimenting with different techniques, the company developed a lightweight wig fiber that looked like straightened black hair and did not have to be set. The fiber was patented and trademarked under the name Presselle, and the first line of the Naomi Sims Collection went into production.

For the first three years, Sims designed all the wig styles herself. "Basically, we duplicated the styles that were popular—what black women in the street were wearing, and combined that with my fashion sense," Sims told *Black Enterprise*. She also wrote and designed the advertisements and traveled the country promoting her wigs.

Initially, store buyers were skeptical about the need for Sims's product, not understanding the difference between black hair and Caucasian hair. Customers could certainly tell the difference, though: in the first year, sales of Sims's wigs reached $5 million. By 1979, when the Naomi Sims Collection was spun off into a separate division, it was generating the majority of Metropa's sales.

Wrote Books for Black Women

During this time, Sims also launched a career as an author. Her first book, *All about Health and Beauty for the Black Woman,* was published in 1976. As well as beauty tips, the book included information on nutrition, disease prevention, common health problems, fashion, and etiquette. "I had originally planned to call this book *The Beautiful Black Woman,* but as my thinking and reading plunged me into all areas of our black female ethic, I soon realized that this ap-

proach was too one-dimensional," Sims wrote in the book's preface. The book sold well, and three years later was in its tenth printing.

In 1979 Sims published her second book, *How to Be a Top Model.* Three years later, she published two more books: *All about Hair Care for the Black Woman,* and *All about Success for the Black Woman.* In *All about Success,* Sims was able to draw on her own experience as an entrepreneur, offering advice about landing a job, dealing with corporate politics, and juggling a career, marriage, and motherhood. In a review of the book for *Black Enterprise,* Phil W. Petrie wrote, "I am going to ignore the reference to gender in the title of this book and give it to my sons."

Launched Second Company

Meanwhile, beginning in the early 1980s, Sims gradually expanded her business interests to include perfume, skin care products, and cosmetics for black women. Her signature fragrance, Naomi, was launched in 1981. Four years later she founded her own company, Naomi Sims Beauty Products Ltd.

In 1987 the company introduced a line of skin-care products, with Sims as the spokesmodel. "One of the things people notice about me is the quality of my skin," Sims told Anne-Marie Shiro of the *New York Times.* "We decided I was the best person to advertise my products." Alfred Edmond Jr. of *Black Enterprise* concurred. "Her look—clean, simple, and elegant—conveys sophistication, class and power." Edmond continued, "It's the look the company is selling—and the public is buying." Shortly afterward, Sims added cosmetics to the mix. By 1989 Naomi Sims Beauty Products was grossing $5 million, and its products were distributed not only across the United States, but also in Africa, the Caribbean, and Canada.

From the beginning, all of Sims's products were marketed as luxury items at high price points. When Naomi Sims wigs were first introduced, they were considered expensive at $20 to $30; and when Naomi perfume was launched in 1981, it cost $100 an ounce. The pricing policy was deliberate, Sims told *Black Enterprise*: "When I started my business I insisted that my wigs not be put on sale … [because] it would cheapen the image. I know as a black consumer that we will go out of our way to pursue the best products—no matter what the cost, we buy quality."

By the late 1980s, Sims's firm was being challenged by larger, white-owned firms, who wanted a share of the African-American cosmetics market. By 2001 nearly all the major cosmetics companies offered products developed for African-American women. Nonetheless, Sims' company remained competitive, and in 2009 Naomi Sims Beauty Products was still active, with Sims' brother-in-law Alexander Erwiah as its president.

While Sims's accomplishments as an entrepreneur are truly impressive, she has been criticized by some feminists, who have accused her of making money from women's insecurities about their own attractiveness. Sims brushed off these criticisms, however: "I am sure I have my share of black female critics and enemies," she was quoted as saying in *African American Business Leaders*. "It doesn't matter. I adore women and I know I am a woman's woman. ... I would be nowhere if it weren't for black women."

Died of Breast Cancer

Sims died on August 1, 2009, from breast cancer at the age of sixty-one. At the time, two images of her were part of a New York Metropolitan Museum of Art exhibition entitled "The Model as Muse: Embodying Fashion." The curators of the exhibition wrote a short tribute to Sims in the exhibit catalog that was reprinted in her *New York Times'* obituary: "The beautifully contoured symmetry of Sims' face and the lithe suppleness of her body presented on the once-exclusionary pages of high-fashion journals were evidence of the wider societal movement of Black Pride and the full expression of 'Black Is Beautiful'." Moreover, Naomi Sims—supermodel and skilled entrepreneur—was an important force in that movement, not just evidence of it.

Selected writings

All about Health and Beauty for the Black Woman, Main Street Books, 1976.

How to Be a Top Model, Doubleday, 1979.
All about Hair Care for the Black Woman, Doubleday, 1982.
All about Success for the Black Woman, Doubleday, 1982.
All about Health and Beauty for the Black Woman, revised edition, Main Street Books, 1986.

Sources

Books

African American Business Leaders, Greenwood Press, 1994.

Periodicals

Black Enterprise, March 1989, p. 42; July 1979, p. 41.
Fortune, November 9, 1987, p. 162.
Mademoiselle, August 1974, p. 296.
New York Times, May 15, 1987, p. A20; August 4, 2009, p. A21.
Jet, August 24, 2009, p. 36.
Washington Post, August 5, 2009, p. B5.

Online

Duke, Alan, "Naomi Sims, Pioneering Black Model, Dies at 61," CNN.com, August 4, 2009, http://edition.cnn.com/2009/SHOWBIZ/08/04/obit.naomi.sims/ (accessed November 16, 2009).

—Carrie Golus and Sandra Alters

The Sugarhill Gang

Rap group

In the late summer of 1979, three unknown young men came together as The Sugarhill Gang at a New Jersey recording studio to make "Rapper's Delight," the first commercially successful rap single. Those original members were Henry Jackson, Guy O'Brien, and Mike Wright, who used the professional names Big Bank Hank, Master Gee, and Wonder Mike for the fourteen-minute single that gave birth to the rap and hip-hop record industry. It was "the catalyst for what would arguably become the cultural revolution of our times," noted *Vanity Fair*'s Steven Daly in 2005. "Rock creationists can debate long and hard about which records heralded the advent of rock 'n' roll in the 1950s; recorded hip-hop began with a stark and solitary statement: 'Rapper's Delight'."

Daly chronicled the history of "Rapper's Delight" in a nine-thousand-word article for the magazine that focused less on the talents of the budding emcees than on the business acumen of Sylvia Robinson, a music industry veteran who owned All Platinum Records in Englewood, New Jersey. All Platinum was the predecessor of Sugar Hill Records, launched by Robinson and her husband in 1979. Robinson had had a couple of hits as a performer earlier in her career and went on to become a songwriter and record producer after her last hit, 1973's "Pillow Talk." Six years after that, she discovered a burgeoning new style of dance music in the African-American communities of Harlem, the Bronx, and Brooklyn which was gradually making its way across the Hudson River to her New Jersey community. "Rapping," as it was called, relied on emcees who delivered freestyle rhymes over records spun by disc jockeys at nightclubs and underground dance events.

Recruited Literally off the Street

Robinson enlisted her son Joey Jr. to help her find some homegrown talent in Englewood. Joey contacted a local emcee who went by the name of Casper, but Casper did not show up at the studio at the appointed hour after his father reportedly warned him against doing business with the Robinsons, who had a reputation for unscrupulous business practices. Robinson, her son, and his friend Warren Moore drove around trying to find Casper until the boys thought of Henry Jackson, a Bronx native who managed a local pizzeria. A former wrester, Jackson had worked as a bouncer at two Bronx discos, Sparkle and Disco Fever, and also managed an act called the Cold Crush Brothers. At the time, Jackson was working at Englewood's Crispy Crust Pizza to pay off a loan he owed to his parents after buying a sound system. He auditioned for the woman known in the neighborhood as "Mrs. Rob," then closed up the shop early to head to the Robinsons' studio on West Avenue.

According to Daly, who interviewed by Sylvia Robinson and Joey Jr., Mark Green heard the audition in the parking lot and told the Robinsons that his friend Guy O'Brien, who had been rapping with Englewood's One on One crew, could do better. O'Brien, too, auditioned on the spot and passed muster. At that point, six-foot-six-inch Mike Wright approached the car and said he could rap, too. Wright was an associate of Casper's and had only started rapping a few months earlier. "In May 1979, I didn't even know what rap was," Wonder Mike recalled years later in an interview with the *News & Record* of Piedmont Triad, North Carolina, about that Friday in August. "My cousin invited me to a show, I

At a Glance . . .

Members are Big Bank Hank (born Henry Jackson in 1956, in Bronx, NY); Master Gee (born Guy O'Brien); Wonder Mike (born Michael Anthony Wright on April 30, 1957). *Education:* Jackson earned an associate's degree from Bronx Community College.

Career: Group formed in August of 1979 in Englewood, New Jersey, to record the single "Rapper's Delight" for Sugar Hill Records.

Addresses: *Office*—c/o Sugar Hill Records Ltd., 96 West St., Englewood, NJ 07631.

liked what I heard, then I went home and wrote some of my own rhymes and joined the group."

Wright, who had worked with his cousin's DJ group, Sound on Sound, did not impress the Robinsons on his first try. He told them he was an asthma sufferer and asked for another chance, and on his second attempt was much more impressive in delivering his rhymes to the cassette backing tape playing in Joey's Oldsmobile. Sylvia Robinson then brought the three to the studio and drew up a contract. They were signed as The Sugarhill Gang and told to return on Monday for the recording session. Wright, as Wonder Mike, opened "Rapper's Delight" with the immortal line: "I said a hip hop, the hippie the hippie, to the hip hip hop, and you don't stop." When it was done, the song clocked in at fourteen minutes and thirty-seven seconds, and the Robinsons released it on the newly created Sugar Hill Records because their previous incarnation, All Platinum, had filed for bankruptcy.

Became Overnight Sensations

"Rapper's Delight" debuted at number eighty-four on the Billboard Hot 100, and soon the trio was opening for George Clinton's Parliament Funkadelic. "I thought it would be big in Connecticut, New Jersey and New York, but then three months after its release I was on the Champs-Elysees in Paris," Wonder Mike recalled in the *News & Record* interview. The single reached number thirty-six on the U.S. singles chart and the number four position on *Billboard*'s R&B chart. The group filmed a video to promote it on the European market, where dance singles consistently dominated the charts. In it, the trio is surrounded by disco dancers in matching outfits, and "the clip reflected the record in all its incongruous glory," wrote Daly in *Vanity Fair*. "The three … look as if they haven't seen one another since their single recording session together." Wonder Mike opens the song, sporting sideburns and a beige V-neck sweater, trades off to the portly Big Bank Hank, and then Master Gee, wearing a turtleneck and cardigan, takes over. Daly asserted that Big Bank Hank was the star of the video, the pizzeria manager wearing a too-tight T-shirt and sunhat who "sells this number as if his life depended on it," wrote Daly. "Not even the hired crowd of disco-dancing extras can diminish the palpable energy that crackles around Sylvia Robinson's ill-matched trailblazers."

The Sugarhill Gang became superstars. "Girls were chasing us down the street, tearing our clothes off," Wonder Mike recalled in the *News & Record*. Robinson's label issued The Sugarhill Gang's debut LP, which featured six tracks including another version of "Rapper's Delight," but the trio's credibility was disputed almost from the start. Big Bank Hank, for one, had borrowed the notebook of one of the Cold Crush Brothers he managed, Grandmaster Caz, and the freestyle rhymes he delivered were reportedly the work of Caz, which was short for "Casanova"; Big Bank Hank even introduces himself as "Casanova" in the song. Interviewed by Daly, Grandmaster Caz said he was stunned by Big Bank Hank's treachery. "The story that he told at the end? 'Since I was six years old I knew never let an M.C. steal my rhyme'? He's stealing a line about stealing a rhyme!" Caz said. Big Bank Hank, however, has always insisted that he and Caz wrote rhymes together.

"Rapper's Delight" was The Sugarhill Gang's only major hit. They toured with Rick James, Teena Marie, and Cameo, and recorded another studio record for the Sugar Hill label, *Eighth Wonder,* in 1982. The Robinsons had signed Grandmaster Flash and the Furious Five, who had been active in the Bronx music scene for several years by then, and scored major hits with "The Message" and "White Lines (Don't Do It)." Master Gee left the group and was replaced by Joey Robinson Jr.; he reportedly moved to Chicago and started a marketing firm. Wonder Mike was in the construction business and eventually settled in Farmingdale, New York. Writing in *Vibe* magazine on the fifteenth anniversary of "Rapper's Delight" in 1994, Harry Allen noted that what became "the single most important release in hip hop history" has a dubious reputation and is not very good, "but it's the only record after which, no matter who you were or what you did in hip hop, *everything* was different. It changed the rules of the game."

In 2009 Big Bank Hank still lived in the Bronx and was the sole original member of The Sugarhill Gang who was still with the group. Joey Robinson Jr. and Warren Moore, the friend who drove around in the Oldsmobile looking for rappers, also performed under The Sugarhill name. Wonder Mike and Master Gee, however, were required to bill themselves as "Wonder Mike and Master Gee of the Original Sugarhill Gang." In 2008 Wonder Mike and Master Gee filed suit in U.S. District Court in Manhattan to retain The Sugarhill name and to receive royalty payments from the Robinsons.

Selected discography

LPs

Sugar Hill Gang, Sugar Hill Records, 1980.
Eighth Wonder, Sugar Hill Records, 1982.
Jump on It, Rhino Records, 1999.

Singles

"Rapper's Delight," Sugar Hill Records, 1979.
"Rapper's Reprise (Jam Jam)," Sugar Hill Records, 1980.
"Apache," Sugar Hill Records, 1981.
"Kick It Live from 9 to 5," Sugar Hill Records, 1983.

Sources

Books

Watkins, S. Craig, *Hip Hop Matters: Politics, Pop Culture, and the Struggle for the Soul of a Movement,* Beacon Press, 2006, pp. 12–20.

Periodicals

News & Record (Piedmont Triad, NC), June 29, 2000, p. 6.
New York Times, October 12, 1980, p. D30; June 15, 1997; December 18, 2001.
Remix, February 1, 2006.
Vibe, December 1994, p. 71.
Vanity Fair, November 1, 2005, p. 250.

Online

Larson, Erik, "'Sugarhill Gang' Sues over Royalties, Stage Names (Update1)," Bloomberg.com, November 14, 2008, http://www.bloomberg.com/apps/news?pid=20601110&sid=aXePN0DykBkM (accessed September 25, 2009).

—Carol Brennan

Baratunde Thurston

1977—

Political editor and blogger, comedian

Baratunde Thurston is a self-described "vigilante pundit." A stand-up comedian, blogger, and Web site editor, he is known for his witty, well-informed analyses of politics and technology. In the summer of 2009 he began hosting his own television series, *Popular Science's Future Of,* on the Science Channel.

Relatively few details of Thurston's early life are available. He was born Baratunde Rafiq Thurston on September 11, 1977, in Washington, DC, and was raised there by his mother, a computer programmer for the U.S. Treasury Department. In a 2009 interview with Gillian Reagan of Observer.com, the Web site of the *New York Observer,* Thurston noted that he grew up at a time when Washington faced rising crime rates and other social ills. His mother, however, worked hard to insulate him from these problems, enrolling him in a wide variety of extracurricular activities, including music lessons and martial arts classes. He also attended private school, where his grades proved strong enough for admission to Harvard University.

It was at Harvard that Thurston, a philosophy major, began establishing himself as a commentator on politics, technology, and culture. He did so primarily through his work on the campus newspaper, the *Harvard Crimson.* As the *Crimson*'s technology editor, he oversaw the development of its Web site as well as its coverage of topics such as computing and personal electronics. He also found time to compose satires on college life. Those dual interests—satire and technology—later became major components of his career.

After receiving his bachelor's degree in about 1999, Thurston worked as a consultant for a variety of well-known corporations, notably telecommunications giants Verizon and AT&T. Finding the work unfulfilling, however, he left the corporate world in 2007 to become a stand-up comedian. The opening lines of his monologue, later quoted on ComedyCentral.com and other Web sites, proved particularly popular. "My full name is Baratunde Rafiq Thurston," he told audiences. "Baratunde is a Nigerian name meaning 'one with no nickname.' Rafiq is an Arabic name meaning 'really, no nickname.'"

Even as he worked long hours to establish himself in the notoriously competitive and demanding field of stand-up, Thurston was pursuing other opportunities. In the fall of 2007 he became Web and politics editor for *The Onion,* arguably the most prominent satirical publication in the country. He also devoted considerable time to JackAndJillPolitics.com, a blog he helped start in 2006. Providing an African-American perspective on contemporary politics, the site quickly became one of the most popular of the so-called "black blogs." In September of 2009 its front page featured posts on health-care reform, climate change, and Newark, New Jersey, mayor Cory Booker. Several of these threads were started by Thurston, using the pen name Jack Turner. A review of his author archive revealed hundreds of posts, often as many as four per day. He has also been a guest contributor to HuffingtonPost.com, a widely read site with a liberal orientation on national and international issues.

At a Glance . . .

Born Baratunde Rafiq Thurston on September 11, 1977, in Washington, DC. *Education:* Harvard University, BA, philosophy, 1999(?).

Career: Consultant for a number of major corporations, 1999(?)–2007; independent blogger, 2006—; stand-up comedian, 2007—; *The Onion,* Web and politics editor, 2007—; *Popular Science's Future Of* (television program), host, 2009—.

Awards: Iowa State University, Champion of the First Amendment, 2000s; Bill Hicks Award for Thought Provoking Comedy, 2000s.

Addresses: *Agent*—DGS Talent Management, 25 Bank St., #2, Stamford, CT 06901. *Web*—http://www.baratunde.com/.

As blogs grew dramatically in popularity in the months following JackAndJill.com's founding, broadcast networks and other major media interests began to take notice. Thurston's unusual combination of talents proved particularly attractive to these organizations: while witty and perceptive writers were easily found online, few possessed his charisma, a quality he continued to hone in his onstage performances. In addition to the brief nightclub appearances that sustain most stand-up comedians, Thurston was increasingly successful in finding work as an emcee. In 2006 and 2007, for example, he hosted the YearlyKos, an annual convention associated with the liberal blog DailyKos.com. He has since performed similar duties at the South by Southwest (SXSW) music festival in Austin, Texas, and the National Conference for Media Reform.

Impressed by his performance in these venues, the Science Channel, a prominent cable broadcaster, recruited Thurston to host a new program focused on emerging technologies and their capacity to transform the future. Entitled *Popular Science's Future Of,* it debuted in August of 2009. In each episode, Thurston interviewed scientists and then experimented with their inventions. Featured technologies have included, according to the program's Web site, "computerized contact lenses, invisibility cloaks, [and] floating cities." In an interview posted on PopSci.com just before the airing of the first episode, Thurston told Natalie Avon that one of his favorite segments involved an aerodynamically designed aquatic fin that enabled swimmers to reach speeds of eight miles per hour, more than twice the pace of the fastest athletes in the world. "This could change the whole landscape for adventure," he

noted, adding that using the fin himself made it "one of the few pieces from the future that I could really, really feel."

One of the most innovative aspects of Thurston's program has been the way it has incorporated social media services, notably Facebook and Twitter. Much of *Future Of*'s pre-debut promotion was accomplished through Facebook groups, many of them associated with Thurston's personal page. Twitter, meanwhile, was incorporated into the program's structure to give viewers a way to send questions and comments as soon as they arose. Thurston's responses to those communications—and his own comments—have given *Future Of* a distinctive, highly interactive tone. Twitter has also played a role in some of Thurston's other work. In January of 2009, for example, ComedyCentral.com hired him to be its "Twitter correspondent" at the inauguration of U.S. President Barack Obama.

As of September of 2009 Thurston had written and self-published three books: *Better Than Crying: Poking Fun at Politics, the Press & Pop Culture* (2004), *Keep Jerry Falwell Away from My Oreo Cookies* (2005), and *Thank You Congressional Pages (For Being So Damn Sexy!)* (2006). He also maintained a prominent presence in the stand-up world, with regular appearances as the host of a weekly program at New York City's Sage Theater. NYCGo.com, a site belonging to the city's tourism department, has called the event "a fail-proof solution for the lack of funny in your life."

Selected works

Books

Better Than Crying: Poking Fun at Politics, the Press & Pop Culture, self-published, 2004.
Keep Jerry Falwell Away from My Oreo Cookies, self-published, 2005.
Thank You Congressional Pages (For Being So Damn Sexy!), self-published, 2006.

Television

Popular Science's Future Of, Science Channel, 2009—.

Sources

Online

"About Baratunde," Baratunde.com, http://www.baratunde.com/about/ (accessed November 13, 2009).
Avon, Natalie, "Baratunde Thurston: Correspondent of the Future," PopSci.com, August 5, 2009, http://www.popsci.com/events-and-promotions/article/2009-08/baratunde-thurston-correspondent-future (accessed November 13, 2009).

Baffour, Fritswa, "Free in NYC: Events," http://www. nycgo.com/?event=view.article&id=195422 (accessed November 13, 2009).

"Baratunde Thurston," ComedyCentral.com, http://comedians.comedycentral.com/baratunde-thurston/ (accessed Novmeber 13, 2009).

"Jack and Jill Politics," JackAndJillPolitics.com, http://www.jackandjillpolitics.com/ (accessed November 13, 2009).

Modell, Josh, "*The Onion*'s Web Editor to Host New TV Show, Premiering Tonight!" AVClub.com, August 10, 2009, http://www.avclub.com/articles/the-onions-web-editor-to-host-new-tv-show-premieri,31517/ (accessed November 13, 2009).

"*Popular Science's Future Of,*" Discovery.com, http://science.discovery.com/tv/pop-sci/pop-sci.html (accessed November 13, 2009).

Reagan, Gillian, "Baratunde Thurston Explains the Future of … Lots of Things!" Observer.com, August 17, 2009, http://www.observer.com/2009/media/baratunde-thurston-future (accessed November 13, 2009).

—R. Anthony Kugler

Channing H. Tobias

1882–1961

Educator, civil rights advocate

Educator and administrator Channing H. Tobias played a leading role in the civil rights movement for half a century. An ordained minister, he spent several decades with the Young Men's Christian Association (YMCA) before moving on to a variety of prominent positions with the federal government, the Phelps Stokes Fund, and the NAACP. A moderate consensus builder, he counted Indian leader Mahatma Gandhi, whom he once met, among his greatest influences.

Channing Heggie Tobias was born on February 1, 1882, in Augusta, Georgia. His parents, coachman Fair J. Tobias and housekeeper Clara Belle Robinson Tobias, had likely been born slaves. Education, particularly religious education, was a priority in the devout, close-knit family, and Tobias's performance in school and church was closely monitored. At a preparatory school attached to Augusta's Paine Institute (later Paine College), he quickly proved himself an exceptional student. His undergraduate work, also completed at Paine, culminated in a BA in 1902. He then entered New Jersey's Drew Theological Seminary, which granted him a bachelor of divinity degree three years later. By that time he was already serving as a minister, having been ordained by the Colored Methodist Episcopal Church (later the Christian Methodist Episcopal Church) while still at Paine.

After Drew, Tobias returned to Georgia, where he accepted a job at his alma mater as a professor of biblical literature. He remained there for the next six years. In 1911 he left at a mentor's urging to become student secretary of the International Committee of the

YMCA, one of the world's largest social service non-profits. His job, in essence, was to represent the organization in countries around the globe. That task brought him to a number of international conferences, among the most prominent of which was the Second Pan-African Congress. Held in Europe in 1921, it was an early effort to build unity among those of African descent. Tobias soon became a sought-after speaker at such events, thanks in part to the rhetorical training he had gained in the ministry.

In 1923 Tobias moved from the YMCA's International Committee to its National Council, becoming senior secretary of the latter's Colored Men's Department (CMD). While most of the YMCA's international affiliates did not practice racial segregation, the U.S. branch did. For the next twenty-three years Tobias worked tirelessly from within to change that policy; it was at last rescinded in 1946, his final year with the organization.

In 1936 Tobias traveled to India to take part in a YMCA conference. It was there that he encountered Gandhi, already well known for his nonviolent approach to the issues of racism, colonialism, and political oppression. The two had a long private meeting. Deeply impressed by the older man's humility and determination, Tobias returned to the United States with renewed faith in the principles of nonviolence and civil disobedience.

With the country's entry into World War II in 1941, Tobias shifted some of his focus from the YMCA to the federal government's mobilization efforts. As a member of the National Advisory Committee on Selective

At a Glance . . .

Born Channing Heggie Tobias on February 1, 1882, in Augusta, GA; died November 5, 1961, in New York, NY; son of Fair J. Tobias (a coachman) and Clara Belle Robinson Tobias (a housekeeper); married Mary C. Pritchard, 1908 (died 1949), Eva Arnold, 1951; children: two daughters. *Religion:* Methodist. *Education:* Paine College, BA, 1902; Drew Theological Seminary, BD, 1905.

Career: Paine College, professor of biblical literature, 1905–11; YMCA, student secretary of the International Committee, 1911–23, senior secretary of the Colored Work Department, 1923–46; Phelps Stokes Fund, director, 1946–53; NAACP, chair, 1953–59, chair emeritus, 1959–61.

Memberships: National Advisory Committee on Selective Service, early 1940s; Joint Army and Navy Committee on Welfare and Recreation, early 1940s; President's Committee on Civil Rights, 1946–47; U.S. Delegation to the United Nations, alternate representative, early 1950s; served on the board of many schools, community organizations, and corporations.

Awards: Gammon Theological Seminary, honorary doctorate, 1924; Harmon Foundation, Harmon Award, 1928; NAACP, Springarn Medal, 1948.

Service, he helped manage the implementation of the massive wartime draft. He also served on the board of the Joint Army and Navy Committee on Welfare and Recreation. In both of these roles, he pressed the military to begin integrating its facilities. His efforts in this regard drew the attention of President Truman, who appointed him shortly after the war to a new advisory body, known as the President's Committee on Civil Rights (PCCR). The group's final report, issued in 1947, urged the government to dismantle the legal framework underpinning segregation.

Tobias's work with the PCCR coincided with his move from the YMCA to the Phelps Stokes Fund, founded in 1911 to improve educational facilities for minorities. His arrival as director in 1946 marked a turning point in the organization's history, as his predecessors, without exception, had been white. He remained with the Phelps Stokes Fund until 1953, when he left to become chair of the NAACP, a role he held for the next six years. During that time he helped to orchestrate the group's response to one of the most important events

in the history of the civil rights movement: the U.S. Supreme Court's 1954 decision in *Brown v. Board of Education* outlawing segregation in public schools. As heated debate began over the decision's implementation, Tobias urged all sides to show moderation and restraint.

In 1959 Tobias stepped down as NAACP chair; he was then named chair emeritus. He remained active, however, in the struggle for civil rights and education, serving as a trustee for dozens of nonprofit organizations. Among these were the Hampton Institute, the Palmer Memorial Institute, Howard University, the Field Foundation, the Jessie Smith Noyes Foundation, and the National Council of Churches of Christ in the U.S.A. He also served on several corporate boards and was an alternate delegate for the United States at the Sixth General Assembly of the United Nations in 1951–52.

Tobias received a number of honors and awards in his lifetime. The best known of these was the 1948 Springarn Medal, the NAACP's highest honor. According to the organization's Web site, the Springarn "is awarded annually to the man or woman of African descent and American citizenship who shall have made the highest achievement in the previous year or years in any honorable field of human endeavor." Other recipients have included the Rev. Dr. Martin Luther King Jr. (1957), musicians Duke Ellington (1959) and Leontyne Price (1965), and writer Maya Angelou (1994). Tobias was chosen by the Springarn Committee of Awards "in recognition of his consistent role as a defender of fundamental American liberties." Tobias died in 1961 at the age of seventy-nine.

Sources

Periodicals

New York Times, November 6, 1961, p. 37.
Pittsburgh Courier, November 18, 1961.
Time, November 17, 1961.

Online

"Black History Month: Channing Tobias," NBCAugusta.com, February 21, 2009, http://www.nbcaugusta.com/story5/40034312.html (accessed November 13, 2009).
"Channing H. Tobias: An Inventory of His Papers," University of Minnesota, 2003, http://special.lib.umn.edu/findaid/html/ymca/yusa0007.phtml (accessed November 13, 2009).
"The NAACP Springarn Medal," NAACP.org, http://www.naacp.org/events/spingarn/index.htm (accessed November 13, 2009).
"Springarn Medal Winners," NAACP.org, http://www.naacp.org/events/spingarn/past/index.htm (accessed November 13, 2009).

—R. Anthony Kugler

James Ulmer

1942—

Jazz and blues guitarist

Ulmer, James, photograph. Douglas Mason/Getty Images.

Guitarist James "Blood" Ulmer has been at the forefront of both jazz and the blues for more than half a century. His highly original compositions have often featured a guitar tuned to a single note—an unusual technique known as "unison tuning." Critic Peter Watrous of the *New York Times* once described the South Carolina native as "a great American expressionist," adding, "He seems as if he sprang, fully formed, from a mythical Parts Unknown, guitar and personality in hand."

James Ulmer was born February 2, 1942, in St. Matthews, South Carolina, a rural hamlet some thirty-five miles south of Columbia, the state capital. He received his nickname, a shortened version of "Youngblood," as a teenager. Music attracted him from his earliest days, and he was performing on stage with his father's gospel group, the Southern Sons, as early as the age of seven. It was not gospel, however, but the blues that he found most thrilling. By high school he was increasingly focused on mastering the blues guitar, and there was little doubt that music would be his profession.

In 1959 when he was just seventeen, Ulmer moved to Pittsburgh, Pennsylvania, to join that city's vibrant music scene. While supporting himself with guitar work for a variety of pop groups, he fell increasingly under the sway of jazz. The innovations of fellow guitarist Wes Montgomery in that genre influenced him deeply, as did jazz organist Jimmy Smith, with whom he sometimes played.

After roughly four years in Pennsylvania, Ulmer moved west to Columbus, Ohio, where he began collaborating with another organist, Columbus native Hank Marr. The two played dozens of gigs together, including several in Europe, and then entered the recording studio. Marr's album *Sounds from the Marr-ket … Place* brought Ulmer his first major recording credit. Within weeks of its release in 1967, he left Marr and moved to Detroit, Michigan, then a magnet for musicians interested in blending jazz with other genres. In that respect the city was an ideal headquarters for Ulmer, whose plans for a unique style of blues-inflected jazz had begun to take shape. A major component of those plans was unison tuning. In the course of his experiments in this area, he formed an avant-garde quintet called Focus Novii; he also had a more traditional group called the James Ulmer Trio.

At a Glance . . .

Born on February 2, 1942, in St. Matthews, SC; children: at least one.

Career: Independent performer and recording artist, 1959—.

Awards: *Talent Deserving Wider Recognition, Down Beat* magazine, 1980; Grammy Award nomination, 2002, for *Memphis Blood: The Sun Sessions*; Blues Foundation, Blues Music Award nomination, 2006, for *Birthright.*

Addresses: *Office*—c/o Hyena Records, 105 15th St., Suite 3L, Brooklyn, NY 11215. *Web*—http://www.myspace.com/jamesbloodulmer.

Despite steady work in some of Detroit's most famous clubs, including the Bluebird and the 20 Grand, Ulmer moved on in 1971, this time to New York City. His work there brought him into contact with drummers Art Blakey and Rashied Ali, and he played a major role in the success of the latter's 1973 album, *Rashied Ali Quintet.* It was through Ali that Ulmer met saxophonist Ornette Coleman, one of the pioneers of what had come to be known as free jazz. Coleman's work in "harmolodics"—his term for mixing melody and harmony—fit well with Ulmer's unison tuning, and the two began a period of intense collaboration that included a number of gigs with Coleman's group Prime Time. Inspired by that experience, Ulmer decided to record an album of his own. Released on the In & Out label in 1977, *Revealing* was, in the words of AllMusic.com's Thom Jurek, "a solid jazz date with visionary players taking a new turn with the music and seeing how fast they can drive it down the road."

In the decades since, Ulmer has released albums at an impressive pace. Many of these, including three well-known works on the Columbia label (*Free Lancing,* 1981; *Black Rock,* 1982; and *Odyssey,* 1984), have been issued under his own name. Others, however, have been released as cooperative projects, including *In Touch* (1988), a highly regarded work by a group Ulmer and his band mates called Phalanx.

A major force in 1980s free jazz, Phalanx coexisted for several years with an Ulmer-led group called the Music Revelation Ensemble. The latter was still releasing albums in the 1990s, more than fifteen years after its 1980 debut, *No Wave.*

By the late 1980s, Ulmer was turning increasingly to the blues. On solo albums such as 1990's *Black and Blues* and 1998's *Forbidden Blues,* he used the instrumental techniques he had developed to interpret traditional blues arrangements, adding his own gravelly vocals in the process. He did not, however, abandon jazz; on the contrary, his work in the mid-1990s with Third Rail, a jazz-funk group he formed in 1993 with bassist Bill Laswell and drummer Ziggy Modeliste, attracted enthusiastic crowds in New York and elsewhere.

The early 2000s were marked by increasing recognition of Ulmer's talents among fans and critics worldwide. A pivotal moment in this regard came with the 2001 release of *Memphis Blood: The Sun Sessions,* which was nominated for a Grammy Award. Completed at the historic Sun Studio in Memphis, Tennessee, the album of blues standards was produced by fellow guitarist Vernon Reid, best known for his work with the rock band Living Colour. Reid also produced 2003's *No Escape From the Blues: The Electric Lady Sessions* and 2005's *Birthright.* The latter received a Blues Music Award nomination from the Blues Foundation.

Hurricane Katrina's devastation of New Orleans, Louisiana, in September of 2005 affected Ulmer deeply, and he spent several years writing music to commemorate the storm's victims. Those efforts resulted in *Bad Blood in the City: The Piety Street Sessions,* released on Hyena Records in 2007. Working once again with Reid, Ulmer took pains to record the album in New Orleans. In comments quoted on Hyena's Web site, Bill White of the *Seattle Post Intelligencer* called *Bad Blood* "the blues album of the decade."

In June of 2009, Ulmer was featured on an episode of *American Routes,* a weekly music program on National Public Radio. He also continued to appear in concerts around the country.

Selected discography

Hank Marr, *Sounds from the Marr-ket ... Place,* King, 1967.
Rashied Ali, *Rashied Ali Quintet,* Survival, 1973.
Revealing, In & Out, 1977.
Tales of Captain Black, DIW, 1978.
Are You Glad to Be in America? Rough Trade, 1980.
Music Revelation Ensemble, *No Wave,* Moers, 1980.
Free Lancing, Columbia, 1981.
Black Rock, Columbia, 1982.
Odyssey, Columbia, 1984.
Phalanx, *Got Something Good for You,* Moers, 1985.
America: Do You Remember the Love? Blue Note, 1986.
Phalanx, *In Touch,* DIW, 1988.
Music Revelation Ensemble, *Music Revelation Ensemble,* DIW, 1988.
Blues All Night, In & Out, 1989.
Black and Blues, DIW, 1990.

Music Revelation Ensemble, *After Dark,* 1992.
Harmolodic Guitar with Strings, DIW, 1993.
Music Revelation Ensemble, *Knights of Power,* DIW, 1996.
Third Rail, *South Delta Space Age,* Polygram, 1997.
Reunion, Knitting Factory, 1998.
Forbidden Blues, DIW, 1998.
Memphis Blood: The Sun Sessions, Label M, 2001.
No Escape from the Blues: The Electric Lady Sessions, Sindrome, 2003.
Birthright, Hyena, 2005.
Bad Blood in the City: The Piety Street Sessions, Hyena, 2007.

Sources

Periodicals

New York Times, February 1, 1988, p. C28.

Online

Gross, Jason, "James Blood Ulmer" (interview), Furious.com, April 1998, http://www.furious.com/perfect/bloodulmer.html (accessed November 13, 2009).

"James Blood Ulmer," HyenaRecords.com, http://www.hyenarecords.com/jamesbloodulmer (accessed November 13, 2009).

"James Blood Ulmer," MySpace.com, http://www.myspace.com/jamesbloodulmer (accessed November 13, 2009).

Jurek, Thom, "*Revealing*: Review," AllMusic.com, http://allmusic.com/cg/amg.dll?p=amg&sql=10:fvfpxqygldae (accessed November 13, 2009).

Kelsey, Chris, and Thom Jurek, "James Blood Ulmer: Biography," AllMusic.com, http://allmusic.com/cg/amg.dll?p=amg&sql=11:fpfpxqt5ld6e (accessed November 12, 2009).

—R. Anthony Kugler

Ebonya Washington

1973(?)—

Economist

Ebonya Washington is the Henry Kohn Assistant Professor of Economics at Yale University. One of the few African-American women academics in her field at the Ivy League level, Washington specializes in public finance and political economy. In one study she demonstrated that in U.S. elections, having an African-American Democrat on the ballot serves to increase turnout among voters of both parties. In another she explored how faithfully African-American elected officials represent their minority constituents. Gender issues also interest Washington: in a landmark study she determined that male legislators with daughters are more likely to cast votes for liberal causes than their colleagues who have only sons.

Washington graduated from Brown University in Rhode Island in 1995 with an honors degree in public policy. She went on to the Massachusetts Institute of Technology for a doctorate in economics, which she earned in 2003. Along the way she was a graduate research fellow with the National Science Foundation and also at Boston College's Center for Retirement Research. She joined the faculty of Yale University in 2004, and four years later she was named the Henry Kohn Assistant Professor of Economics. She also teaches classes in political science.

In 2006 Washington's name appeared in the media in conjunction with two newly published academic papers. The first, entitled "Female Socialization: How Daughters Affect Their Legislator Fathers' Voting on Women's Issues," was published by Yale's Economics Department. Washington began by analyzing the Congressional voting records of male lawmakers from 1997 to 2004 on issues including equal pay, workplace discrimination, and reproductive rights. Washington determined the number of children each lawmaker had, whether they were sons or daughters, and where the legislators stood on the political spectrum, from conservative to liberal. Her analysis concluded that "conditional on total number of children, each daughter increases a congress person's propensity to vote liberally, particularly on reproductive rights issues." The legislators also tended to vote more liberally on issues related to labor and health. One question Washington's study did not resolve was why men tended toward more liberal views the more daughters they had. "I believe, although I have no evidence, that it's actually through parent-child interaction," Washington told Cathy Shufro in the *Yale Alumni Magazine*. "To the extent that men participate more in child-rearing, you can imagine that this might be likely to happen."

Washington's second 2006 study, entitled "How Black Candidates Affect Voter Turnout," appeared in the *Quarterly Journal of Economics*. The study, which examined voting patterns in Congressional and gubernatorial races from 1982 to 2000, demonstrated that having black Democratic candidates on the ballot tends to boost voting among both Democrats and Republicans by two to three percentage points. The effect is apparent among both black and white voters. The same increase was not seen when black Republican candidates appeared on the ballot.

Washington has also examined the purchasing patterns of consumers receiving government food assistance. In

At a Glance . . .

Born 1973(?). *Education:* Brown University, BA (with honors), 1995; Massachusetts Institute of Technology, PhD, 2003.

Career: Massachusetts Institute of Technology, Department of Economics, postdoctoral lecturer, 2003–04; National Bureau of Economic Research (NBER), faculty research fellow, 2004—; Yale University, Departments of Economics and Political Science, assistant professor, Yale University, 2004–08, Henry Kohn Assistant Professor of Economics and assistant professor of political science, 2008—.

Memberships: National Economic Association; American Economic Association.

Addresses: *Office*—Department of Economics, Yale University, P.O. Box 208264, New Haven, CT 06520-8264.

"The First of the Month Effect: Consumer Behavior and Store Responses," Washington and her co-author, Justine Hastings, compiled data from three grocery store chains in Nevada on purchases made by customers using the electronic debit card system that replaced food stamps in most states in the 1990s. Their analysis debunked the commonly held perception that government aid recipients "splurge" on extravagant items during the first week of the month, when aid is disbursed. While it was true that aid recipients spent more early in the month, they simply purchased less food—not lower-quality food—later in the month.

Washington has been a faculty research fellow at the National Bureau of Economic Research (NBER) and a visiting scholar at Harvard University. Her work is published regularly in the *Journal of Human Resources* and the *Quarterly Journal of Economics.*

Sources

Periodicals

Washington Post, April 14, 2006.
Yale Alumni Magazine, July/August 2008.

Online

Ananat, Elizabeth Oltmans, and Ebonya Washington, "Segregation and Black Political Efficacy"), NBER Working Paper No. 13606, http://www.econ.yale.edu/faculty1/washington/research.htm (accessed September 20, 2009).

"Ebonya Washington Appointed the Henry Kohn Assistant Professor," Yale University Office of Public Affairs, June 13, 2008, http://opa.yale.edu/news/article.aspx?id=5879 (accessed September 20, 2009).

Gelman, Andrew, "Having Daughters Rather Than Sons Makes You More Liberal," FiveThirtyEight: Politics Done Right, May 19, 2009, http://www.fivethirtyeight.com/2009/05/having-daughters-rather-than-sons-makes.html (accessed September 20, 2009).

Washington, Ebonya, and Justine Hastings, "The First of the Month Effect: Consumer Behavior and Store Responses," Yale University, Department of Economics, April 2009, http://www.econ.yale.edu/faculty1/washington/research.htm (accessed September 20, 2009).

Other

Economics Department Working Paper No. 15, Yale University, Department of Economics, May 2006.

—Carol Brennan

Margaret Bush Wilson

1919–2009

Attorney, civil rights leader

Margaret Bush Wilson was a lifelong advocate for civil rights, both in her hometown of St. Louis and on the national stage. She is best remembered as the first African-American woman elected to chair the national board of directors of the National Association for the Advancement of Colored People (NAACP), a position she held for nine terms, from 1975 to 1983. Wilson's diminutive stature and quiet, unassuming manner belied a deeply held passion for social justice and an unwavering commitment to stand up for what she believed was right—qualities that earned her the nickname "Mary Poppins … with a Razor Blade." An attorney who specialized in real estate law, Wilson worked throughout her career to ensure that African Americans had fair and equal access to good jobs and quality housing. Although an internal dispute with the NAACP's executive director and board of directors resulted in her ouster in 1983, the affair did not diminish her reputation as one of the "giants" of the civil rights movement.

Focused on Education

Margaret Berenice Bush was born on January 30, 1919, in St. Louis, Missouri, the second of three children of James and Margaret Bush. Both of her parents were active members of the NAACP in St. Louis and worked to further the civil rights cause. Her father was one of the first successful black real estate agents in St. Louis; in the 1940s he helped organize black realtors in a legal battle against racially exclusive covenants that barred black families from purchasing homes in whites-only neighborhoods—a case that his daughter would be a part of. Her mother, an elementary school teacher, served on the executive committee of the local NAACP chapter and attended the organization's national conference as a delegate in the 1920s. The Bushes encouraged their children to focus on education, and to envision a brighter future for themselves unrestricted by the boundaries of race and gender.

After being graduated with honors from Sumner High School, one of two segregated public high schools in St. Louis, Margaret Bush Wilson attended the historically black Talladega College in Alabama. Although her father encouraged her to pursue a career in teaching or nursing, she chose instead to study economics and mathematics. "I went to college without really knowing what I wanted to do with my life, but I knew what I didn't want to do," Wilson told the *Crisis* in 2007. "I didn't want to be a teacher. I didn't want to be a nurse. I didn't want to be a social worker, and I didn't want to be a librarian. I realize now that I was eliminating all these female careers." During her senior year in college, Wilson received a fellowship to study at Visva Bharati College in India, where she met Indian leader Mohandas K. Gandhi and Nobel Prize–winning poet Rabindranath Tagore.

Wilson received her bachelor's degree from Talladega College in 1940 and went on to study at the Lincoln University School of Law. The school had been established in response to the U.S. Supreme Court's ruling in *Gaines v. Canada* (1938), which ordered the state of

At a Glance . . .

Born Margaret Berenice Bush on January 30, 1919, in St. Louis, MO; died on August 11, 2009, in St. Louis; daughter of James Bush (a mail clerk and real estate broker) and Margaret Casey Bush (a teacher); married Robert E. Wilson Jr. (an attorney), 1944 (divorced, 1968); children: Robert E. Wilson III. *Politics:* Democrat. *Religion:* Episcopal. *Education:* Talladega College, BS, economics, 1940; Lincoln University School of Law, JD, 1943.

Career: U.S. Department of Agriculture, Rural Electrification Administration, attorney, 1943–45; Wilson & Wilson, partner, 1947–65; State of Missouri, assistant attorney general, 1961–62; Missouri Office of Urban Affairs, 1965–67; Missouri Department of Community Affairs, 1967–68; St. Louis Lawyers for Housing, 1969–72; Wilson & Associates, senior partner, 1972–2009; St. Louis University, Council on Legal Opportunities, law faculty, 1973; National Association for the Advancement of Colored People, national board of directors chair, 1975–83.

Memberships: Alpha Kappa Alpha; American Bar Association; President's Commission on White House Fellowships; board of trustees: St. Augustine's College, Talladega College, and Washington University in St. Louis.

Awards: Bishop's Award, Episcopal Diocese of St. Louis, 1963; Louise Waterman Wise Laureate Award, National Women's Division, American Jewish Congress, 1975; Democracy in Action Award, St. Louis Council of the American Jewish Congress, 1978; Woman of the Year Award, *St. Louis Daily Record,* 2000; Spirit of Excellence Award, American Bar Association, 2008; Lifetime Achievement Award, St. Louis Community Empowerment Foundation, 2009; numerous honorary degrees.

Missouri to either admit black students to the law school at the University of Missouri or offer them a comparable education at a separate in-state institution. Wilson completed her law degree in 1943. She was among the first women to be graduated from the Lincoln University School of Law and the second African-American woman ever to be admitted to the Missouri state bar.

Fought Racial Discrimination in Housing Practices

As a young lawyer, Wilson was recruited to work for the U.S. Department of Agriculture's Rural Electrification Administration in 1943, helping to organize farmers into cooperatives in order to bring electricity to farms. The following year she married fellow Lincoln University law student Robert E. Wilson, and in 1947 the couple formed the firm Wilson & Wilson in St. Louis. She often quipped that because she had passed the bar before her husband, "Technically, I was the senior partner. But, I never raised that question," she told the *Crisis.*

In the 1940s, Margaret Wilson, a specialist in housing law, worked with the Real Estate Brokers Association, an organization of black realtors founded by her father, helping the group obtain a charter and serving as its counsel. James Bush was then representing a black family who wished to purchase a home in a whites-only neighborhood in St. Louis but were prevented from doing so by a restrictive covenant—a legal agreement that barred minorities from owning the home. Wilson was part of the legal team that contested such racially based covenants as part of an NAACP test case. The case, *Shelley v. Kraemer,* went to the U.S. Supreme Court, which issued a landmark ruling in 1948 that declared restrictive covenants unconstitutional. That year, Wilson ran an unsuccessful campaign for a seat in Congress on the Progressive Party ticket, the first black woman in Missouri to run for congressional office. Thereafter, she was a lifelong member of the Democratic Party.

Though she had been a member of the NAACP since her youth, Wilson began to take on a leadership role in the organization in 1956, when she helped organize the Job Opportunities Council in St. Louis, which encouraged the hiring of African-American employees. Two years later, she became the president of the St. Louis chapter of the NAACP, and in 1962 she headed the conference overseeing all of the chapters in Missouri. In 1963 she was elected to serve on the NAACP's national board of directors and participated in the March on Washington.

During the 1960s and 1970s, she headed task forces on housing and urban reform as part of President Lyndon B. Johnson's War on Poverty, served as treasurer of the NAACP's National Housing Corporation, and took part in the successful campaign to desegregate public schools in Atlanta, Georgia. In 1973 Wilson was chosen as the permanent chair of the NAACP's annual convention, a key policy-making post.

Became First Black Woman NAACP Chair

The death of NAACP chairman Bishop Stephen G. Spottswood in December of 1974 necessitated an election to choose his replacement the following January. Wilson was chosen over three other candidates in a "practically unanimous" vote, making her the first black woman to be appointed as chair of the NAACP. Speaking of her election, one board member commented, "It's tremendous that the country's oldest civil rights organization, whose history is rooted in fighting race and sex discrimination, would pioneer in choosing a black woman to lead it—particularly now in these days of affirmative action," the January 14, 1975, *Washington Post* reported.

Although some detractors alleged that Wilson fit the bill simply because she was a woman, she countered, "I assume they elected me because I'm competent and professional," she told the *Pittsburgh Post-Gazette* in 1975. "My sex and race are accidents of my birth. I take them for granted." During her tenure as chair, Wilson focused on bringing more young people into the NAACP, improving the organization's management, and stabilizing its finances.

In 1983 Wilson was involved in a public dispute with NAACP executive director Benjamin L. Hooks that resulted in her ouster from the organization. Accusing Hooks of mismanagement and insubordination, Wilson fired him without consulting the rest of the board of directors. The board immediately reversed her decision, rehiring Hooks and stripping Wilson of her responsibilities. She was denied a chance to speak at the NAACP's annual convention the following month, and when she stood for reelection six months later, the sixty-four-member board instead elected a dead man. Wilson claimed that her dismissal had been motivated by gender discrimination. "We have all had our moments of truth about sexism, about male chauvinism, and about disrespect and disregard for women as equals," she said in an interview with Jacqueline Trescott of the *Washington Post* in 1983. "What has happened to me has been my moment of truth."

Following her expulsion from the NAACP, Wilson returned to private practice in St. Louis, heading the law firm Wilson & Associates until two months before her death. She died of multiple organ failure at age ninety on August 11, 2009, in St. Louis.

Wilson received many accolades in recognition of her outstanding work, including the Bishop's Award from the Episcopal Diocese of St. Louis (1963), two awards from the American Jewish Congress (1975, 1978), the *St. Louis Daily Record*'s Woman of the Year Award (2000), and the American Bar Association's Spirit of Excellence Award (2008). She received honorary degrees from Alabama State University, Boston University, Kenyon College, Smith College, St. Paul's College, Talladega College, Washington University.

Sources

Periodicals

Crisis, March/April 2007, p. 27.
Ebony, April 1975, pp. 88–92.
New York Times, August 14, 2009, p. B13.
Pittsburgh Post-Gazette January 15, 1975, p. 22.
St. Louis Beacon, August 14, 2009.
Washington Post, January 14, 1975, p. A3; November 28, 1983, p. C1; August 14, 2009.

Online

"Margaret Bush Wilson," interview with Christine Lamberson, American Lives Project, Washington University in St. Louis, August 25, 2003, http://amlives.artsci.wustl.edu/transcripts/full/912.pdf (accessed October 15, 2009).

—Deborah A. Ring

Rod Woodson

1965—

Professional football player, television analyst

Woodson, Rod, photograph. Al Messerschmidt/Getty Images.

In his seventeen seasons in the National Football League (NFL), Rod Woodson distinguished himself as one of the most talented, versatile, and enduring defensive players in the game. He is best known for his decade-long stint as a cornerback with the Pittsburgh Steelers in the late 1980s and early 1990s, and then as a key member of the Baltimore Ravens defense during its Super Bowl XXXV championship season in 2000–01. In his career, Woodson totaled 71 interceptions, third all-time in NFL history, and had 1,483 yards in returns and 12 touchdowns on interceptions, both league records. He was named to the Pro Bowl eleven times at three different positions—cornerback, free safety, and kick returner—a record for a defensive back. In retirement, Woodson launched a successful career in television, appearing as an analyst on the NFL Network and the Big Ten Network. He was inducted into the Pro Football Hall of Fame in 2009.

Roderick Kevin Woodson was born on March 10, 1965, in Fort Wayne, Indiana, the youngest of three sons of James and Linda Jo Woodson. Growing up in a mixed-race family—his father was black and his mother was white—Woodson often endured taunts from schoolmates of both races. "The whites would call me mulatto, nigger, zebra and half-breed," he told *Sports Illustrated* in 1992. "The blacks would call me yellow boy, white boy or mixed breed." The experience instilled in Woodson a deep sense of pride in his individuality, and a fearlessness that later would prove invaluable on the gridiron. "I was taught never to back down," he said. "When you're mixed, you have three options: stay in the middle, pick a side, or stand on your own. My parents let me know I didn't have to pick a side, because I always had a friend in my family. I learned to stand up for myself and to never be afraid."

Excelled at Gridiron and Track

Woodson attended R. Nelson Snider High School in Fort Wayne, where he excelled at football, basketball, and track. He made the all-conference basketball team in his senior year, and twice won the state championship title in the low and high hurdles. On the football team, he played a variety of positions, and in his senior year, he was named an All-American player by *Parade* magazine. Heavily recruited by college football

At a Glance . . .

Born Roderick Kevin Woodson on March 10, 1965, in Fort Wayne, IN; son of James Woodson and Linda Jo Doerflein Woodson; married Nickie Theede; children: Marikah, Demitrius, Tia, Jairus, Nemiah. *Education:* Purdue University, BS, criminal justice, 1987.

Career: Pittsburgh Steelers, 1987–96; San Francisco 49ers, 1997; Baltimore Ravens, 1998–2001; Oakland Raiders, 2002–03; NFL Network, analyst for *NFL Total Access*; Big Ten Network, analyst.

Awards: Pro Bowl, National Football League, 1990–95, 1997, 2000–03; NFL Defensive Player of the Year, 1993; Defensive Player of the Year, American Football Conference, 1994; NFL 75th Anniversary All-Time Team, 1994; Intercollegiate Athletics Hall of Fame, Purdue University, 2003; Pro Football Hall of Fame, 2009.

Addresses: *Office*—c/o NFL Network, 280 Park Avenue, New York, NY 10017-1206.

coaches, Woodson chose Purdue University in nearby West Lafayette—allowing him to stay close to his family—and received a full scholarship.

At Purdue, Woodson played mainly as a defensive back, safety, and kick returner, but he was so versatile that he occasionally played offensive positions as well, filling in as a running back and wide receiver. He was a four-year starter for the Boilermakers, playing 44 consecutive games and setting 13 individual records, including 11 interceptions and 320 solo tackles. In 1985 and 1986, he was named an All-American defensive back, and was selected for the All–Big Ten first team three times. Woodson's final game at Purdue was particularly memorable: He played tailback and cornerback, returned kickoffs and punts, and covered kicks for the special teams units—138 plays in all, rushing for 93 yards, catching 3 passes for 67 yards, making 10 tackles, and returning 3 punts for 30 yards. That year, Woodson finished second in voting for the Jim Thorpe Award, which recognizes the top collegiate defensive back in the country.

In addition to his accomplishments on the football field, Woodson also stood out as a track and field athlete at Purdue, setting school records in the 60- and 110-meter hurdles. In 1984, at age nineteen, he qualified for the Olympic trials in the 100-meter hurdle but

declined the opportunity in order to focus on football. In the summer of 1987, he ran the 110-meter hurdles for the Los Angeles Track Club on the European track circuit in 13.29 seconds, tying the fourth-best time in the world. Although Woodson considered sticking with track as an amateur athlete, a career in professional football beckoned.

Joined the "Blitzburgh" Defense

In the 1987 NFL draft, Woodson was chosen by the Pittsburgh Steelers in the first round as the tenth pick overall—a pleasant surprise for Steelers coach Chuck Noll and defensive coordinator Tony Dungy, who had expected Woodson to be one of the top-five picks. In his first season, Woodson played defensive backup and kick returner, making his first career interception on November 22, 1987, when he picked off a pass thrown by Boomer Esiason of the Cincinnati Bengals. By 1989 Woodson had settled into the position of cornerback, leading the NFL in kick returns with a 27.3-yard average and earning the first of eleven trips to the Pro Bowl.

Under Steelers head coach Bill Cowher, who took over the team in 1992, Woodson began to see more contact with the ball and became a key player in the "Blitzburgh" defense, which dominated the NFL. In 1993 he made eight interceptions, earning the NFL Defensive Player of the Year title and helping the Steelers clinch a playoff berth as the wild-card team, although they quickly were eliminated by the Kansas City Chiefs. The next year, the Steelers defense ranked second in the NFL, and Woodson put in another strong performance, with 83 tackles, 3 sacks, 4 interceptions, and 23 pass defenses. He was one of only five active players named to the NFL's 75th Anniversary All-Time team and earned the American Football Conference Defensive Player of the Year award.

In 1995 Woodson suffered a torn anterior cruciate ligament in the opening game, forcing him to miss all of the regular season. Most players require at least a year to recover from such an injury, and up to two years to return to peak form. But as the Steelers went on an incredible eight-game winning streak at the end of the season, Woodson vowed that he would rejoin the team for the playoffs—just four months after surgery. "The doctors tell me I'm crazy. The players tell me I'm crazy. Everybody tells me I'm crazy.... But I know I'd be going crazy if I didn't have this," he told the Associated Press in November of 1995, according to the August 5, 2009, *Fort Wayne News-Sentinel.*

Coach Cowher, who had kept a roster spot open for just such a possibility, played Woodson in Super Bowl XXX against the Dallas Cowboys. Woodson would have to wait for a championship ring, however, as the Steelers fell to the Cowboys 27–17. He returned to Pittsburgh for the 1996 season—his last with the team—but was felled by injury again in the postseason and underwent knee surgery a second time. The Rooney family, owners of the Steelers, elected not to renew Woodson's contract, citing a pay dispute.

Sought a Super Bowl Championship

Now a free agent, Woodson looked for a team that could take him back to the Super Bowl. He played for a single season with the San Francisco 49ers before signing in 1998 with the Baltimore Ravens, recruited by defensive coordinator Marvin Lewis. Under head coach Brian Billick, the thirty-three-year-old Woodson transitioned from cornerback to safety, a position he had played in college. "Very few players are as complete a player as Rod Woodson," Billick said, according to the August 6, 2009, *News-Sentinel.* "You see that in something as simple as the transition from corner to safety. Corner is a very instinctive, physical position. Safety requires a certain vision and intelligence to play. He made the transition seamlessly." The change paid off, and Woodson's veteran leadership helped the Ravens to their first-ever championship title, defeating the New York Giants 34–7 in Super Bowl XXXV in 2001. Woodson finally had the prize he had longed for.

Woodson finished out his career with the Oakland Raiders, joining the team as one of six veteran players over the age of thirty-five. He led the NFL in interceptions, with eight, for the first time in his career, and made his final championship appearance in Super Bowl XXXVII in 2003 against the Tampa Bay Buccaneers, in which the Raiders lost 48–21. Woodson was released by Oakland in July of 2004 after he failed to pass a physical.

In retirement, Woodson launched a second career in television, appearing as an analyst on the program *NFL Total Access* on the NFL Network and providing color commentary on the Big Ten Network. Since 1994 he has operated the annual Woodson/Fabini Football Camp on the grounds of Snider High School, his alma mater in Fort Wayne, and in 2009 he hosted a charity dinner and auction to benefit the Valley Christian schools in Dublin, California, where he is a defensive coach. Woodson was inducted into the Pro Football Hall of Fame in 2009, selected on the first ballot.

Sources

Periodicals

Fort Wayne (IN) News-Sentinel, August 3, 2009; August 5, 2009; August 6, 2009.
Pittsburgh Post-Gazette, June 28, 2009.
Sporting News, November 29, 1993.
Sports Illustrated, September 7, 1992, p. 58.

Online

"Former Boilermaker Rod Woodson Elected to Pro Football Hall of Fame," Purdue University, news release, January 31, 2009, http://www.purdue sports.com/sports/m-footbl/spec-rel/013109aab. html (accessed September 14, 2009).
Labriola, Bob, "Hall of Fame: Woodson's Greatness Went Beyond Stats," Pittsburgh Steelers, January 31, 2009, http://news.steelers.com/article/1027 46/ (accessed September 14, 2009).
"Rod Woodson," Pro Football Hall of Fame, http:// www.profootballhof.com/hof/member.aspx?PLAY ER_ID=282 (accessed September 14, 2009).

—Deborah A. Ring

Cumulative Nationality Index

Volume numbers appear in **bold**

Cumulative Occupation Index

Volume numbers appear in **bold**

Art and design

Abele, Julian **55**
Aberra, Amsale **67**
Adjaye, David **38, 78**
Allen, Tina **22, 75**
Alston, Charles **33**
Amaki, Amalia **76**
Amos, Emma **63**
Anderson, Ho Che **54**
Andrews, Benny **22, 59**
Andrews, Bert **13**
Armstrong, Robb **15**
Ashford, Calvin, Jr. **74**
Bailey, Preston **64**
Bailey, Radcliffe **19**
Bailey, Xenobia **11**
Baker, Matt **76**
Barboza, Anthony **10**
Barnes, Ernie **16, 78**
Barthé, Earl **78**
Barthe, Richmond **15**
Basquiat, Jean-Michel **5**
Bearden, Romare **2, 50**
Beasley, Phoebe **34**
Bell, Darrin **77**
Benberry, Cuesta **65**
Benjamin, Tritobia Hayes **53**
Biggers, John **20, 33**
Biggers, Sanford **62**
Blackburn, Robert **28**
Bond, J. Max, Jr. **76**
Brandon, Barbara **3**
Brown, Donald **19**
Brown, Robert **65**
Burke, Selma **16**
Burroughs, Margaret Taylor **9**
Camp, Kimberly **19**
Campbell, E. Simms **13**
Campbell, Mary Schmidt **43**
Catlett, Elizabeth **2**
Chase-Riboud, Barbara **20, 46**
Colescott, Robert **69**
Collins, Paul **61**
Cortor, Eldzier **42**
Cowans, Adger W. **20**
Cox, Renée **67**
Crichlow, Ernest **75**
Crite, Alan Rohan **29**
De Veaux, Alexis **44**
DeCarava, Roy **42**
Delaney, Beauford **19**
Delaney, Joseph **30**
Delsarte, Louis **34**

Donaldson, Jeff **46**
Douglas, Aaron **7**
Driskell, David C. **7**
du Cille, Michel **74**
Dwight, Edward **65**
Edwards, Melvin **22**
El Wilson, Barbara **35**
Ewing, Patrick **17, 73**
Fax, Elton **48**
Feelings, Tom **11, 47**
Fine, Sam **60**
Freeman, Leonard **27**
Fuller, Meta Vaux Warrick **27**
Gantt, Harvey **1**
Garvin, Gerry **78**
Gilles, Ralph **61**
Gilliam, Sam **16**
Golden, Thelma **10, 55**
Goodnight, Paul **32**
Green, Jonathan **54**
Guyton, Tyree **9**
Hammons, David **69**
Harkless, Necia Desiree **19**
Harrington, Oliver W. **9**
Harrison, Charles **72**
Hathaway, Isaac Scott **33**
Hayden, Palmer **13**
Hayes, Cecil N. **46**
Holder, Geoffrey **78**
Honeywood, Varnette P. **54**
Hope, John **8**
Hudson, Cheryl **15**
Hudson, Wade **15**
Hunt, Richard **6**
Hunter, Clementine **45**
Hutson, Jean Blackwell **16**
Jackson, Earl **31**
Jackson, Mary **73**
Jackson, Vera **40**
John, Daymond **23**
Johnson, Jeh Vincent **44**
Johnson, William Henry **3**
Jones, Lois Mailou **13**
Jones, Paul R. **76**
King, Robert Arthur **58**
Kitt, Sandra **23**
Knight, Gwendolyn **63**
Knox, Simmie **49**
Lawrence, Jacob **4, 28**
Lee, Annie Frances **22**
Lee-Smith, Hughie **5, 22**
Lewis, Edmonia **10**
Lewis, Norman **39**
Lewis, Samella **25**

Lovell, Whitfield **74**
Loving, Alvin, Jr., **35, 53**
Manley, Edna **26**
Marshall, Kerry James **59**
Mayhew, Richard **39**
McCullough, Geraldine **58, 79**
McDuffie, Dwayne **62**
McGee, Charles **10**
McGruder, Aaron **28, 56**
Mitchell, Corinne **8**
Moody, Ronald **30**
Morrison, Keith **13**
Motley, Archibald, Jr. **30**
Moutoussamy-Ashe, Jeanne **7**
Mutu, Wangechi **44**
Myles, Kim **69**
Ndiaye, Iba **74**
Neals, Otto **73**
N'Namdi, George R. **17**
Nugent, Richard Bruce **39**
O'Grady, Lorraine **73**
Olden, Georg(e) **44**
Ormes, Jackie **73**
Ouattara **43**
Perkins, Marion **38**
Pierre, Andre **17**
Pindell, Howardena **55**
Pinder, Jefferson **77**
Pinderhughes, John **47**
Pinkney, Jerry **15**
Piper, Adrian **71**
Pippin, Horace **9**
Pope.L, William **72**
Porter, James A. **11**
Prophet, Nancy Elizabeth **42**
Puryear, Martin **42**
Reid, Senghor **55**
Ringgold, Faith **4**
Roble, Abdi **71**
Ruley, Ellis **38**
Saar, Alison **16**
Saint James, Synthia **12**
Sallee, Charles **38**
Sanders, Joseph R., Jr. **11**
Savage, Augusta **12**
Scott, John T. **65**
Sebree, Charles **40**
Serrano, Andres **3**
Shabazz, Attallah **6**
Shonibare, Yinka **58**
Simmons, Gary **58**
Simpson, Lorna **4, 36**
Sims, Lowery Stokes **27**
Sklarek, Norma Merrick **25**

Sleet, Moneta, Jr. **5**
Smith, Bruce W. **53**
Smith, Marvin **46**
Smith, Morgan **46**
Smith, Vincent D. **48**
Steave-Dickerson, Kia **57**
Stout, Renee **63**
Sudduth, Jimmy Lee **65**
Tanksley, Ann **37**
Tanner, Henry Ossawa **1**
Thomas, Alma **14**
Thrash, Dox **35**
Tolliver, Mose **60**
Tolliver, William **9**
Tooks, Lance **62**
VanDerZee, James **6**
Verna, Gelsy **70**
Wagner, Albert **78**
Wainwright, Joscelyn **46**
Walker, A'lelia **14**
Walker, Kara **16**
Washington, Alonzo **29**
Washington, James, Jr. **38**
Weems, Carrie Mae **63**
Wells, James Lesesne **10**
White, Charles **39**
White, Dondi **34**
White, John H. **27**
Wiley, Kehinde **62**
Williams, Billy Dee **8**
Williams, Clarence **70**
Williams, O. S. **13**
Williams, Paul R. **9**
Williams, William T. **11**
Wilson, Ellis **39**
Withers, Ernest C. **68**
Woodruff, Hale **9**

Business

Abbott, Robert Sengstacke **27**
Abdul-Jabbar, Kareem **8**
Abiola, Moshood **70**
Adams, Eula L. **39**
Adams, Jenoyne **60**
Adkins, Rod **41**
Ailey, Alvin **8**
Akil, Mara Brock **60**
Al-Amin, Jamil Abdullah **6**
Alexander, Archie Alphonso **14**
Allen, Byron **24**
Allen-Buillard, Melba **55**
Ames, Wilmer **27**
Amos, Wally **9**
Archer, Lee, Jr. **79**

Pitta, Celso 17
Poitier, Sidney 11, 36
Ramaphosa, Cyril 3
Rawlings, Jerry 9
Rawlings, Nana Konadu Agyeman 13
Roberto, Holden 65
Robinson, Randall 7, 46
Sampson, Edith S. 4
Sankara, Thomas 17
Sankoh, Foday 74
Savimbi, Jonas 2, 34
Sawyer, Amos 2
Senghor, Augustin Diamacoune 66
Senghor, Léopold Sédar 12, 66
Simpson-Miller, Portia 62
Sirleaf, Ellen Johnson 71
Sisulu, Walter 47
Skerrit, Roosevelt 72
Skinner, Kiron K. 65
Smith, Jennifer 21
Soglo, Nicephore 15
Soyinka, Wole 4
Spencer, Winston Baldwin 68
Tandja, Mamadou 33, 78
Taylor, Charles 20
Taylor, John (David Beckett) 16
Todman, Terence A. 55
Touré, Amadou Toumani 18
Touré, Sekou 6
Tsvangirai, Morgan 26, 72
Tutu, Desmond (Mpilo) 6, 44
Van Lierop, Robert 53
Vieira, Joao 14
Wade, Abdoulaye 66
Weah, George 58
Wharton, Clifton R., Jr. 7
Wharton, Clifton Reginald, Sr. 36
Williams, Eric Eustace 65
Wiwa, Ken 67
Yar'adua, Umaru 69
Zuma, Jacob G. 33, 75
Zuma, Nkosazana Dlamini 34

Government and politics--U.S.

Adams, Floyd, Jr. 12
Alexander, Archie Alphonso 14
Alexander, Clifford 26
Allen, Claude 68
Allen, Ethel D. 13
Allen, Eugene 79
Archer, Dennis 7, 36
Arrington, Richard 24
Avant, Clarence 19
Baker, Thurbert 22
Ballance, Frank W. 41
Baltimore, Richard Lewis, III 71
Barbee, Lloyd Augustus 71
Barden, Don H. 9, 20
Barrett, Andrew C. 12
Barrett, Jacqueline 28
Barry, Marion S. 7, 44
Bass, Karen 70
Bell, Michael 40
Bellamy, Terry 58
Belton, Sharon Sayles 9, 16
Berry, Mary Frances 7
Berry, Theodore M. 31
Bethune, Mary McLeod 4
Bing, Dave 3, 59, 78
Blackwell, Kenneth, Sr. 61
Blackwell, Unita 17
Bond, Julian 2, 35

Booker, Cory Anthony 68
Bosley, Freeman, Jr. 7
Bowman, Bertie 71
Boykin, Keith 14
Bradley, Jennette B. 40
Bradley, Thomas 2
Braun, Carol Moseley 4, 42
Brazile, Donna 25, 70
Brimmer, Andrew F. 2, 48
Brooke, Edward 8
Brooks, Tyrone 59
Brown, Anthony G. 72
Brown, Byrd 49
Brown, Byron W. 72
Brown, Cora 33
Brown, Corrine 24
Brown, Elaine 8
Brown, George Leslie 62
Brown, Jesse 6, 41
Brown, Lee Patrick 24
Brown, Les 5
Brown, Ron 5
Brown, Willie L., Jr. 7
Bruce, Blanche K. 33
Bryant, Wayne R. 6
Buckley, Victoria (Vicki) 24
Bunche, Ralph J. 5
Burke, Yvonne Braithwaite 42
Burris, Chuck 21
Burris, Roland W. 25, 75
Butler, Jerry 26
Butts, Cassandra 78
Caesar, Shirley 19
Campbell, Bill 9, 76
Cardozo, Francis L. 33
Carson, André 69
Carson, Julia 23, 69
Carter, Pamela Lynn 67
Carter, Robert L. 51
Chavis, Benjamin 6
Chisholm, Shirley 2, 50
Christian-Green, Donna M. 17
Clay, William Lacy 8
Clayton, Eva M. 20
Cleaver, Eldridge 5
Cleaver, Emanuel 4, 45, 68
Clemente, Rosa 74
Clyburn, James E. 21, 71
Clyburn, Mignon 78
Cockrel, Kenneth V., Jr. 79
Cockrel, Kenneth Vern, Sr. 79
Coleman, Mary 46
Coleman, Michael B. 28, 79
Coleman, William T. 76
Collins, Barbara-Rose 7
Collins, Cardiss 10
Colter, Cyrus J. 36
Connerly, Ward 14
Conyers, John, Jr. 4, 45
Cook, Mercer 40
Cose, Ellis 5, 50
Craig-Jones, Ellen Walker 44
Crockett, George W., Jr. 10, 64
Cummings, Elijah E. 24
Cunningham, Evelyn 23
Currie, Betty 21
Currie, Ulysses 73
Davis, Angela 5
Davis, Artur 41
Davis, Benjamin O., Jr. 2, 43
Davis, Benjamin O., Sr. 4
Davis, Danny K. 24, 79
Davis, Gordon J. 76

Davis, James E. 50
Days, Drew S., III 10
Delany, Martin R. 27
Delco, Wilhemina R. 33
Dellums, Ronald 2
Diggs, Charles R. 21
Dinkins, David 4
Dixon, Julian C. 24
Dixon, Sharon Pratt 1
Dixon, Sheila 68
Dougherty, Mary Pearl 47
Du Bois, W. E. B. 3
Dudley, Edward R. 58
Dukes, Hazel Nell 56
Dunbar-Nelson, Alice Ruth Moore 44
Dymally, Mervyn 42
Easley, Annie J. 61
Edmonds, Terry 17
Edwards, Donna 77
Elders, Joycelyn 6
Ellison, Keith 59
Espy, Mike 6
Farmer, James 2, 64
Farrakhan, Louis 2
Fattah, Chaka 11, 70
Fauntroy, Walter E. 11
Felix, Larry R. 64
Fenty, Adrian 60
Ferguson, Roger W. 25
Fields, C. Virginia 25
Fields, Cleo 13
Fisher, Ada M. 76
Flake, Floyd H. 18
Fleming, Erik R. 75
Fletcher, Arthur A. 63
Flipper, Henry O. 3
Ford, Harold E(ugene) 42
Ford, Harold E(ugene), Jr. 16, 70
Ford, Jack 39
Ford, Johnny 70
Fortune, T. Thomas 6
Foster, Ezola 28
Franklin, Shirley 34
Franks, Gary 2
Frazer, Jendayi 68
Fudge, Marcia L. 76
Fulani, Lenora 11
Gantt, Harvey 1
Garrett, Joyce Finley 59
Garvey, Marcus 1
Gibson, Johnnie Mae 23
Gibson, Kenneth Allen 6
Gibson, William F. 6
Goode, W. Wilson 4
Gravely, Samuel L., Jr. 5, 49
Gray, William H., III 3
Grimké, Archibald H. 9
Guinier, Lani 7, 30
Haley, George Williford Boyce 21
Hamer, Fannie Lou 6
Harmon, Clarence 26
Harris, Alice 7
Harris, Patricia Roberts 2
Harvard, Beverly 11
Hastie, William H. 8
Hastings, Alcee L. 16
Hatcher, Richard G. 55
Hawkins, Augustus F. 68
Hayes, James C. 10
Henderson, Thelton E. 68
Henry, Aaron 19
Herenton, Willie W. 24

Herman, Alexis M. 15
Hernandez, Aileen Clarke 13
Hill, Bonnie Guiton 20
Hilliard, Earl F. 24
Hobson, Julius W. 44
Holder, Eric H., Jr. 9, 76
Holmes, Amy 69
Holt Baker, Arlene 73
Ifill, Gwen 28
Irving, Larry, Jr. 12
Irvis, K. Leroy 67
Jackson, Alphonso R. 48
Jackson, Frank G. 76
Jackson, George 14
Jackson, Jesse 1, 27, 72
Jackson, Jesse, Jr. 14, 45
Jackson, Lisa 77
Jackson, Mae 57
Jackson, Maynard 2, 41
Jackson, Shirley Ann 12
Jackson Lee, Sheila 20
Jacob, John E. 2
James, Sharpe 23, 69
Jarrett, Valerie 73
Jarvis, Charlene Drew 21
Jefferson, William J. 25, 72
Johnson, Eddie Bernice 8
Johnson, Harvey, Jr. 24
Johnson, James Weldon 5
Johnson, Jeh C. 76
Johnson, Katherine (Coleman Goble) 61
Johnson, Kevin 70
Johnson, Norma L. Holloway 17
Johnson, Robert T. 17
Jones, Elaine R. 7, 45
Jones, Emil, Jr. 74
Jordan, Barbara 4, 78
Jordan, Vernon 3, 35
Kelley, Cliff 75
Kennard, William Earl 18
Keyes, Alan L. 11
Kidd, Mae Street 39
Kilpatrick, Carolyn Cheeks 16
Kilpatrick, Kwame 34, 71
Kincaid, Bernard 28
King, Martin Luther, III 20
Kirk, Ron 11, 75
Lafontant, Jewel Stradford 3, 51
Langford, Larry P. 74
Lee, Barbara 25
Leland, Mickey 2
Lewis, Delano 7
Lewis, John 2, 46
Love, Reggie 77
Majette, Denise 41
Mallett, Conrad, Jr. 16
Mallory, Mark 62
Marsh, Henry, III 32
Marshall, Bella 22
Marshall, Thurgood 1, 44
Martin, Louis E. 16
Martin, Ruby Grant 49
McCall, H. Carl 27
McGee, James D. 74
McGee, James Madison 46
McKinney, Cynthia 11, 52, 74
McKissick, Floyd B. 3
Meek, Carrie 6, 36
Meek, Kendrick 41
Meeks, Gregory 25
Meredith, James H. 11
Metcalfe, Ralph 26

White, Reggie **6, 50**
White, Walter F. **4**
White, Willye **67**
White-Hammond, Gloria **61**
Wideman, John Edgar **5**
Wilkins, Roger **2**
Wilkins, Roy **4**
Williams, Armstrong **29**
Williams, Evelyn **10**
Williams, Fannie Barrier **27**
Williams, George Washington **18**
Williams, Hosea Lorenzo **15, 31**
Williams, Maggie **7, 71**
Williams, Montel **4, 57**
Williams, Patricia **11, 54**
Williams, Robert F. **11**
Williams, Stanley "Tookie" **29, 57**
Williams, Walter E. **4**
Williams, Willie L. **4**
Wilson, August **7, 33, 55**
Wilson, Margaret Bush **79**
Wilson, Phill **9**
Wilson, Sunnie **7, 55**
Wilson, William Julius **22**
Withers, Ernest C. **68**
Wiwa, Ken **67**
Wolfe, George C. **6, 43**
Woodson, Robert L. **10**
Worrill, Conrad **12**
Wright, Charles H. **35**
Wright, Louis Tompkins **4**
Wright, Nathan, Jr. **56**
Wright, Richard **5**
Wyatt, Addie L. **56**
X, Malcolm **1**
Xuma, Madie Hall **59**
Yancy, Dorothy Cowser **42**
Yarbrough, Camille **40**
Yeboah, Emmanuel Ofosu **53**
Yoba, Malik **11**
Young, Andrew **3, 48**
Young, Jean Childs **14**
Young, Whitney M., Jr. **4**
Youngblood, Johnny Ray **8**
Zulu, Princess Kasune **54**

Sports

Aaron, Hank **5**
Abdul-Jabbar, Kareem **8**
Abdur-Rahim, Shareef **28**
Adams, Paul **50**
Adu, Freddy **67**
Alexander, Shaun **58**
Ali, Laila **27, 63**
Ali, Muhammad **2, 16, 52**
Allen, Marcus **20**
Amaker, Tommy **62**
Amos, John **8, 62**
Anderson, Elmer **25**
Anderson, Jamal **22**
Anderson, Mike **63**
Anderson, Viv **58**
Anthony, Carmelo **46**
Artest, Ron **52**
Ashe, Arthur **1, 18**
Ashford, Emmett **22**
Ashford, Evelyn **63**
Ashley, Maurice **15, 47**
Baines, Harold **32**
Baker, Dusty **8, 43, 72**
Banks, Ernie **33**
Barber, Ronde **41**
Barber, Tiki **57**

Barkley, Charles **5, 66**
Barnes, Ernie **16, 78**
Barnes, John **53**
Barnes, Steven **54**
Barney, Lem **26**
Barnhill, David **30**
Baylor, Don **6**
Beamon, Bob **30**
Beasley, Jamar **29**
Bekele, Kenenisa **75**
Bell, James "Cool Papa" **36**
Belle, Albert **10**
Bettis, Jerome **64**
Bickerstaff, Bernie **21**
Bing, Dave **3, 59, 78**
Bivins, Michael **72**
Black, Joe **75**
Blair, Paul **36**
Blake, James **43**
Blanks, Billy **22**
Blanton, Dain **29**
Bogues, Tyrone "Muggsy" **56**
Bol, Manute **1**
Bolt, Usain **73**
Bolton-Holifield, Ruthie **28**
Bonaly, Surya **7**
Bonds, Barry **6, 34, 63**
Bonds, Bobby **43**
Bowe, Riddick **6**
Brand, Elton **31**
Brandon, Terrell **16**
Branham, George, III **50**
Brashear, Donald **39**
Brathwaite, Fred **35**
Briscoe, Marlin **37**
Brock, Lou **18**
Brooks, Aaron **33**
Brooks, Derrick **43**
Brown, James **22**
Brown, Jim **11**
Brown, Mike **77**
Brown, Sean **52**
Brown, Willard **36**
Bruce, Isaac **26**
Bryant, Kobe **15, 31, 71**
Buchanan, Ray **32**
Bush, Reggie **59**
Butler, Leroy, III **17**
Bynoe, Peter C.B. **40**
Campanella, Roy **25**
Carew, Rod **20**
Carnegie, Herbert **25**
Carter, Anson **24**
Carter, Butch **27**
Carter, Cris **21**
Carter, Joe **30**
Carter, Kenneth **53**
Carter, Rubin **26**
Carter, Vince **26**
Cash, Swin **59**
Catchings, Tamika **43**
Chamberlain, Wilt **18, 47**
Chaney, John **67**
Charleston, Oscar **39**
Cheeks, Maurice **47**
Cherry, Deron **40**
Cheruiyot, Robert **69**
Christie, Linford **8**
Claiborne, Loretta **34**
Clay, Bryan **57, 74**
Clemons, Michael "Pinball" **64**
Clendenon, Donn **26, 56**
Clifton, Nathaniel "Sweetwater" **47**

Coachman, Alice **18**
Coleman, Leonard S., Jr. **12**
Cooper, Andy "Lefty" **63**
Cooper, Charles "Chuck" **47**
Cooper, Cynthia **17**
Cooper, Michael **31**
Copeland, Michael **47**
Corley, Tony **62**
Cottrell, Comer **11**
Crennel, Romeo **54**
Crooks, Garth **53**
Croom, Sylvester **50**
Culpepper, Daunte **32**
Cunningham, Randall **23**
Dandridge, Ray **36**
Dantley, Adrian **72**
Davis, Ernie **48**
Davis, Mike **41**
Davis, Milt **74**
Davis, Piper **19**
Davis, Shani **58**
Davis, Terrell **20**
Dawes, Dominique **11**
Day, Leon **39**
DeFrantz, Anita **37**
DeGale, James **74**
Delaney, Joe **76**
Devers, Gail **7**
Dibaba, Tirunesh **73**
Dickerson, Eric **27**
Dixon, George **52**
Doby, Lawrence Eugene, Sr. **16, 41**
Doig, Jason **45**
Dorrell, Karl **52**
dos Santos, Manuel Francisco **65**
Drew, Charles Richard **7**
Drexler, Clyde **4, 61**
Drogba, Didier **78**
Dumars, Joe **16, 65**
Duncan, Tim **20**
Dungy, Tony **17, 42, 59**
Dunn, Jerry **27**
Durant, Kevin **76**
Dye, Jermaine **58**
Edwards, Harry **2**
Edwards, Herman **51**
Edwards, Teresa **14**
Elder, Lee **6**
Ellerbe, Brian **22**
Elliott, Sean **26**
Ellis, Dock **78**
Ellis, Jimmy **44**
Ervin, Anthony **66**
Erving, Julius **18, 47**
Eto'o, Samuel **73**
Ewing, Patrick **17, 73**
Farr, Mel **24**
Faulk, Marshall **35**
Felix, Allyson **48**
Fielder, Cecil **2**
Fielder, Prince Semien **68**
Flood, Curt **10**
Flowers, Vonetta **35**
Ford, Cheryl **45**
Foreman, George **1, 15**
Forrest, Vernon **40, 79**
Foster, Andrew **79**
Fowler, Reggie **51**
Fox, Rick **27**
Frazier, Joe **19**
Frazier-Lyde, Jacqui **31**
Freeman, Cathy **29**
Freeman, Marianna **23**

Fuhr, Grant **1, 49**
Fuller, Vivian **33**
Futch, Eddie **33**
Gaines, Clarence E., Sr. **55**
Gaither, Alonzo Smith (Jake) **14**
Garnett, Kevin **14, 70**
Garrison, Zina **2**
Gaston, Cito **71**
Gebrselassie, Haile **70**
Gentry, Alvin **23**
Gibson, Althea **8, 43**
Gibson, Bob **33**
Gibson, Josh **22**
Gibson, Truman K., Jr. **60**
Gilliam, Frank **23**
Gilliam, Joe **31**
Gooden, Dwight **20**
Gorden, W. C. **71**
Goss, Tom **23**
Gourdine, Meredith **33**
Gourdine, Simon **11**
Granderson, Curtis **66**
Grand-Pierre, Jean-Luc **46**
Gray, Yeshimbra "Shimmy" **55**
Green, A. C. **32**
Green, Darrell **39, 74**
Green, Dennis **5, 45**
Greene, Joe **10**
Greene, Maurice **27, 77**
Gregg, Eric **16**
Gregory, Ann **63**
Grier, Mike **43**
Grier, Roosevelt **1**
Griffey, Ken, Jr. **12, 73**
Griffith, Yolanda **25**
Griffith-Joyner, Florence **28**
Gumbel, Bryant **14**
Gumbel, Greg **8**
Gwynn, Tony **18**
Hamilton, Lewis **66**
Haney, Lee **77**
Hardaway, Anfernee (Penny) **13**
Hardaway, Tim **35**
Harris, James **79**
Harris, Sylvia **70**
Harrison, Alvin **28**
Harrison, Calvin **28**
Haskins, Clem **23**
Hayes, Bob **77**
Heard, Gar **25**
Hearns, Thomas **29**
Henderson, Rickey **28, 78**
Henry, Thierry **66**
Hickman, Fred **11**
Hill, Calvin **19**
Hill, Grant **13**
Hillary, Barbara **65**
Hilliard, Wendy **53**
Hines, Garrett **35**
Holdsclaw, Chamique **24**
Holland, Kimberly N. **62**
Holmes, Kelly **47**
Holmes, Larry **20, 68**
Holyfield, Evander **6**
Hopkins, Bernard **35, 69**
Horton, Andre **33**
Horton, Suki **33**
Howard, Desmond **16, 58**
Howard, Juwan **15**
Howard, Ryan **65**
Howard, Sherri **36**
Hunter, Billy **22**
Hunter, Torii **43**

Cumulative Subject Index

Volume numbers appear in **bold**

Cumulative Name Index

Volume numbers appear in **bold**